MW01258444

PR/
ROSEMARY, NOW AND THEN

"My mother in the grips of dementia, it was hard looking after her. This book gave clarity to what I felt, and detailed the life of a person on her final journey."

— Wanda Strike, minister for United Church of Canada (Brighton)

"An honest, intimate look at management of severe medical conditions, its mystical revelations, premonitions, and near-death experiences intertwine scientific and spiritual understanding, seeking to understand the delicate balance between life and afterlife, and the compassionate care that connects us all."

– K. Michael Dürr Specht, MD, PhD

"A must-read for deep understanding of dementia's intense effects, the enduring strength of love, and mysteries of the great beyond. Meet unforgettable Rosemary, a beloved and eccentric mother whose energy, creativity, and quirks shine despite her decline. An intimate exploration, entwining heartbreak and astonishing joy as it scrutinizes the gap between life and death."

– Tonya Dalhaus, University of Colorado Adjunct Faculty,
Emerald Coast Writers president

"My mom had to transition from assisted-living to memory care. Thankfully, Rosemary's story offered our family great comfort and taught valuable things for this season of life."

– Lynn Schneider, MS, CPCM
(certified professional contracts manager)

"*Rosemary, Now and Then* promises to be a tour de force from a unique and compassionate voice. Written by a gifted and soulful human being, this book is uncompromising, authentic, deep and true. Anyone who invests in this project won't be disappointed."

– Michael DeMaria, Bestselling author of *Peace Within*
and four-time Grammy nominee

"When Rosemary Baker gets hit with multiple strokes, her wit spars with dementia in a body reduced to the function of a toddler. Her daughter, Chris, a retired paramedic, cares for Rosemary to the end. Robin to Rose's Batman, Chris enables her mother in her darkest hours to jab humorous comebacks at the ultimate trickster. Refusing to go gently anywhere, Rose gets the last laugh."

— Katherine Nelson Born, Emerald Coast Writers' Poet laureate

"Making the most of life in the face of it all, Rosemary sets an example for every one of us. She dabbles her toes into eternity, splashes about in laughter, and then wades in, leaving vital inspiration in her wake."

– Michael Dowd, author of *Thank God for Evolution*

"More than a daughter's loving tribute, *Rosemary, Now and Then* offers a glimpse of a sparkling and compassionate mind, impaired but not extinguished by debilitating strokes."

– Janet Kivisto, RN

"I love the criteria Rosemary set as her definition of life worth living: recognizing herself and her daughter. Taking detours in stride, having fun with mental mayhem, the mother/daughter sleep deprivation triathlon, the nursing home descriptions, the coincidence of the dog's stroke decades before, and the many creative ideas—like giving Rose a pen and paper to jot down the answers to her own questions—make this a most memorable book on memory loss, a testament of loving care in desperate circumstances."

— Christine Ziebold, M.D., Infectious Disease Pediatrician

ROSEMARY, NOW AND THEN

ROSEMARY, NOW AND THEN

A Multidimensional Memoir

CHRISTINA LARSON

Rosemary, Now and Then: A Multidimensional Memoir

© 2025 by Christina Larson

Library of Congress Control Number: 2024920495
ISBN: 978-1-964686-19-6 (paperback)   978-1-964686-20-2 (ebook)

This book is based on true events reflecting the author's memory of them. Some names and characteristics may have been changed, and some events compressed.

Editors: Mary Ward Menke, Linda Dessau, Deborah Froese
Cover and Interior Design: Emma Elzinga

Printed in the United States of America

First Edition

3 West Garden Street, Ste. 718
Pensacola, FL 32502
www.indigoriverpublishing.com

Ordering Information:

Quantity sales: Special discounts are available on quantity purchases by corporations, associations, and others. For details, contact the publisher at the address above.

Orders by U.S. trade bookstores and wholesalers: Please contact the publisher at the address above.

With Indigo River Publishing, you can always expect great books, strong voices, and meaningful messages. Most importantly, you'll always find . . . *words worth reading.*

To my inimitable mother

ROSEMARY JANE MARTIN
a 1948 glamore photo paid for with a 50 cent coupon

CONTENTS

START HERE

Clouds of the past, oceans of the future form,
in moment-to-moment drops, day-by-day downpours.
– ROSEMARY, 1963

ROSEMARY'S BRAIN IS LIKE LACE." A clever nurse translated the dementia diagnosis into poetic imagery for the sake of our concerned family. That lacey depiction replaced brain scan jargon that had reduced the patient to a dysfunction. Fine threads of brilliance continued to weave intricate Irish-veil thoughts through my mother's filigree mind.

As Rosemary's middle child and a paramedic, I assumed responsibility for her from then on. Based on what I knew of dementia, I expected a slow, meaningless decline. That is *not* what happened. Although strokes eroded my phenomenal mom's cognition, dementia uplifted her spirit—compelling me to reconsider mental disorder in particular, and the nature of death in general.

At first, her brain lost white matter, the part that connects ideas into recognizable reality. Memory swatches unraveled at their adjoined seams, but her gray matter smarts remained unscathed. She recalled family traditions, South Jersey colloquialisms, word games, and loving relationships. Holes between cognitive functions widened with each stroke, while steadfast parts of her smarts stayed intact and oh-so-animated.

Mind-altered adventures took Rosemary to places far beyond the confines of conventional reality. Dementia proved no match for her exceptional insight, let alone her fabulous sense of humor, as the hard line between life and death dissolved into a permeable membrane. Unhinged, she traveled back and forth through the mortal veil and described otherworldly perceptions. Delusions? Too dismissive. These excursions brought uplifting joy comparable to hearing Barber's *Adagio for Strings'* crescendo, or gazing into the eyes of a smiling baby, or dozing off to soothing sleep. Strokes battered Rosemary's brain, yet dementia sparkled her twilight years with awe. Here-and-now grounding gave way to there-and-then awareness. Remarkable coincidences connected the dots of existence. Rosemary's odyssey epitomized creative living and dying for the rest of us mortals.

In my mother's late eighties, I began to keep notes of her knee-slapping anecdotes along with challenges of caregiving. Behind the scenes, 24/7 ups and downs mounted. So did Rosemary's whimsical remarks as family and friends joined me in jotting her words on any handy scrap of paper. Like a dismantled crazy quilt cluttering her well-organized home, cue card reminder notes kept track of her, and kept her on track. Fireflies in the dark, these memos illuminated the final pages of my mother's life.

Longing for distant loved ones—departed or far-flung on the planet—Rosemary rode her bemused nostalgia like a chariot on voyages to otherworldly realms, somewhere way over the rainbow. These mental excursions didn't always make sense to anyone, including herself. But what appeared pure fantasy became more salient as her fascination with living made dying an exquisite, meaningful adventure.

STROKES OF GENIUS, NOW AND THEN

Thumbing through the local daily news,
at last she locates the crossword puzzle.
"Oh, here it is in the sports section—
I feel so athletic."
– ROSEMARY, 2009, AGE 81

INTRODUCTION TO AN END-OF-LIFE ADVENTURE

Every tick-tock of
"My Grandfather's Clock"
charts bountiful things
as the pendulum swings.
– ROSEMARY, 2018, AGE 90

FRESHER THAN FLOWERS, with more punch than an obituary and more gravity than a grave, welcome to the enchanting, final years of Rosemary Baker. That's my mother, unpretentious matriarch of the extended, extensive Martin family of her origin. She answers to an array of nicknames dubbed by loved ones: Re, Mom, Gram, Ro, Aunt Rosie, Mumz, Mrs. B, Rosey, Ma, Posey . . . If endearing aliases were wildflowers, Rosemary—by any name—would be a handpicked bouquet, more exquisite than a blooming botanical garden.

Rosemary recognizes herself as part of nature and accepts death as the natural conclusion to life . . . just not yet. Oddly, her dementia averts the Grim Reaper. For now, she delights in the splendid moments each breath affords.

During my years of service as a paramedic, I cared for stroke patients at the initial event and also those with subsequent dementia. Bouts of uncontrollable violence left family aghast. Emergency calls rang each time Granny Mae (pseudonym) inflicted bodily injury on someone. And whenever Amos (pseudonym) escaped the nursing home, we would find him dehydrated, confused, and in a state of utter contempt.

But exceptions to dementia's grim rule occur. Sylvia (pseudonym) maintained her pleasant disposition, although aphasia left her with a single-word vocabulary: "no." And retired English professor Dr. Reeves (pseudonym) hobbled to the end with her kind dignity sufficiently intact to bestow a repetitive blessing: "Peaceful repose throughout the universe."

Much to the relief of our family, Rosemary seldom experiences post-stroke emotional volatility. All things considered, my mother laughs, cries, and laughs some more for good reason. Over time, I realize why: short-term memory loss thwarts her recall of suffering. Days fill with exquisite one-liners, joyful revelations, and endearing tenderness. Although dementia tests my caregiving endurance and pillages my mother away piece by piece, it also obliterates her sorrow.

Until the strokes, Rosemary had typical ups and bleak downs. Throughout her earlier life, she greeted creative highs with calm satisfaction. Decades ago, young mother Rose painted happy mercurochrome faces on skinned knees, encouraging her children to face tumbles undaunted. Like great artists who alter their mistakes until the results appear intentional, Rosemary had a nonchalant knack for taking detours in stride—the definition of a life well lived. But stormy moods and dreary nightmares of the soul would cast her better nature into despair. Dostoevsky understood this propensity for melancholy in people like Rosemary, with vast intellect and generous hearts, who suffer depths of sadness. Then along came the strokes.

Ministrokes impose temporary mental loss on Rosemary, like digging holes, then filling them back in. No harm done. But the transient version foretells worse things to come. Full-blown strokes plow permanent pits through her brain. It takes extended periods of time for her circuitry to rebuild bridges over cognitive craters. With strokes a leading cause of severe disability and death in the United States, uncommon Rosemary becomes a common statistic.[1] *My phenomenal mom deserves fireworks, not a fizzle out*, I tell myself.

Abrupt transitions in this story's narrative, from the caregiving present to past-tense memories, mirror my mother's elusive grasp on reality. Following her train of thought, unbidden mental excursions derail from chronological order. Disjointed leaps in time and space reflect the psychological gymnastics necessary to keep pace with dementia. These now and then hops also lighten intensity for readers, just as they did at the time for caregivers.

A huge plus comes with Rosemary's dementia. Hardships dissolve from her mind like Polaroid pictures developing in reverse. One piercing example is dwindling memories of her son's premature death.

At age forty-four and in his prime, my brother Martin developed a splitting headache and was diagnosed with the most lethal form of brain cancer.

"Glioblastoma multiforme," his neurosurgeon said, "the cancer that gives cancer a bad name."

Mom and I cared for Marty during his rapid decline. Regretfully, my paramedic background proved a hindrance. Skills for rescuing people from the brink of death conflict with the empathy needed to say goodbye to someone precious. During my brother's final months, efficient medical treatment masked my anguish over his pending, mortal demise. Like every dying person, what Marty needed most was compassion. He received this in spades from others, less so from me, numbed and robotic. The best parting gift I could have offered Marty was my love. In the end, death ushered him on . . . only love survived.

In contrast to my stunned care for Martin during his plummet toward death, I vow to stay engaged as our mother shuffles to the grave. My emotional vulnerability transforms into purposeful energy. Every spoon-fed sip of soup, every diaper change, and every walk holding hands becomes an opportunity to honor our relationship.

Her mind travels to historic South Jersey, the Garden State she calls home, to a bicycle railway through the Pine Barrens and walks over Clements Bridge, where retreating British soldiers once discarded their muskets. She recalls William Penn's respect for Indigenous people and the Philadelphia statue of him visible down the train tracks, across the Delaware River. Filling in present-tense gaps left by strokes, I keep my mom apprised of current events here in the Florida Sunshine State. On occasion, stories of past and present coalesce in her mind, like a broken glass thermometer's mercury she let us view as children—"Look, but don't touch." She recounts vivid details . . . until daily distractions once more scatter her attention into fragmented reality.

Each cognitive insult transforms Rosemary in unexpected ways, as if absent brain cells open portals to secret, sacred places. Psychologies meet philosophies. Rosemary knows full well that you cannot put your thoughts into the same stream of consciousness twice: William James meets Heraclitus. And she appreciates kindness as pragmatic: Carl Rogers meets Aristotle. My mom interprets the Golden Rule—a standard moral code of religions—as nature's law of interconnectedness. "Hate him, hate yourself," she interjects over a mean-spirited remark on TV.

Basic abilities fade, but not her encyclopedic vocabulary or astute thoughts. Unburdened by drudgeries of normalcy imposed on functional adults, a bright, youthful Rosey comes out to play. Bliss fills the void of vaporized brain matter. Rosemary's mind flies free, on mystic escapades beyond the bars of reality.

Dementia proves no match for my mom's sense of humor. The neurologist dismisses her witty remarks as denial, a way to cover for confusion. That may be true; the specialist knows his stuff. But he does not know my mom's decisive honesty. Rather than deceit, jocularity is a courteous gesture, her gift to weary listeners. Mirth is how she chooses to ride this ailment out. More power to her for making fun of mental mayhem. Wit is her poke in the shoulder of woe. Cheers for the palliative power of snappy retorts and hearty laughter. As strokes course through her skull, my mom becomes a standup comedian . . . except perhaps for the standup part.

Rosemary's stroke-tilled brain flourishes with savvy and endearing traits seeded in her youth. Memory loss makes way for ever-broadening amazement. Her three-year-old self, Rosey revives, bedazzled by the flutter of leaves in the breeze. A golden silk orb spider's finesse brings her to a captivated halt. And the upside-down antics of a nuthatch on the dogwood animate Rosemary's hands and feet—traces of her tree-climbing years. Flashes of her childlike enchantment and sage-like wisdom sparkle to the end.

Challenges of life naturally ended for Rosemary with her passing. Though her body died, her influence lingered as I retraced my mother's strokes over her final years. But this story does not end with death.

Two final chapters further connect reality's dots of what is and is to be. One chapter follows survivors through the realities of postmortem care. Then in the last chapter, an astounding pandemic twist entices intrigue over how afterlife perspectives form. As a parting gift, the Rosemary story concludes with her own epitaph, and the recipe for her signature cinnamon buns to share with loved ones . . . as she would do.

My mother once spoke of vanished memories, obsolete lifestyles, and loved ones passed: "How fortunate to experience something so precious, that you can agonize over the loss." On the upside, in celebration, I raise a toast to Rosemary, her love of life, and to the wonder of existence. May her story from the enigmatic edge magnify life's fleeting miracles, happening right under our noses.

STROKE 1

BACKWARD IN STEP, STYLE, AND STANCE

A situation is never a single thread, but a web.
– **ROSEMARY**, circa 1990

THE FIRST STROKE THAT POPS into Rosemary's head—in September 2014—does not come with classic, one-sided symptoms. So like her unconventional approach to things.

Wafting from her front door come aromas of fresh-baked cinnamon buns, simmering spaghetti sauce, and an invigorating kick of lemon rinds boiling for iced tea. Rosemary's unforeseen first stroke minutes away, she pauses at the dining room table to grab a jigsaw puzzle piece with her free hand and locates its rightful place in the big picture. The other arm balances a laundry basket on her hip. Inaudible *Weather Channel* forecasts mutter background accompaniment to Rosemary's voice reciting the prelude to Longfellow's epic poem, "Evangeline." A befitting soliloquy, "This is the forest primeval . . . " resounds over an ancient woodland scene assembling beneath her searching fingers.

"Hi, Ma," I call. Her front door closes behind me as she shoves a bite of cinnamon bun into my willing mouth. I hand over the laundry detergent she requested, brought from my home around the corner. The satisfaction of living nearby goes beyond convenience; shared experiences deepen our relationship.

She catches my eyes with a knowing look and forms a crooked, half-smile fraught with significance. "Every time someone says hi, I picture the "H" and "I" Scrabble tiles."

"I understand, Mom."

October 8, 2001, the day after my brother Marty died in his Newport, Rhode Island home, our mother vacuumed his dining room to forge her anguish into some semblance of purpose. Finding the "H" tile on the floor, at first Rosemary was scandalized by such carelessness. Avid Scrabble players, our family took great care to store the alphabet tiles in their drawstring bag after each game. Cleaning further, Mom then spotted the "I" in close proximity and handed it to me. The unmistakable salutation from Marty gave us immense comfort.

Back in Florida, fond memories of Marty keep her company as I walk back home. Laundry soap in hand, Rosemary starts a load of wash. Hunched over the machine, she finds herself mesmerized by the back-and-forth sashay of clothes. All at once, her feet take charge and dance her backward, in step with the agitating rhythm of the washer. Forced against a nearby wall, her renegade feet keep marching. Like a pair of determined soldiers with no sense of what they are doing or why, her feet follow orders from her hapless brain. Astonished, Rose drops the empty laundry basket, grasps the flip phone dangling from her neck by its lanyard, and pushes speed dial to summon me back.

"Chris, I'm in the laundry room walking into the wall. My feet have a mind of their own. This sort of thing never happened with my mom's wringer washer."

Thus, my mother begins her journey to elsewhere, escorted by a rather eccentric series of strokes. I return lickety-split. Sure enough, backed against the wall, she runs in place, as if determined to keep the house upright. The hospital only a few minutes' drive away, we decide to forego an ambulance. As we manage our way to the car in an ungainly fashion, her feet stop their misbehavior. We hightail it to Fort Walton Beach Medical Center's emergency department to wind our way through the labyrinth of twenty-first century medical protocol. The ER doctor diagnoses a minor stroke and follows standard procedure. Medicare requires a full, three-night hospital stay for observation before insurance will cover inpatient therapy at a rehabilitation center. God help families who do not know this and push for an earlier transfer. Rosemary only complains over the interference with her plans to share cinnamon buns at church on Sunday.

The fourth hospital day arrives, and an ambulance transports her a few blocks away for inpatient therapy at Fort Walton Beach Rehabilitation Center. By amazing coincidence, Rosemary's assigned room happens to be directly across the hall from her old friend, Ruth, who was her neighbor, right across the street, for twenty-six years.

Ruth and Rosemary lived in Elliot Point—a modest subdivision, nestled between Choctawhatchee Bay and Good Thing Lake. A frequent guest at Rosemary's table from 1982 to 2008, Ruth shared stories of her profession as a World War II nurse. She pined over the loss of her husband, haunted by the knowledge that bleeding ulcers later became readily treatable. Ruth confided in Rosemary about her struggles as a widowed parent. Prompted by my mother, our family coordinated with the Center for Independent Living and replaced Ruth's unsafe stepping stones with a sidewalk.

In 2008, my mother made the harrowing decision to leave her once-cozy neighborhood—defiled by unsupervised teens and feral cats. Tearfully, she traded her half-century-old house filled with married-life memories for the comfort of living near family, eight miles away in Shalimar.

Neighbors once more, Ruth and Rose delight in the serendipity of their rehab room assignments. Ruth's health declines, but she dies in good company. Rosemary recuperates and graduates from wheelchair to walker. To quicken her pace, she holds the adaptive device in midair. The nurses catch this and allow supervised strolls in the corridors without the aid of what Rose calls "confusing contraptions."

Rosemary regards rehab as an opportunity to socialize. Congenial to everyone—staff, patients, and physicians alike—it fails to faze her that unresponsive people may be oblivious to her pleasantries. Doctors pressed for time barely bother with the common courtesy of a response to her salutations.

"Ma, I don't think anyone's paying attention." Clutching her arm to prevent a fall, I cannot write down her comment verbatim but recall the gist.

"It doesn't matter." With a shrug, she reminded me that people possess untold worth, whether they know it or not. Rosemary values each encounter as a chance to connect. Sometimes her words click, even for those she greets with mouths agape who seem comatose. Glimmers of awareness sparkle in the eyes of disengaged people.

A nurse with a warm smile admires my mother's friendliness but speaks to me, not her patient. Rose overhears the compliment and pipes in. She credits her affable nature to her parents' fine example.

Rosemary's parents, Anna and William Martin, opened the doors of their Audubon, New Jersey, home to "visiting firemen." An obsolete custom, locals once offered free room and board to out-of-town firemen (males only in those days) who volunteered in emergencies. Hospitality toward strangers was so common that the term was extended to any overnight company.

Rosemary's folks hosted countless guests. A talented Pennsylvania sculptor, Edgar Wilson, needed a night's stay. Impressed by their kindness, the man gifted the Martin family one of his original, limited edition Pippin tree lamps.

Over the years, Rose read more than books in the lamp's light. The depiction portrayed by the lamp design piqued her curiosity. Did the ornery boys in tattered clothes resemble her brothers by sheer coincidence or only in her mind? Chased by the farmer's dog, she admired their cooperation, helping one another climb the tree. Would the hatful of gathered apples abandoned on the ground be left to spoil? Rosemary viewed the lamp as a talisman for close, supportive relationships.

My mother wants to befriend everyone at the rehab center. In the cafeteria, patients who possess the ability to choose for themselves may sit wherever they please. Paused at the entryway, Rose scans the room, and her smile falters.

"Where would you like to sit, Mom?" *And what upset you?* I wonder, oblivious to the ethnicity and gender barriers that segregate the diners.

"At *that* table." She points with indignation. Then off she goes to a spare seat where a couple of Black men await their meals. I scurry to keep up.

The fellows grow animated as Rosemary approaches. She asks permission to join them and they greet her with reciprocal smiles, one genuine, the other leery. The cheerful man tips an imaginary hat with a "how-do." The wary gentleman scooches an empty chair out from the table for their new lunch companion. I leave to fill out forms. Over my shoulder, I hear my mother initiate conversation. Her voice breaks with stifled emotion.

"A toast to the witnesses."

The men raise their plastic tumblers in response. Clink-clunk-clink.

After lunch, I fetch my mother and inquire about the "witnesses" she toasted.

"Longfellow," is all she says.

Clueless, I write it off as an indecipherable dementia remark. *So many incidental comments she makes fly over my head unnoticed, like migrating flocks of magnificent frigate birds.*

On to the next subject, I ask why she selected that particular table. Rosemary gazes into the unseen distance and cocks her head. Her mouth twists and eyes narrow to a squint. I worry she's in pain or on the verge of another stroke. Instead, she launches into resolute suffragette mode.

"I refuse to be party to any sort of segregation." The best she knows how, Rosemary had staged a one-woman crusade for racial and gender equality. But her unconditional respect goes beyond a mere luncheon gesture.

It is impossible to be untouched by the water in which we wallow. To swim against the current of drowning injustice is never futile. If enough people act, civility survives. Every effort has a cumulative effect. Years after my mother's death, I will better appreciate her cafeteria rebellion. Thumbing through the crumbled pages of her Longfellow poetry book, I come upon "The Witnesses," about enslaved people whose skeletons, still shackled, watch from the ocean floor.

From an early age, Rosemary developed the heart of a Samaritan and a sense of civic responsibility. My mother balked at elitist differentiations made between flowers and weeds, between various cultural ethnicities, and between economic castes. At the sight of bullying, she intervened. Her soothing words disarmed the vitriol of cruel parents, defusing volatile situations. Rosemary left public places nicer than she found them: she picked up broken glass on beaches, disposed of cigarette butts left littering parks, and, in restrooms, she put sloppy people's used paper towels into waste cans.

Not goody-two-shoes, these were her simply expressions of respect for Mother Nature. "Pay the toll," said Rose. Contribute to the common good and civilization advances in incremental, if not discernible, ways.

In a high school report about colonial times, Rosemary cited six-foot, twenty-five pound lobsters and foot-long oysters in abundance.[2] From then on, with any mention of environmental exploitation, Rose cited the contrast between 1600s shellfish and current catches-of-the-day. Rebalance occurs with determination. Who knows? Rose's remarks may have influenced the fishing industry to a modest degree. Her chastising letters to Monsanto may have dissuaded another Agent Orange catastrophe. It's possible that broken glass she removed from beaches spared harm to bare feet. And plastic circles snipped with scissors before tossed in the recycle bin may have saved some sea turtles.

As she matured, matters of fairness and safety moved Rosemary to voice her concerns to government officials through letters, calls, and at public meetings. She told county commissioners about the harm stray cats inflict on native wildlife. She informed state representatives of wasteful expenditures and challenged the White House over the country's system of wrongful imprisonment. She penned a missive to Lady Bird Johnson in gratitude for the first lady's efforts to preserve native wildflowers along highways. In the1970s, during Rosemary's lunch breaks from work, she visited dying patients at a nearby Philadelphia hospital and returned to her file clerk job exhausted, dozing between floors on the crowded elevator. In the 1980s, neo-Nazis requested a parade permit in Fort Walton Beach, Florida; Rose suggested that kindness advocates line the street with their backs turned to the hatred mongers. A decade later, my mother helped save the heritage trees from development along Highway 98 in Mary Esther, Florida and on 17th Avenue in Pensacola. In letters to the editor, she bid a fond farewell to the community-spirited Albertsons' grocery store manager, wrote a tribute to the trees that saved the barrier islands from Hurricane Opal, and encouraged protection of Indian Temple Mound historic sites.

After my dear father died in 1992 from complications of his second open-heart surgery, Mom volunteered with the American Cancer Society for eleven years. She clocked over 5,000 miles transporting people for treatment and retained cordial memories of each person, as if they were family members. In a letter to Florida congressman Joe Scarborough, Rosemary expressed concern for constitutional protocol over summarily ejecting officials. She concluded with a broad perspective: "More than a public office is at stake." Representative Matt Gaetz got calls from her, admonishing his support of fracking. And Rose hounded newspaper editors weekly over her pet peeve, published grammatical errors and typos.

As September falls to October, Rosemary resumes finding newspaper typos as she makes progress at the rehab center. Her undaunted spirit leaves vivid impressions. Therapists light up when it's their turn to work with Rose. Blank faces revitalize at the sound of her voice.

"I never met anyone like your mother," the nurse supervisor tells me.

Rosemary's quick recovery and sharp mind convince the doctor to release her from rehab. Although social interaction with folks her age has been a welcome change, she celebrates the return to her own digs. The physician orders home health care to provide additional watchful eyes. Rosemary counts the steps from her front door to ours just around the corner—240, her favorite number. Close proximity to my husband Robert and me put all three of us more at ease.

Back in our woodsy neighborhood, before bedtime, we pick up my mom and drive to Longwood Park to view the blood moon rising. The splendid lunar sky above reflects in Garnier Bayou below.

Batammaliba African people regard such an eclipse as a time to resolve conflicts. The struggle between the sun and moon reestablishes natural order. Familiar routines regain balance. On this momentous evening, dolphins break the surface, scattering water around them like falling stars, and Rosemary jumps for joy.

A solar eclipse marked the 1963 start of Rosemary and Herman's hunt for a larger home to better accommodate the family and aid my sister in her social needs. Mom was enthralled with the new place in Oaklyn, New Jersey because of its magnificent oak tree out back. For her, the house was of secondary importance.

Our parents enticed our anticipation for the move. In order of age, each of us kids got to select our own bedroom. Eleven-year-old Beth chose the one with red linoleum flooring that she

Freedom, under a full blood moon

found beautiful. The middle child at age nine, I liked the one with the unique bay window, unaware it was the largest. Six-year-old Marty selected the back bedroom for its view of the old-growth oak and nearby train tracks with daily rail traffic that rattled the windows. That left the tiniest room for our parents. But no hint of regret ever came from the doting duo, nestled in the room overlooking lilies of the valley in the yard below. Painting their bedroom to baptize it their own, Mom liked blue and Dad liked red. They compromised on lavender and dubbed the cramped space "cozy."

Beyond the sprawling oak out back, a good-sized concord grapevine made its way along the fence. Rosemary would spread an old quilt on the ground for evening gatherings whenever the forecast promised meteor showers. Like watching Fourth of July fireworks—minus the manmade pollution—meteorites arced across the heavens. Celestial displays replaced television on those nights. We snacked on grapes, connected the dots of constellations, and pointed out every fiery white streak, the atmosphere punctuated by "ooohs" and "aaaahs."

Free from rehab, Rosemary regards every outing as an adventure. A simple excursion for fresh vegetables elicits her "ooohs" and "aaaahs" at carrots, peppers, and potatoes.

Accompanied by my husband and me to church, she finds a comfortable chair behind the congregation to avoid the hard wooden pews. After the service, a young couple, pleased to see her, invites Rose to hold their newborn son. Parishioners pass by, coo at the infant in her arms, and welcome my mother back, amazed at her quick recovery.

"Great to see you, Rose."

"Wow, look at you, up and about."

Always ready with a snappy retort, the antiquated Madonna quips, "And you thought I was hospitalized for having a stroke."

After a quizzical pause, laughter erupts from the gathered congregants. Oh, yes. Rosemary is back.

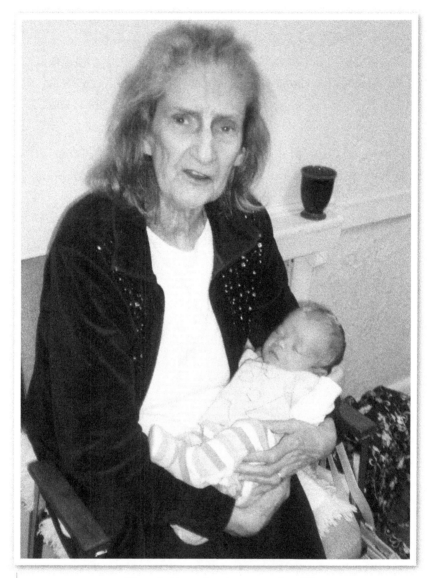

Thought I was having a stroke, eh?

STROKE 2

WHAT'S IN A NAME

Thoughts on Life ... and Death

Freedom is knowing yourself.
Freedom is accepting yourself.
Freedom is liking yourself.
Freedom is cleansing yourself of that
which you cannot like, accept, or know
– **ROSEMARY, OCTOBER 1991**

ABOUT A YEAR LATER in December 2015, the second stroke seizes control of Rosemary's feet. Similar to the first one, it walks her backward through her kitchen. Crossing the dining room in reverse, she grabs hold of a sturdy post and manages to maintain position while her feet continue their attempt to stride elsewhere. When the madcap ordeal abates a few minutes later, she calls me for help. Knowing many days may pass before she can return home, my mother insists we tidy the house before leaving for the hospital. It is useless to argue, and her feet are calm. So, I grab the jigsaw box to put away the puzzle she almost completed. Her face remains stoic as she shoves her hand through the tranquil cardboard scene. "Rothemary" is a lisping Godzilla, rising from a stream, unwittingly smashing the covered bridge depicted in the picture. I snap a quick photo that portrays her mental havoc with more passion than any words in her expansive vocabulary.

Godzilla and the Covered Bridge

At the hospital, a baffled emergency physician assumes Rosemary's described bilateral symptoms must be seizure activity. After the doctor wanders off, behind the curtained cubicle on the gurney, Rose's feet kick up a jig again, tossing the bottom half of her sheet about. She grabs the top seam to prevent the flimsy cover from escaping and leaving her exposed to the cold room. I push the nurse call button; no one comes. Twenty-two minutes later, Rose's feet relax again. No one official witnessed the telltale behavior so the doctor orders a follow-up neurology appointment, writes a prescription for who knows what, and sends her home. Stopping at the pharmacy, we grab a shopping cart for her to lean on. As I pay for the medication, Rosemary's feet take control again, and she begins walking the cart backward at a furious pace. Good fortune prevails, and the burly fellow next in line catches her before she falls or, in full throttle reverse, demolishes any store displays.

This time, the ER doc sends her straight to the neurologist, across the street from the hospital. This doctor takes a close look at her brain scan and determines that, yes, she has had another stroke. The damaged cells centered on her brain explain the signs and symptoms on both sides of her body. He points to the top of her head, the exact spot she keeps hitting on a particular kitchen cabinet door whenever she leaves it open and stands up. The doc dismisses the notion that her stroke could be trauma-induced. I imagine my mother's subcranial dead zone as a halo, encircling her precious mind.

The doctor first regards this as an expansion of last year's stroke, but reconsiders. Additional brain areas show signs of death. He orders a Montreal Cognitive Assessment, which the physician's assistant conducts right away. He asks my mom questions and has her make simple drawings. The neurologist compares her responses to damage evident on the scan. Rosemary's high level of function astonishes him.

Mom reminds the doc of her do-not-resuscitate order. To emphasize her desire for minimal intervention, she offers to have DNR tattooed across her forehead. Since her backward gallivanting has ceased, the neurologist shakes his head, stifles a snicker, and acquiesces to Rosemary's desire to return home. He increases the dosages of anticoagulants and such, prescribes additional home health nursing with speech therapy for her new "lithp," and sends her off.

First things first, we pad the kitchen cabinet door where she hits her head. A dangling towel from its knob acts as a warning flag. Next, we broach the subject of her moving in with us. Prior to the first stroke, Robert and I renovated our house in preparation for my mother moving in as her health deteriorates with age. The new bedroom faces west, and we call it the West Wing to make her feel extra special. But she voices the cliché of self-effacing resistance, "I don't want to be a burden." In all honesty, no one *wants* to feel burdened, not even by loved ones. But life without challenges, responsibilities, and duties falls meaningless. A bigger question arises: can dedication keep pace with obligation?

For now, she's just around the corner in the house she moved to seven years ago on her eightieth birthday. Daily visits between the households become routine. Sometimes she strolls the short distance to our home. Using her wheeled walker like a scooter, neighbors report Rose sometimes puts one knee on the padded seat and rides the slight descent downhill. As the device picks up speed, it wiggles something fierce, a signal for Rosemary to act her age.

The bumpy jaunt reminds her of Sunday outings when the Martins drove on Camden, New Jersey's hilly dirt track, designed for bumpy amusement. A short-lived attraction, passengers jostled about as car owners wore out their shock absorbers . . . and Herman flirted with Rosemary.

Rosemary and "Her man" forever

Rosemary first met the love of her life, Herman John Baker Jr., in the mid-1940s at an Artisans Insurance meeting in her parents' cellar. She found the twenty-year-old redhead fetching with his impish jokes, sparkly blue eyes, and dimpled chin. Instantly smitten by eighteen-year-old Rosemary's bright wit, Herman admired her stunning intellect. She marveled at his common sense. Both were able to recognize virtues in each other, not apparent to themselves.

During their courtship, Rosemary grew fond of Herman's sisters, but not their father. After the wife abuser's spouse died, Herman Sr. aimed his drunken violence at his only surviving son. Rosemary refused to call her beau by his given name. She nicknamed her future husband Blackie, an endearing, nonsensical reference to his red hair. They married on October 22, 1949, with the wedding reception at her parents' Audubon home at 240 West Atlantic. Longing for his departed mother, Herman embraced the harmonious household atmosphere, grateful to join Rosemary's family. The couple's boundless love grew. And every Christmas, they organized a big family reunion that was joined by his sisters' families as well. Rosemary made sure both sides of the family got acquainted.

Christmas 2015 approaches, and my mom feels well enough to invite folks over for the tradition she calls "rounding up the strays." Rosemary cannot bear the thought of people left lonely on a holiday. Two solitary souls join the three of us. Our Swedish friend, Lars, and Father Sebastian, a retired priest who arrives in St. Nick regalia. Mom and I orchestrate a festive feast of shrimp, ham, creamed peas, sweet potatoes stuffed into Florida orange halves, mashed potatoes, cranberry delight, apple pie, pistachio cake, and homemade whipped cream. After dinner, the five of us convene in her backyard abutting Choctawhatchee National Forest, for some semi-sedentary play. Bubble wands fly through the air, each orb filled with our wishes, prayers, and hopes. The floating talismans burst from sight, releasing their infusions into the world.

Orbs filled with hopes and prayers, set free

Mounting evidence of my mother's mental impairment becomes more obvious as we bid farewell to 2015. She phones family and friends across the country to extend "Happy New Year!" greetings, but flusters, unable to remember whom she already called. Her once well-organized desk clutters. An avid cook, she leaves the stove on full blast and forgets. Noisy kitchen timers bellow unheard alarm as she naps. Burnt meals happen often, and we suggest she keep the timer with her. Despite the danger of burning the house down with her in it, she declines to move in with us. Her courteous, "I don't want to be a burden" screams impracticality. Our daily visits increase. At least three times a day we find excuses and stay longer.

Awakening from a nap, Rosemary chats about high school classmates. She nicknamed Margaret Roth "Moth." "Maggie was short for Ann McGee. Patsy became Pat, named after her father, Frank. Your middle name, Elinor, is after your godmother, Pat."

As the calendar relinquishes its hold on January, Robert and I sit down with my mom for a serious conversation. We need to know her wishes as her health in general, and mental health in particular, continue to deteriorate. In response, she writes a directive with a simple gauge for the quality of life she wishes to keep. That lucid letter becomes invaluable as a way to honor my mother's end-of-life wishes, when she can no longer speak for herself. Specifically, she indicates that she will be content so long as she knows her own name and can recognize me.

Rosemary Jane Martin was born at home in Audubon, New Jersey, on April 12, 1928. She never understood why her parents named her after an herb. The family's modest dwelling still stands on Davis Avenue at the corner of Nicholson Place. Over the years, each time the town reorganized, the house number changed from three to six to eleven. Although never fond of her given name—Latin for dew by the sea—Rosemary appreciated the bushy, Mediterranean evergreen's savory aroma and purported health benefits as an antibacterial and antioxidant. In deference to her parents' chosen name, she grew rosemary in her garden.

We play Scrabble daily in 2016. She builds F-R-A-G-R-A-N-C-E onto my R-A-G. Our mother/daughter roles shift, and the table turns on pastime entertainment. In my teens, Mom initiated word games to build my abysmal spelling ability and address my undiagnosed dyslexia. Now, I use Scrabble to evaluate her physical and mental well-being. The search for words stimulates her mind and continues to expand my vocabulary through her exceptional language skill. Regardless of what the strokes take away, my mother's presence always constitutes a learning experience.

True to character, Rosemary interprets official game rules as mere guidelines. If badminton birdies fly the coop, improvise with ping-pong or wiffle balls. Rule books occupy one of her bookshelves: *According to Hoyle: The World-Famous Book on Rules of Games, Official Rules of Card Games, The Scrabble Brand Games Word Guide* . . . Their instructions blow the starting whistles for socializing fun to begin. Rosemary combines games to resolve disputes over what to play. Try hide-and-seek tag, Twister Simon Says, chess/checkers, and board games played from finish to start. An inventive nap time device, she looks at the ceiling, imagines the house upside down, chest deep in water, and swims from room to room.

Rosemary decrees the twofold object of any game: enjoyment and basking in good company. In the best games, *everyone* wins, for example, cooperative musical chairs as Robert Fulghum describes in his 1993 book, *Maybe, Maybe Not.* We joke that if both football teams were given their own ball, they wouldn't have to tackle one another and get hurt. For cooperative tennis, we count volleys and try to beat our highest score. Only one parameter applies: if it bounces, it counts.

In accordance with Rosemary's Scrabble rules, we join forces to cover all the red, triple-score squares. Rather than stump the opposition, players help each other make clever words. Whoever draws the *Q* announces it, and other players try to place a convenient *U.* If someone can use all seven tiles, we reserve an opportune space on the board. Toying with the English language, we invent new words. Concocted definitions convince other players the innovation warrants printing on the inside of the Scrabble game lid. Our fabricated wordishes include *shirtwide* (bodice width), *goofling* (a small klutz), *tulipee* (a spring flower recipient), *vialents* (test tubes used as weapons), *shalting* (proclaiming mandates), *wordist* (Scrabble player), and *grayhood* (old age).

My mother always loved literature, Scrabble, and etymologies. Never pedagogical, her eloquence administered blood transfusions to mediocrity. Even in casual conversation, she used her expansive vocabulary with proficiency. Her English mastery had a strong impact on my siblings and me.

At age six, I taught my four-year-old brother the thrill of compound words. Neither of us understood why an ink implement, an adult male, and a seaworthy vessel combined to mean writing quality. But Marty became the kindergarten kid who could spell "pen-man-ship," instilled with self-confidence for the rest of his education.

In Rosemary's company, language surpassed superficial communication. There's more to speech than any dictionary can convey. "You don't have to be a linguist to take pleasure in the way certain words roll off your tongue." Ethiopia, iconoclast, onomatopoeia, and sprocket turn your mouth into a pronunciation playground.

My mother's fascination with the world extended beyond the limits of language. She recognized that no religion can encompass divine nature and that sciences only skim the surface. Experience is our litmus test for personal relevance. One need not be a physicist to appreciate the paisley patterns of fractals, to sense the vibrations of string theory, or marvel at the transitional phenomenon of matter and energy. My mother's nonchalant awe was contagious.

Months since Rosemary's last stroke, the debilitating affects take indelible form. I open her kitchen drawer to a surprising sight. Instead of using the handy self-stick labels to note what leftovers her storage containers hold, she has written their temporary contents in permanent ink, directly on the plastic lids. I point the overlapping scribbles out to her. She laughs with keen awareness of the demented absurdity. "Remember the writing on the walls before your father wood-paneled over the crumbling plaster?"

Dad was a wanna-be carpenter with a fondness for the smell of sawdust and a tempered thrill at the sight of shaven wood curls. In the early 1960s, he decided to tackle the home improvement task on our new abode in Oaklyn, New Jersey. We were school-aged kids at the time and mom gave us permission to sign the old walls before Dad paneled over them. As major household projects go, the work took longer than expected. Weeks turned to months as uncles and VFW (Veterans of Foreign Wars) buddies came to help. The guys weren't just playing Tiddlywinks either. They tackled the task with inventive determination. Mom's canning pot steamed long strips of wood that they bent into contoured archways.

Wall signatures expanded to art doodles and homework math calculations. Those who happened by–friends, the paperboy, solicitors, the milkman, neighbors–added their John Hancocks, words of wisdom, inspirations, and illustrations. Eight-year-old Marty climbed a chair he'd balanced on the couch to write a joke over one arch. It cracked us up: "Old Farmer Brown kicked the bucket; he died of a broken toe." Our walls were a neighborhood sensation.

Until her strokes, Rosemary's generous meals were a Florida neighborhood attraction. But cooking issues continue to worsen. Would-be meals char. Casual drop-ins escalate to urgent interventions. Smoke alarms blare while Rosemary naps in oblivion. The occupational therapist urges me to forbid my mother from cooking without supervision. The advice hits with a double blow. *How does a daughter halt her mother from doing what she loves?* Meal preparation, once a part of her identity, is fading away.

Rosemary's kitchen clutters with automatic timers, gifts from friends concerned over the risky situation. Mom agrees to call me before using the stove. I become her backup. When it's time to turn off the heat, I call. If she doesn't answer, I sprint over. Routine strolls around the corner become dashes of trepidation.

Since young Rosey could lift a skillet, she catered to others. Like homecomings, her best childhood memories formed around neighborhood meals her parents organized during Depression-era shortages.

Matriarchal *Großmuter* (German for grandmother) grew plentiful victory gardens. And Rosemary's Irish Uncle Tom always came prepared to cook with his own set of carving knives. Appreciative guests hailed Chef Thomas McGlynn at renowned venues where he presided: Philadelphia's Bingham House, Duke of Gloucester's Washington Park Hotel, and South Mountain Manor in the Poconos. Rosemary accompanied her family on rare outings to these glamorous retreats, joined by characters like Johnny Engstrom who relished "beans-on-a-stick" (corn on the cob) and Henry Beck, author of *Forgotten Towns of Southern New Jersey* (1936).

Asked to draw a tree, adult Rosemary drew a telling rendition "loaded with fruit to nourish passing people." As a senior, she served Saturday meals to hungry family, "old codgers," and visiting firemen. After my father died, cooking gave Mom a sense of purpose that coaxed her out of her mournful shell. Rosemary meals were as much about good company as good food.

My mom's apple pie put every other one I've tasted to shame. Winesaps and Braeburns unavailable, she used Granny Smiths. Crisp, slightly sweet, tart fruit hunkered inside a flaky crust. Fresh-baked, the aroma beckoned passersby. Her signature cinnamon buns were worth writing home about. And her spaghetti sauce–made with Jersey tomatoes–was unsurpassed. Rosemary was no gourmet cook, but she loaded her meals with TLC (tender loving care). What her feasts lacked in finesse, she made up for in devotion to the mouths she fed, catering to dietary restrictions. Fat-free, reduced salt, nondairy, no pork, vegetarian, vegan . . . she customized every banquet to her guests.

Never squeamish, Rose would cut her fingers mincing celery, garlic, or onions and shrug off the weeping wound. "A bit of added protein in the sauce shows you put your heart into it."

In her eighties now, Rosemary's dining table holds more puzzles than meals. Two-thousand-piece jigsaws sit incomplete for months instead of days. On her desk, overdue notices stack like playing cards with less than a full deck.

Previously conscientious at keeping her financial affairs in order, my mother asks for help with bills. I streamline her financial ledger. Holding a full house of past due bills, I put her expenses on automatic payment. Name variations on envelopes signify how long since updated. Most say "Herman" or "Mrs. Herman Baker." One reads "HermanRoseB." Regardless the circumstances, this Rose—by any name—is forever my sweet Mom.

Mother's Day, Rosemary receives customary greeting cards. She knows this isn't supposed to be a celebration of motherhood. Like other national holidays, World War II distorted the peacemaking aspirations of its founder.

The original intent of Mothers' Peace Day (not to be confused with its distortion into Mother's Day) honored the humanity of people who were deemed enemies. Its founder—remembered for her pro-war song, "The Battle Hymn of the Republic"—Julia Ward Howe had second thoughts. The Civil War taught her the costs of combat, and she channeled her visceral disdain for war into the motherhood proclamation. A call for worldwide disarmament, the 1870 proclamation beseeched every mother on Earth to discourage their men from participating in violence. Recognizing "enemies" as human—not as adversaries, but as other mothers' beloved family members—curbs the savage proclivity to kill. Julia tapped into an institution more powerful than politics: motherhood.

Rosemary regards no one as an enemy, although she disdains her father-in-law's drunken abuse, neighbor Bill's blatant bitterness toward his stepdaughter, bullies who torment, and politicians who usurp power for personal gain. "They deserve annoying mosquito bites." That's the worst Rose wishes on them. Hearing a fisticuffs brawl on TV gets her goat: "For God's sake, use your words." Dreadful misdeeds raise Rosemary's hackles to threats of stern conversation: "I have a bone to pick with that person." Her confidence in others' humanity prevails, even if they forget it themselves.

Early one morning, I awaken to furious knocks on our front door. A neighbor informs us that Rosemary fell. I sprint over and launch up the driveway. Holding my breath, as if to freeze time, I brace for what awaits. Neighbor Tim kneels beside her in the garage.

"Chris?" My mom sprawls in a heap on the two cement steps that led up from the garage into her kitchen. The door open, she rests half in and half out of the house.

Conscious, the paramedic in me notes, heaving a sigh of relief. "Don't move, Mom." Checking her vital signs, I search for injuries. Tim reports she staggered and collapsed, but it was not a hard fall.

Rose confirms. "Nothing hurts. I got the trash cans to the curb. Coming back, my knees buckled. I was too tired to climb the steps, so I flopped down." Her cheek rested on the kitchen floor, and she complains how dirty it looks from that angle. "I just mopped here yesterday."

Tim helps me get her inside before he leaves for work. I call my sister Beth in New Jersey for moral support. She rises to the occasion and orders a wagon for our mother to cart the trash cans.

A week later, the wheeled conveyance arrives, and neighbor Randy assembles it for Rosemary. Her strength regained, she bakes cinnamon bun "thank-yous" for our helpful neighbors. The wagon reminds us of Beth's thoughtfulness. Mom finds it convenient for yardwork, a practical "pick-up-sticks" tote.

Summer in Florida cranks up to a slow sizzle as June advances toward July. My mother's health remains precarious with day-to-day ups and downs. Robert and I keep fit with frequent jogs to her home. The changes in seasons and months that Rosemary once clocked like an efficiency expert now pass by her unnoticed.

"I'm having an absent-minded morning. I forget, and then forget I forgot, so it doesn't matter." Rosemary takes dementia in stride, rejecting prospects of moving in with us. No way.

STROKE 3
SISYPHEAN REHAB:
A PERPETUAL PURSUIT
OF HEALTH

Stalactites form
on drip nodules of paint
in manmade subway caverns.
– ROSEMARY, 1970S

THE THIRD STROKE BEGINS WITH a few ministrokes. Under the summer sun, Rosemary dons her "Old Broad Power" tank top. Her speech suddenly slurs with a ministroke, then another, but each subsides within minutes. No dancing feet this time. Last episode, the ER doc sent her to the neurologist, so we beeline straight to his office. The specialist looks her over, detects another full-blown stroke occurring, and sends us across the street to the hospital. The medical cycle commences once again, and Rosemary winds up back in rehab.

Although ominous, strokes become routine to my mother. By no fault or choice of her own, Rosemary embodies Sisyphus, pushing post-stroke boulders uphill. Eager to please and to recover, she puts her heart into every rehabilitation exercise. Hard work pays off; Rosemary recuperates more each day. Fine motor control improves with occupational therapy.

Her penmanship nears legible once more. The lisp vanishes and proper pronunciation returns with speech therapy. Physical therapists determine she can now get up from the floor on her own.

After each stroke to date, however, before Rosemary reaches peak function, another one hits, and she must begin again from even further downhill.

Brace for impact, I tell myself with every stroke, in anticipation of my mother's death. Unexpected fatalities—like my brother's brain cancer—hit like lightning bolts. In contrast, dementia trickles Rosemary away like rain. Weight drops, anemia worsens. Her complexion resembles once-colorful fabric, blanched with bleach, and hung over brittle twigs. Episode upon episode, year by year, my mother dissipates before my eyes.

Twenty-four/seven dementia caregiving redefines what constitutes a challenge. Running is a breeze compared to circling the block in tiny, snail's pace steps. Forget crocheting an afghan or French braiding hair; try getting a mother's wayward arm through a sleeve. No finish line in sight, it seems unlikely that the finale will be in any way beautiful. But we'll just see about that.

Rosemary's introduction to motherhood in the early 1950s caught her off guard. Their beautiful firstborn's enlarged thymus forced the young couple to stay with her parents for several years. Bethany's illness caused projectile vomiting and cyanosis. Two years later and still alarmed over Beth's infirmity, Rose gave birth to a second daughter, me. My wide-set eyes filled Rosemary with misplaced trepidation that this baby had Down syndrome. Those first years, her daughters were in the care of a mom aghast by motherhood.

Stroke number three leaves Rosemary as befuddled as early parenthood. Nevertheless, she recognizes the rehabilitation center and understands its significance. Her gait less confident, she shuffles along the hallways. This time her walker never leaves the floor. As we pass rooms once occupied by people we knew and loved, she recalls everyone else who had spent time here, except herself.

"This is Uncle Ho's old room. Homer sure belly laughed when he read the comics. Over there is where Ruth died. She should never have tried to lift that sewing machine by herself. This is the room where we visited your cousin's wife. What was she doing here so young? Here's the hall where our neighbor Joe stayed when he could no longer care for himself. Didn't he start the local Audubon Society chapter?" Her mind plays tricks on her, but Rosemary's memories of her people remain as vivid as her heart is big.

Passing the therapy wing, she pauses. "That's not right. Where's the bear grass?" A few questions later, I realize she recalls the building when it was new, this entire section once a field of lush trees and vegetation.

Decades ago, Fort Walton Rehabilitation Center was constructed as a nursing home. On moving day 1987, when the doors first opened, our able-bodied family members helped transport patients from the previous place—the old, repurposed Fort Walton hospital (where a pair of drinking fountains sported creepy labels "Colored" and "White")—to this shiny new facility on the rural outskirts at that time, off Old Dump Road. My parents, husband, and I drove back and forth shuttling residents to the new place.

Many patients were stroke survivors. A good-natured wheelchair user I'll call Sylvia could only say, "No, no, no, no, no, no, no," always sung seven times in the same pleasant tone. And poor Betty (pseudonym) seemed plagued by her remaining vocabulary, limited to

A mother/daughter mind meld

the alphabet, but without the letter *H* and ending with an annoyed expletive, "You GDSOB," before beginning again in rapid succession. Despite their frustrations, when moving day arrived, the "no nos" rang with heightened exuberance, and the alphabet resounded with uncommon cheer. As Rosemary wheeled her old neighbor Joe in from the car, he identified killdeer plover scurrying through bear grass on land that would one day become the therapy wing.

Back home from rehab after this third stroke, daily functions pose greater challenges. Rosemary still keeps a tidy household but requires more adaptations. Colorful Post-it Notes festoon her home: "Call Chris before cooking" beside the stove, "Brush your teeth" on the bathroom mirror, "Put phone in your pocket" stuck to the charger on her dresser. Her wheeled walker sports a basket for carting things from room to room—dishes, a short-handled dustpan and its brush, birthday cards to send this month, and a notebook. The pages keep track of needed groceries and record her fleeting thoughts. She wraps a needle, thread, and scissors in garments to mend, peeking over the no-frills basket rim.

Like her seamstress mother, Rosemary made her children's outfits. Lacking technical skill, she compensated with designer joie de vivre. Any Halloween costume we chose, she made. Over the years, I was Little Bo-Peep, an elephant, a box turtle . . . Daughter Beth did a stint as a princess, wearing Mom's tiara. Marty was a fully set dining room table—dishes, silverware, napkins—in anticipation of his favorite holiday, Thanksgiving.

My sister and I wore school outfits lined with love. Granny also designed apparel for our dolls. No disproportioned Barbies, my Tammy, Ted, Toni, Shirley, Penny, Betsy, and Freckles all got outfits. Even my trolls received tiny garments, fashioned from remnants.

For winters, Mom transformed a moth-eaten, Persian lamb coat into muffs for her girls. Leftover swatches became stuffed animals for newborns in the extended family. Summer 1958, Rosemary made Tarzan-style leopard swimsuits for our family. We only wore them once, due to uncomfortable design flaws and terrycloth's absorption when wet. Exiting the Atlantic Ocean, Dad had to hold up his drawers. But those bathing suits left a sense of close-knit family worth every stitch.

1958: Baker family "down the shore" in Avalon, NJ

Always accommodating, Rosemary begins welcoming a succession of tenants, church members, and active-duty air force recruits into her home. In exchange for low rent, meals, and an occasional button sewn back in place, guests pitch in with heavy chores. Live-in helpers oversee her cooking. When renters are away, I remove stove and oven knobs so my mother can't cook without supervision. Robert and I stop by to take out the trash, taste her meals, change light bulbs, ask her advice, play Scrabble . . . any excuse so she doesn't feel intruded upon or, worse, like an inconvenience.

A third line on our family phone plan costs less than one of those "Help! I've-fallen-and-I-can't-get-up!" security buttons. Rosemary now keeps her flip phone on her for emergencies and as a "Help,-I'm-talking-and-I-can't-shut-up!" socializing accessory. She only wears garments with pockets. Stuffed full, they hold the phone, notes to herself, a pen and pad, and many hankies.

In her teens following World War II, Rosemary's nose started running chronically and never stopped. She also developed asthma, but her lungs recuperated decades later when my dad broke his two-packs-a-day cigarette habit. Back then, nicotine addiction and the effects of secondhand smoke were unacknowledged.

Although her lungs cleared, the torrent from her nose continued her entire life. She always had a handkerchief ready in her pocket, shoved up her sleeve, or tucked into her brassiere peeking out of her blouse. As a young mother, she had us spit on a clean hankie to wipe our grimy faces. Until used, the crumpled cloths resembled lovely nosegays.

An impressive hanky collection evolved over the years. In Rose's teens, she washed used hankies twice, fed them through her mother's wringer washer, and then ironed each one. Everything got ironed in those days. Long before recycling gained popularity, she shunned disposable tissues. Over the years, Rose received new hankies for Christmas and birthdays, some with fancy tatted edges, others with beautiful embroidery. But she preferred the oldest, softest ones, hand-sewn from her pop's old shirttails. Threadbare, they gradually disintegrated into more holes than fabric.

Rosemary no longer keeps track of hankies. She resigns herself to blowing that nose of hers into leftover hospital tissues, paper napkins, or a handy square of toilet paper. Even so, that iconic corsage look begs me to tuck a few fabric charms into her pockets every morning. In the stand beside her bed, clean stacks of hankies await her nose's bidding.

Overnight, her flip phone cradles on its charger within arm's reach. Come morning, I safety-pin the phone's lanyard strap under her collar for safe keeping. When someone calls, she reels in the ringing thing like a flopping fish. Hands fumble, trying to open the slippery thing before the caller hangs up. Besides her link to the outside world, the flip phone assures that we can call and track her down if she wanders from home. As we feared, one day a neighbor spots her a block away, staggering along without her walker.

Escorting her home, arm in arm, I listen as Rosemary explains the nature of her escapade: "I heard a noise and wanted to identify the source." The mischievous sparkle in her eyes reveals a deeper motive. She wants to join in whatever fun happens beyond her windows. Seated on a porch chair, she watches box turtles mosey, rabbits sniff, and squirrels hop in the fern. Weather permitting, we vow to take her for daily walks to curtail cabin fever.

Back indoors, an Asimov volume on the bookshelf catches her eye. Dementia-hindered comprehension fails to daunt her. Instantly engrossed, she flips through the pages, determined to understand.

I ask what it's about.

"I'm reading a sci-fi, but it's more sigh than fiction."

Rosemary was a frail, anemic child. At age eight, she weighed only thirty-three pounds. To avoid exposure to illness, her parents kept their youngest out of school the entire third grade. Rosie entertained herself by reading through her parents' bookshelves.

Everything, cover to cover. She read *The Wonderful Wizard of Oz*, a Charles Dickens collection, Edna St. Vincent Millay, Shakespeare, Melville's *The Scrivener*, Erle Stanley Gardner's detective series, *The Sound and the Fury*, *A Farewell to Arms*, *Ulysses*, *Egyptian Queen*, *Little Women*, *The Call of the Wild*, *Walden Pond*, *Tarzan of the Apes . . .*

Friends who stopped by to play after school often found Rosemary's nose in the dictionary. In characteristic reading spots, Rose snuggled into the pocketed wicker chair, journeying through World Book Encyclopedias. Or she'd straddle a weeping willow branch, book balanced on the wide limb. She most treasured her grandmother's 1936 illustrated *Garden Encyclopedia*. Once all were read, Rosey began again.

The magnetic pull of printed words continues to attract adult Rosemary, regardless the source—newspapers, cereal boxes, clothing labels. Asked what books she likes best, autodidactic Rose shows no favoritism. "I'm an omnivorous reader."

The Shakespeare collection's volume seven most captivated her attention as a child, but she cannot recall why. Once, hours of sedentary reading time allowed her eight-year-old body to recuperate from illness. Now reading allows her mind to recuperate from strokes.

Despite her smarts, Rosemary failed to develop an appropriate sense of self-worth. To compensate, she tries to redeem herself through service.

"Everybody takes such good care of me. It's not like I'm an antique that can be cashed in." She has no idea the depth of her value to those who love her.

Adult niece Judy came to visit Aunt Ro in the 1970s and insisted her daughters behave with due respect to their cherished aunt. Turning a blind eye to her own mischievous childhood, Judy reprimanded the girls for running in the house. But rambunctious clamor failed to fray Rosemary's nerves. Truth be told, she celebrated light-hearted commotion. Never one to chastise kids for being kids, she simply requested they "keep it down to a dull roar."

Rose's toddler grandson David, dachshund Emily, and shepherd-mix Aargh joined the chase with grand-nieces Mary and Susan dashing in the back door, out the front, and around the yard, over and over. Gleeful Aunt Ro soothed Judy with a rationalization: the raucous pursuit was not so much running in the house as just passing through.

STROKE 4

THE CHILD
WITHIN

An arm of cloud reaches downward
with clenched fist
and flexes a vaporous bicep.
– ROSEMARY, 1990s

OUR COUNTRY WITNESSES the 2017 presidential inaugu-
ration of Donald Trump in January, an event Rosemary considers
a national calamity, the stress a contributing factor to her fourth stroke.
Heading for the bathroom at dawn, her legs give way and she topples
to the floor. A dear childhood friend, Pat, happens to be visiting, asleep
in the next room. Rosemary, all too familiar with stroke symptoms, calls
out for help.

"I'm having another 'thdroke.'" Lying prostrate on the carpet,
semiconscious Rose struggles to make her lisping mouth cooperate.

Pat dials 9-1-1 and then calls me. I dash around the corner in my
pajamas and find my mother paralyzed on the left side of her body. Torn
between my disciplined paramedic response and my desire to honor my
mom's DNR wish, I ask what she wants us to do for her. She struggles

to respond but cannot. The ambulance arrives, and she regains use of her left side. Just a ministroke? No such luck. Sensation in that hand remains limited, never to return.

Her speech gradually improves with an intermittent lisp. That does not stop Rosemary from speaking her mind, determined to regain control of her tongue.

"My mouth will be the 'lathd' thing to go," she always tells us.

Absurdity never escapes Rosemary's detection. Seated in the ambulance front passenger seat, I hear indecipherable banter in the back. Serious tones from the paramedics alternate with Mom's mumbles and bursts of laughter, no doubt in response to Rose's zingers. Arriving at the emergency room, the paramedics wheel the stretcher in through the automatic glass doors. As the partition closes to the world outside, the attending physician approaches my mother. She addresses him with a comment to cap her condition.

"Whoever coined the phrase 'a stroke of luck' had a warped sense of humor."

Playful wittiness infused my mother's character. One sweltering summer day, she put wet laundry in the freezer for a few hours. Donning a heavy coat, earmuffs, and gloves, she hung the frozen garb on the clothesline to prank our next-door-neighbor. Sweaty in Bermuda shorts, the woman stared nonplused as Rosemary feigned shivering frustration with the icy winter cold.

Frazzled by wayward children, young mother Rose spiced reprimands with irreverent humor: "Stop, or I'll flush you down the toilet with all the other little turds." She expressed disappointment with, "What am I, chopped liver?" and exasperation with "Cripes!" or remnants of a square dance call: "Jesus to Jesus and eight hands around!" Making light of heated issues was Rosemary's refreshing way to cool tempers.

Hospital tests and treatments commence for the fourth stroke, and a strange anomaly occurs. The doctor orders a urinalysis, but Rose cannot produce. She squeezes my hand as the nurse catheterizes her to collect a urine sample. Nothing. Her distended abdomen could indicate a bleed from the fall. But she collapsed onto the carpeted floor before she made it to the bathroom. Surely her bladder remains full. Then, to everyone's surprise, Rosemary coughs and the catheter bag fills. The physician offers no medical explanation, but for months to come, Rose must cough to urinate.

Another curious thing happens with this stroke, something wondrous. Once in a while, a distinct radiance lights Rosemary's face. She downright glows as if I can see her aura.

"Whoa, look at her face. She's literally beaming!" exclaims Robert. *It's not my imagination*, I assure myself. Wide-eyed, Rosey blinks like a child peering through a window at Santa's workshop. The bustling emergency department delights her. An exuberant, little-girl squeal comes from my mother's lips as the automatic blood pressure cuff inflates around her arm.

"Wheeeee!" overrides the mechanical hiss. This stroke revives the blissful child Rosey—stifled for much of her adult life. My mother's enchanting three-year-old self comes out to play.

On the ER stretcher for hours, Rose looks upward. "Great view from here," she comments as if outdoors, discerning cloud formations through willow branches. Eager for whatever happens next, she glances my direction and does a double take. "Chris, why are you wearing owl pajamas?" her motherly voice returns.

She's right. I'd forgotten. My husband brings me clothes and stays with her while I change in the restroom. Five hours pass. I fetch more warmed blankets for my shivering mom. Assorted technicians enter the cubicle, look at her bare wrists, and get the same baffled expression when they find no hospital bracelet.

"I'm an unidentified, lying object," Rosey tells them with a mischievous grin.

1931, Richard, Rosemary, and William Martin

The youngest of the six Martin children, Rosey adored her siblings. The girls—Helen ("Dolly"), Anna Mae ("Annie"), and Regina ("Jean")—loved their baby sister, but a decade older, they disappeared with teens their own age. Next in line, brothers William and Richard shared a close bond with each other. The boys came to expect the undivided attention from their parents, until Rosemary's birth. They found the baby intolerable and referred to her as a "spoiled brat." Young Rosey took their insults to heart and tried to compensate by indulging the duo. Even as a small child, she prepared meals for her big brothers and cleaned up after them, happy to be in their company.

Every night, their Irish pop read bedtime stories to his three youngest. During the day, their German mom donned an apron and kept an efficient, lively household, singing as she worked. The couple cherished each other and expressed affection with loving glances, fond embraces, and passing pecks on the cheek. In Rosey's eyes, her parents were models of an ideal marriage.

Following the ER marathon and admission, Rosemary rests in the relative comfort of a hospital bed. More hungry than tired, she asks about breakfast. Grandniece Erika, who lives in nearby Destin, brings Aunt Rosie her favorite dessert, a raspberry jelly donut. Erika arrives accompanied by the youngest members of her brood, fondly referred to as "the littles."

A sparkle of wonder befalls Rosemary. Watching her playful great-grandnieces, young Rosey resurfaces again. Her eyes twinkle as she goes after the donut. But her desensitized left hand baffles her. She looks at the appendage as if a puppet on the end of her arm. Damaged brain cells do not work well with others. The muted sensation "feels like it's bandaged all over."

Rosemary takes it in stride, stumbling over random thoughts and flapping her hand like a limp noodle. Hunger steers her attention back to food. Pure glee turns the challenge of locating her lips into amusement. The uncooperative hand wavers in the air, trying to find its target. Mouth wide open, her head bobs in anticipation. The kids try to help with the donut's trajectory. Jelly and powdered sugar adorn Rosey's face. Laughter sprinkles every bite. Nurses come to check the patient and join the merriment.

The donut down the hatch, Aunt Rosie needs her teeth brushed. The three- and seven-year-olds, eager to help, have no idea a simple task can be such a chore for someone in bed. With motherly determination, they wipe drool from Rosemary's chin. Cooperative Rose makes it a memorable experience for the little girls attending to their auntie like a baby doll.

Looking elderly, acting girlish, Rosey quotes her mother: "Be true to your teeth and they'll never be false to you." Then with child-to-child approval, she adds, "Thank you for wiping my messy face." Rosemary's admiration for little ones in the family has deep roots.

Until age six, Rose felt lonely and purposeless. That all changed starting in 1934 with the birth of her first nephew. Rosemary expressed unconditional devotion to Buddy, the firstborn of her eldest sister Dolly's fifteen children.

As the extended family grew in age and number, no niece or nephew in Aunt Rosie's presence felt unappreciated. Never condescending, she knew each child on their own terms. At reunions of our expansive horde of relatives—for weddings, baby showers, Christenings, funerals, and holidays—Rose watched over younger family members with an attentive eye. She sterilized glass baby bottles, fed infants, and changed cloth diapers, careful not to impale delicate flesh with safety pins. Dishing toddlers' plates, she responded respectfully to their babble. During a torrential rain, she rushed her orneriest nephew, "Happy," indoors, worried no one else would bother. For the older kids, she improvised games, demonstrated calisthenics, and taught them how to climb trees. Always on the lookout for loose shoelaces or runny noses, she found ways to acknowledge every child's valued existence.

Thirty-three nieces and nephews spanning two generations adored their Aunt Rosie. Lacking spare money for Christmas presents, she handmade gifts for each child. One year, Rosemary sewed cloth dolls for all fourteen nieces, each with hair the color of their own, every strand stitched from scraps of yarn. As they aged and their numbers increased, she managed to afford for each to get a pair of socks with fresh dollar bills in the toes. Later, adult couples received homemade cinnamon buns. Wrapped in plain foil, she decorated with red and green ribbons, curling the strands with a scissors' edge.

Rosemary's assigned hospital room beside the busy nursing station allows close supervision. She mistakes noisy shift change activity for a family reunion. Above boisterous commotion, she beckons me.

"Chris, it sounds like quite a gang. We need plenty of vegetables to feed all these people." Always a diligent host, feeding crowds is part of Rosemary's personality.

Local folks visit Rose in the hospital. Those who live far away send cards and flowers. Hung on her walls, memory-cueing photographs remind her of their love. They also send a subliminal message to medical staff that she is deserving of their care. Compassion is contagious. Patients who receive no cards lie at risk of being treated with inadvertent indifference. For this reason, we share my mother's extra cards—the ones without personalized messages—with neglected, unconscious souls. Rose would approve of the Robin Hood caper.

Transferred to rehab again, Rosemary knows people but not places, and cannot keep track of time. All over the map, she thinks she's in Rhode Island where my brother lived. She then shifts to other locales . . . that don't exist.

"Shalimar, New Jersey. I've been living in Florida for the past few months." No point telling her she's lived here for three decades.

When Rose speaks, you never know what's going to come out. Neither does she.

"My communicator is broken," she sighs. "If anyone wants me to jump tall buildings in a single bound, it'll just have to wait," SuperRose shrugs.

During rare moments, Rosemary sounds like herself. Then she slips off to some other dimension. She notices when disjointed words do not make sense, but can only shrug and go along on the madcap ride.

"My brain is in scraps. My mind is a scrapbook in no coherent order."

Often Rose gets stuck on a subject and becomes repetitious, like a record player needle trapped in a damaged vinyl grove. But she is not alone. Those in her presence get caught in her gravitational pull, circling around and around with her.

During these incessant fugues, singing the first line from her vast repertoire of songs puts her back on track. Her mind holds a storehouse of lyrics, including obscure overtures and forgotten verses. Coaxed into a tune about a jack-of-all-trades, she picks up the cue for "The Old Umbrella Man" and her tattered mind abandons its vicious replay. Melodies guide Rosemary along familiar paths home.

Singing societies were integral to Rosemary's matriarchal family, the Schwab and Kohler branches, in Konstanz, Germany, and later as US citizens in Philadelphia. The patriarchal Irish side gathered at pub sing-alongs. But famine forced their migration to England, where the children found little to sing about working dawn to dusk in Manchester factories. The next generation sought a better life in the United States where they regained their lilts of laughter.

Music permeated Rosemary's childhood. Like generations before, her parents, Anne and William Martin, kept their home melodious. Her pop hummed and whistled while working. Her mother organized Sweet Adelines chapters in South Jersey and Fort Lauderdale. Singing filled Rosemary's world.

For Rosemary's children, standard-issue pianos equipped kindergarten through third-grade classrooms. Bingham Elementary teachers taught lessons through song—everything from seasonal changes to calendar structure to traffic safety. After school, our mom played records on the portable player—33 rpms, small yellow and red 45s, and heavy, black 78s. The little machine had no slow speed for her 16 rpm records; played at 33 , the voices sounded like the Three Chipmunks.

Together, we sang Disney tunes: "I'm a Happy Mouse," "Perri, the Little Girl Squirrel," and "A Rolling Stone." A rapid-paced rendition of "The Three Little Pigs" captivated our attention. Danny Kaye's "Ugly Duckling" reminded us of the Hans Christian Andersen film. Mom's old 78s played "My Grandfather's Clock," "Cement Mixer," "Yankee Doodle," "Hooray, Hooray I'm Goin' Away," "If I Knew You Were Comin' I'd've Baked a Cake," and polkas galore.

Undaunted by damaged record skips, we anticipated redundancy and sang along. "Roll out the barrel, we'll have a ba, a ba, a ba." At age five, Marty knew the trick of balancing coins on the player arm to bypass scratches. A dime would suffice, then it would require a penny, then a nickel, a quarter . . . the method gradually made the vinyl unsalvageable. But sing-alongs etched beautiful memories, second only to breathing . . . and talking.

Strolling past the rehab nurses' station, Rosemary sings "I Love to Walk in the Rain," odd since sunny weather beams through the windows. She clutches tight to my arm to avoid falling. Mental jumble forces her to think through every baby step. Despite the clumsy gait, her stumbling feet lead onward, undeterred.

Rose takes interest in a nurse pulling a small oxygen tank on wheels. "That's a funny-looking dog you've got there, girly."

Over the years, Rosemary housed way more pets than people. Menageries of birdcages, fishbowls, rabbit hutches, and improvised shelters for turtles, frogs, a cecropia moth, hamsters, guinea pigs, crayfish, snails . . . occupied every spare space. We thought of pets as friends, unaware that it is impossible to befriend those held captive. Snuggly dogs and cats were more like family members. But allergies precluded most cats from cohabitation with Rosemary and her children.

Since limited gene pools produce defects, we preferred mixed breeds. A cocker spaniel/Lab puppy, black with a white chest, joined our family when we girls were toddlers. My big sister Beth named the pleasant pooch Charlie, Barley, Buck, and Rye after her favorite nursery rhyme. "Charlie" for short. Over the years, ungainly Aargh waggled into our lives, then Great Dane/ Lab galoot Ben, tail-lost-to-window-slam cat Drusilla, and Lab/ springer spaniel beauty Knickerbocker. And last to win our hearts, astute Aussie/Lab mix Splash enjoyed the shared custody of Rosemary and us.

Although pet therapy is beneficial, all we see at this rehab center are people. Quality care comes in other forms—physical therapy, occupational therapy, and speech therapy five days a week. Staff members who know Rose from previous strokes eagerly work with her. A new nurse reintroduces herself as Barbara and points to the badge affixed to her uniform.

"That must be why they labeled you as such," Rosemary remarks.

At my mother's house, I pack a suitcase for her with some nice outfits, but not too nice. A well-kempt Rosemary will assure staff she is loved, persuading them to respond in kind. But due to nursing home tendencies for things to go missing, I select expendables. After one last look in her closet, I make an exception and grab a brightly colored sweater she likes that I find unbecoming. Its colors bleed into the grayish hue of overcooked vegetables, and the bulky thing hangs on her like wet fur on an unhappy dog.

The following morning at rehab, just as I anticipated, the sacrificial sweater has vanished. A mixture of conflicting emotions overcomes me. My decision to only bring superfluous clothes is validated, but I'm annoyed that someone stole from my sweet mom. There's more. Although ashamed of myself for disrespecting my mother's preference, I'm relieved that the oversized knit is gone. But a deeper sense of loss comes with the garment's disappearance. My mother doesn't care. Except for when Rosey surfaces, the part of her that has preferences has been spirited away . . . just like the sweater.

Rosemary remembers visiting other infirm patients at this rehab facility but, like before, she has no recollection of residing here twice herself. On a curious note, she tells me of occasional visits from people long passed—her parents, my brother Martin, my dad . . . . Often, Rosemary asks about her five deceased siblings.

"Is Dolly still alive? Do Annie and Ho still have their Avalon place? Where does Jean live now? How long does it take them to get here? Are my brothers coming to visit again?"

Skeptics dismiss visits from bygone loved ones as nothing but phantom traces of cerebral collapse. We consult with the death doula hired out of pocket. An emerging profession similar to birth doulas but for end-of-life care, death doulas provide comforting knowledge about dying to people on the verge and their loved ones. Insurance does not yet cover the growing, non-medical field. Even with my paramedic background, I found the service invaluable.

Our death doula Deborah takes a broad view on visits from the dead. As the veil between life and death thins, no one knows with certainty the significance of these common, pleasant calls from loved ones passed. Describing these occurrences with friends, an incident from Rosemary's distant past come to light. Apparently, she experienced a similar vision, long before dementia took its toll.

Grossmom was Rosey's adored maternal grandmother. From age six, Rose shared a bed with the matriarch. Born Ida Helen Schwab of Konstanz, Germany in 1868, she died in 1938 when Rosey was nine. A year later, Rosemary confided to her friend Patsy that Grossmom still paid visits.

"If I tell anyone else, they'll think I'm nuts. But they think that anyway," Pat recalls Rosemary saying as they walked alongside the house by Grossy's orange blossom bush.

"There she is!" Overjoyed, Rosey pointed to the garden. Patsy gasped. Transfixed, both ten-year-olds watched as the elderly apparition, wearing a dark gray dress with an apron, tended the hollyhocks. The girls never forgot that ethereal encounter.

Regaining her grasp on earthly reality, Rosemary works on her diction and swallowing ability. Through speech therapy, her pronunciation improves, but the lisp from this stroke sometimes reemerges.

"My thpeech ith thlurry. I theem to have a thurpluth of etheth." Playful Rosey's self-mockery sets listeners at ease.

A lover of the written word since age eight, Rosemary still reads well and rereads letters people send wishing her a speedy recovery. From my father's death in 1992 until this 2017 stroke, Rose always kept a TV on for company. Now television bothers her. She finds the fast-paced images and rapid speech disconcerting. Even her favorite shows confuse her.

The Weather Channel kept pre-stroke Rose company on a daily basis. National updates helped her keep tabs on extended family's well-being. "Looks like snow for Eileen on Lake Tahoe. Hope Barbara carries an umbrella today in North Carolina. Gusty for Mart in Newport."

Her most prized weekly show was the last few minutes of *Sunday Morning* with its nature scenes and sounds. And she never missed an episode of *Jeopardy* or *Wheel of Fortune*, belting out correct answers before the contestants. Except for inane topics like sports and celebrity trivia, Rosemary latched onto challenging subjects—history, mythology, culture, literature, etymology, geography, science, religion, old films. From the kitchen with dough-covered hands or folding laundry on the dining room table, her voiced responses were echoed by lucky competitors.

Understaffed nursing homes and childcare centers tend to use televisions as babysitters. Not for Rosemary—unable to follow plots, her rehab room's TV remains silent. Her personalized additions to weather forecasts cease.

My husband and I visit daily, call often, and when her disorientation worsens, I spend the night. But we are not alone in our efforts. Like redwood groves sharing nutrients through interconnected roots, friends help oversee Rosemary's care when I cannot be by her side.

It happens again; I grab my camera. Another fleeting moment of Rosey radiance washed over her. Rose appears mesmerized. Her countenance shimmers as she tries to describe beauty beyond colors, smells, tastes, textures, and sounds. Cognitive science professor Donald Hoffman advises we take these perceptual gifts seriously, if not literally, noting that our *fitness function* alters information about the actual structure of the world.[3] Onlookers stop in their tracks at the sight of Rosey's childlike enchantment.

Gaps widen between what Rosemary perceives now and realities she once accepted as fact. Concrete thinking anchors her to life as we know it, but abstract thoughts float freely.

I recall how misapplied behavioral psychology deliberately encourages concrete thinking. Punishment and reward, for example, relies on prods and carrots. Take away the external motivations and conditioned behaviors fall short. In contrast, playing peekaboo with babies and hide-and-seek with children develops their capacity for leaps of faith beyond what they can see. At the far end of life, Rosemary relaxes her grip on certainties and describes things beyond worldly understanding. Less restrained by time and space, reality attains new meaning. As death approaches, her awestruck expression resembles that of an infant seeing life for the first time.

Dementia also opens secret passageways to her past. Long-lost, innocence sparkles Rosey's "Poppy eyes" (a family reference to the smiling Irish eyes of her father). Despite her deteriorating physique, Rosemary's retro realm exudes merriment. Vestiges emerge of an exuberant girl playing hopscotch, jump rope, and One, Two, Three, Alairy. A small voice accompanies her antics.

"Remember the game Russia? Bounce a ball against a wall and the moves keep getting more elaborate. Wanna play?"

"Sure thing, Mumz. Let's play."

It makes no difference that there is no ball, jump rope, or hopscotch. It is truly the thought that counts. Entering her world invigorates her spirit.

The enigma of playing virtual ball with Rosey passes. Instead, my twinkle-eyed mom touches various surfaces within reach. Marvelous textures of her sheet, bedrail, fingers . . . dazzle her. She strokes a loose thread as if touching the delicate fluff of a downy feather.

One sunny day, a neighbor child watched a flitting cardinal behind young Rosemary's house in the field of Queen Anne's lace. Fresh-picked flowers in hand, stout little Patsy's eyes follow the bird off into the distance where she noticed a girl climbing the willow tree in her backyard. As Patsy approached, Rosemary flipped upside down and hung by her knees from a branch.

Startled by the acrobatics, Patsy shrieked, "Whatcha doing?"

"Just hanging around," replied Rosey in characteristic nonchalance. Thus began their lifelong friendship.

Rosey sits on her rehab bed, wondering what the world has in store for her. "My thinker's on vacation," she tells the occupational therapist.

Dutifully, Rosemary flexes her hands open and shut as instructed. "Just exercising," she assures visitors. "I'm not insulting you in sign language."

This fourth stroke hinders her ability to regulate body temperature. Plus, she has a urinary tract infection. Thermostat at eighty-four degrees and wearing three layers, still she feels cold.

"It's so chilly. Next time I want a stroke of warmth. When I die, cremate me, so at least I'll be warm."

A fever-induced chill joins forces with terrible indigestion, a side effect of antibiotics.

"I feel like I swallowed a flare. This is a vacation from fun." Unlike her ailing body, Rose's wit seldom tires. Asked if the probiotic pills ease her discomfort, she responds, "Can't tell. The only help I can give is to open my mouth and swallow."

A nurse offers yet another pill and assures Rosemary it will ease the stomach discomfort. "It may be gas," says the RN.

"Is this the power of positive digestion?" Rose retorts between groans of misery. The topic shift alleviates her suffering as she launches into a story.

"My sister Annie had raucous burps. She could belch out a tune or stop a truck with a good one. She was able to burp the entire alphabet."

Robert empathizes with Rose's pain and tries to distract her attention further. "Rose, you have so many cards from friends because you're a lovely person."

She voices an indignant, "Ha!"

"It's true," Robert persists. "You have a good heart and quick wit."

"Right now, I'd trade them both for a good fart." Serious distress be damned, the droll comments keep coming. One-liners fly from her mouth like birds escaping the petrified forest of her once-lush mind.

Rosemary does her best to cope with here and now. But memory of her current home has vaporized. The years she's lived in Shalimar take both hands to count. Yet, only disjointed recollections remain.

"I'll never forget . . . what's his name," she says of Tim, who lives across the street. "He and I talk a lot. A genial person. And his dog, Penny. But she's dead."

Hoping to distract my mother from her pain, I encourage her to attend a rehab spelling bee. The leader asks, "Can anyone spell donkey?"

My mom leans in and whispers, "My left butt cheek is numb. I feel half-athed, like my panth are cutting me in two."

"That's the stroke, Ma," I remind her.

"Thpeaking of donkey, I gueth I need to get my head out of my ath."

Rose says her left foot feels like something is between her toes, as if wearing thongs. I check. Nothing.

"I never liked the feel of flip-flop thandalth, but I do like to thing thongs," she says, playing along with her lisp.

Humor gives way to pain. Rosemary's inflamed esophagus and stomach drag her back to bed. In the midst of misery, she suffers another brain infarction. The dancing feet of her first two strokes return, but worse.

STROKE 5

PIZZA
RESUSCITATION

Where sets the line between
disinterested and not wanting to know?
– ROSEMARY, 1983

ONE EARLY AFTERNOON IN FEBRUARY 2017, Rosemary experiences an overwhelming sensation. "I feel like I'm flowing out, like I'm dying. Tell everybody I love them. I'm not in pain . . . weak, like I'm fading away."

Her feet commence a relentless dance-a-thon. Color drains from her face, like Photoshop saturation removal or a television reverting to 1950s black and white. I inform rehab staff of her distress. Knowing she has a DNR order, they express satisfaction that family is with her, as if our presence absolves them of alleviating Rosemary's discomfort. Hours pass. No one checks on her. My paramedic training demands action. But what can I do? Daughterly concern intensifies as blasé personnel do nothing to curtail Rosemary's misery.

Six hours later, at 7:00 p.m., she shakes uncontrollably. Unlike a seizure, she is awake and alarmed, riding her body like a bucking bronco.

The quake lasts over an hour. Feet flail, then run in place.

"Why does my mother have my legs?" she asks.

After the brutal tremor subsides, cheerful Rosey emerges. "How did I end up in Marty's room?" My child mom imagines herself in Rhode Island on her son's deathbed.

After eight hours, the ordeal abates. Rosemary reorients to current rehab surroundings and regains a firmer planetary footing.

"I'm coming back down to Earth now." The misadventure concludes like the *Outer Limits* science fiction television show. "We now return control to you, until the next episode," says Rosemary.

This stroke leaves her too mobile for her own good. Although advised to call for aid before getting up, she forgets and stumbles to the bathroom, so far without injury (*knock on wood*). Since she reads everything, we post signs: "Push the button and wait for help." She fails to heed the advice, not out of obstinacy but due to concrete thinking. She interprets things literally as her consciousness readjusts to life. Which button? Wait for whom? Where to wait? We clarify the signs.

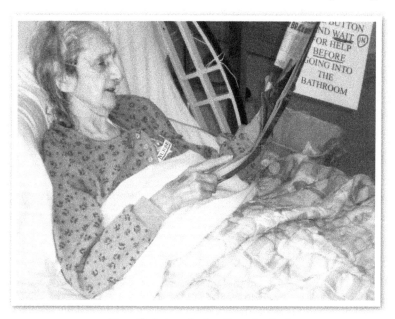

Detailed sign for her literal mind

Rosemary's short-term memory is minimal. Anterograde amnesia prevents the formation of new memories. Retrograde, old memories remain intact, grounding her in the past. Daily living skills drop to preschool level. She requires constant cueing: "Put on your sock, Mom. Point your toes. Pull it up." Toothbrush in hand is not an adequate prompt. "Brush your teeth. Spit. Wipe your mouth." Without cues, she waits in vain for lost brain cells to fire.

Moment-to-moment living has certain advantages. Everything comes as a surprise.

"Are we in the hospital? Was someone hurt? That gal looks polished in her white coat. Oh, are we in a hospital?"

Like a curious child, Rosemary is relentless. She listens, but answers do not gel. On her mental blackboard, she chalks responses, followed close behind by an eraser.

"What is the anticipated outcome of all this?" Her serious expression frames the question in terms of mortality.

We don't know either, Mom. "We'll just have to wait and see, together."

A nurse enters calling, "Knock, knock?"

"Nobody home," retorts Rosemary with sincerity.

Iron pills and B12 shots for anemia don't help. Rosemary's blood count worsens. Normal hemoglobin range is 12+. Hers drops from 9.4 to 8. Grayish tissue paper skin drapes over her scrawny frame.

Friends visit. Clueless who they are, she smiles with polite courtesy. Cards stack in pleasant piles. But bewilderment is no match for her wit. Sitting limp in an activity room wheelchair, she watches residents dance the Hokey Pokey. A smirk tilts one corner of her lips with flashes of her recent ordeal.

"'Shake it all about.' I can do that in my sleep."

The kind pianist asks how she's doing.

"Ups and downs, and a few side-to-sides," Rosemary replies.

She starts singing "Heart of My Heart," and others follows her lead. Oh, how we harmonize. Not. Passersby laugh, cringe, and join in.

Concerned over the insufficient care at this rehab, we check a dozen other facilities and find them all shorthanded, staffed by compassionate but overwhelmed professionals. Researching the cause, I trace the root problem to minimal standards set by law. Inadequate patient/staff ratios compromise care. Impossible workloads allow only a perfunctory lick and a promise by overwhelmed employees. Put an infirm population in an aging building, and things go wrong with inevitable frequency. Understaffed by design, in this place where Rosemary temporarily resides, Murphy's Law overrides legislative law.

Throughout February, the rehab center is plagued with misfortune. A water pipe burst—the very spot where Rosemary sang about walking in the rain—and floods an entire wing.

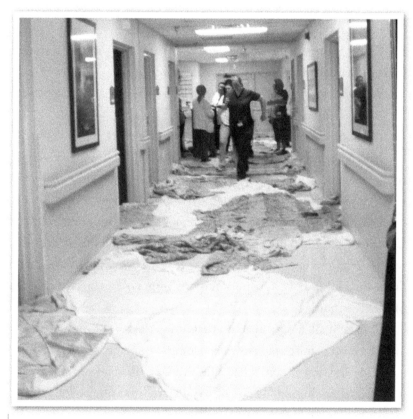

Murphy's Law overrides legislative law

Night after night, fire alarms go off at all hours, awakening patients. No sooner do residents settle back to sleep than the alarms blare again. Firefighters come and go, but the intermittent alarm returns. Mentally unstable patients shriek at a heightened pitch.

Rose made progress with therapy until this month's upheaval. Falls are understandable. But during the mayhem, mishandled incidents mount.

Last night's fall left Rosemary in enough pain to render it memorable despite her addled mind. I arrive along with morning shift. My mother tells us she fell, that she pushed the call button for help and waited, but no one came. Fearing she might wet the bed, she got up, but tumbled to the floor.

"My knees gave way." Dazed and injured, Rosemary says she sat on the cold floor for "a long time," despite the activated nurse call. Eventually, someone showed up and put her to bed with a sore hip and neck, limited range of motion, and bladder still full.

"Falls are to be expected with dementia; we understand that," I tell the unit supervisor.

"Hmm," she mutters to herself. "No incident report was filed." The charge nurse assures that she will check into the matter but focuses on documentation rather than check the patient who fell. That raises my hackles.

Dressing my mother for a scheduled neurology appointment, she grimaces with pain. A wheelchair is needed to get her to the bathroom. Her left hip is red, but no one examines her. At the neurologist's office, the nurse practitioner notes my mother's fall last night. So far as I know, Rosemary is not examined by any medical professional.

Valentine's Day—the holiday to commemorate compassion—Rosemary starts clearing her throat. She blows her nose more often and complains of neck stiffness. The charge nurse shrugs. "No incident report was filed. She probably imagined it." Liability over an undocumented fall matters more than patient care to this RN. So much for basic decency, let alone compassion.

Two days since the fall, the rehab nursing director who denied Rose fell stares at the saucer-size contusion that vindicates Rosemary's story. Annoyance smacks across the woman's face. Without a word, she marches from the room.

I, too, bite my tongue. With my mom at their mercy, nurses need reassurance, not criticism. Rosemary defines tact as knowing what *not* to say. Diplomacy is the filtered part, what we choose to share.

No hip fracture is evident, thank goodness. But Rose develops a fever and empties the tiny tissue box in minutes. We bring large boxes from home. In the waste basket vicinity, used discards resemble a snowy avalanche. We affix a trash bag to the bedrail for easy reach. She misses anyway.

My dad played baseball in the 1950s and taught us kids to catch and throw a ball. Rose couldn't hit the broad side of a skyscraper and acquired a reputation. The family joke was that if Ma got annoyed enough to throw something at us, all we had to do was stand still. Those furious tosses left everyone laughing, especially Mom.

Surrounded by a sea of spent tissues, Rosemary's health continues to deteriorate. Since the fall, she remains too weak for therapy. We ask her to specify what level of medical intervention she wants as her condition worsens. True to form, she answers with enough clarity to be poignant and enough wit to cushion reality. "I would prefer to be with family, but it makes no difference. I'm gonna be horizontal no matter where I am."

We arrange for her to come live with my husband and me. Rehab schedules a home inspection to determine if adaptive equipment is needed.

Rosemary's fever and confusion rise. Before leaving for the night, I caution staff that she is in danger of falling again. No preventative measures are taken—no bed alarm, no safety cushions, no fall precautions whatsoever.

Another day dawns, and Rosemary's constant cough makes her wet the bed. Embarrassed, soggy, and not wanting to inconvenience anyone, she shoves tissues between her legs. She tries to reach the bathroom unassisted and falls again. This gravity-induced collision with the floor is reported. Staff lowers her bed to floor level. This fall leaves her too weak to move. Day shift puts Rosemary in diapers. Congestion hinders swallowing. Food and drink intake virtually cease. Without hydration, her body cannot fight the congestion. A nurse says she will contact the doctor.

By graveyard shift, Rosemary's condition is critical. Propped bolt upright, her chin slumps onto her chest. On ten liters of oxygen by a non-rebreather mask, she remains cyanotic. Although she cannot move, the bed remains at ground level as nursing personnel squat to render aid. Every inhale is desperate. Rosemary cannot speak, and her end-of-life prediction rings in my skull: *My mouth will be the last thing to go.*

The kind night shift supervisor asks what our family wants done. The facility doctor ordered breathing treatments . . . that everyone knows will not arrive until next delivery, perhaps tomorrow. Rosemary is suffering and has the right to die. I shift from lifesaving paramedic to soothing farewell. My throbbing heart does the talking.

"It'll be okay, Mom. Your body is trying to let go. Imagine a big family reunion of people you miss, awaiting your arrival on the other side . . ." Crouched on the floor, holding my father's photo in close view, I ask point-blank, "Are you looking forward to seeing Dad?"

Clinging to life with each gasp, she shakes her head an emphatic NO with force capable of altering wind currents in China.

"Do you want to go to the hospital?"

Suffocating to death with no treatment for anxiety or pain proves too much. She contradicts her previous wishes and responds with a vigorous head nod—YES.

An ambulance scurries Rosemary to the hospital.

Revived by IV treatment en route, Rose asks, "Is this the morgue?" Hearing the straight-faced doctor's assurance that it's the hospital, she retorts, "Then, relatively speaking, I must be doing well."

Diagnosed with pneumonia, Rosemary's grip on life strengthens with IV-infused hydration and antibiotics. In medical circles, pneumonia is called "the old man's friend" as oxygen-starved patients lose consciousness and die peacefully. Not so for Rose. The respiratory therapy mask cannot conceal the expression of relief on her prune-ified face.

No matter how dire the circumstances, the world pauses for no one. Rosemary at the hospital, guests arrive from all over the country to celebrate Robert's eightieth birthday. While I deal with my mother's urgent matter, friends decorate the reserved restaurant. Then Deborah, our death doula, stays with Rosemary in the ER so I can make an appearance at my husband's party.

Planned for months, my aching heart wells with joy to find Robert surrounded by fifty-eight caring people at the festive Aegean Restaurant luncheon. Seated in a place of honor, my darling looks like a good-natured Zeus with whirling curls of cumulus-cloud hair. The rhythm of his paisley print shirt carries through in songs by a guitar-playing priest. Overlapping conversations, poetry, laughter, and a delectable Greek banquet continue as I bid farewell and return lickety-split to Rosemary.

Back at the hospital, the physician reports no available beds. I must choose between the overpacked hospital or deficient rehab. She could wait days on the hard gurney before a bed opens here, and her bony butt remains sore from falling. Rehab has great therapy, but perilous understaffed nursing, questionable management, and medication delays. Since she is perky, I opt for rehab, hoping therapy will strengthen her enough to return home . . . a decision doomed to haunt.

Doula Deborah brings a set of flickering LED candles to set a tranquil tone in Rosemary's rehab room. Volunteers take turns watching over my mother when I cannot be there. Guardian angel friends read to her, reminisce, and sing old, sweet songs.

Certain melodies remind Rosemary of specific people. "All Aboard for Blanket Bay" salutes our Runnemede neighbor Dona, who called the lullaby "Wet Blanket." "Heart of My Heart" takes Rose back to gatherings in her parents' cellar. "We'll Meet Again" hearkens to her childhood chum, Maggie. And "I'll Be Seeing You" draws memories of my dear dad.

Rosemary breathes easy now, and confesses that she decided not to die today because it would interfere with Robert's birthday. The struggle with pneumonia leaves her further confused and too weak to be out of bed. An aide brings a bedpan and tries to mount Rose on, but the thing scoots away like an uncooperative horse.

Rosemary's mind gallops elsewhere, far beyond her weathered body. Calling from some alternate realm of existence, a calm prophetic voice parts her lips. Arms extended, index fingers pointing outward with palms down, she declares, "Sending." Then she rotates her palms upward, closes her hands and bends her elbows. Wrists overlapped close to her core, she announces, "Receiving." Like a sage, she repeats, "Sending. Receiving. Sending . . ."

Gleeful Rosey reports her magic carpet bed has arrived in the Barrington, New Jersey post office. Looking around at her cards, letters, and mail, Rosemary tries to figure out her role.

"I trust I'm providing some useful filing service here."

When Rosemary's children reached their teens, she began work as a file clerk at N.W. Ayer & Son advertising company in Philadelphia. A confident bounce in her stride, she hustled off each weekday to her first paid job. Her organizational skills impressed management, matched only by her eager-to-please enthusiasm.

Back home, whenever something in the house disappeared, she reminded us, "Good filing is an efficient system of retrieval—remember Aunt Jenny's dress."

The reference was to an inexplicable conundrum. Elderly Aunt
Jen lived in our attic for a while. Amid Christmas decorations,
paper dolls, toy trains, Easter baskets, and empty luggage, Jen's
dress vanished, never to be seen again. From then on, if something
went missing, we surmised it must be with Aunt Jenny's dress—lost
forever in life's perpetual churning.

Rosemary's vitality returns along with memories of Batsto, an
eighteenth-century, South Jersey village. She recalls making candles,
something we learned there decades ago. Her mind travels through the
stunted pine forest of Wharton Tract. She traces routes through historic
wooded towns—Tom's River, Double Trouble, and Long-A-Coming
(Berlin, New Jersey's original name).

"Not many people inhabited rural South Jersey, just little settlements.
In the Pine Barrens near Smithville, a company manufactured calico
curtains, I think. Workers could peddle to their job on a bicycle railway."

Lying flat on her back, Rosemary stares upward in fascination,
semi-focused on the rehab ceiling. Gestures accompany her thoughts.

"A *National Geographic Magazine* photo shows an ancient Egyptian
statue. A turbaned woman sits just so." Demonstrating the position, she
bends her knees in the air, straightens her back, and flexes her elbows
as if her forearms rest on chair arms.

Our friend Elena stops to visit. For the woman's sake, Rose repeats
herself.

"That seating position still exists. Anyone can do it. See?" She models
the pose and points overhead to the pharaoh's wife, a step-shaped fire
sprinkler.

Head out of the clouds, Rosemary looks down and frowns at the
bedspread. "We'd better not use this. It looks like clenched knuckles."
Assured it is a leaf pattern, she squints one eye, cocks her head like

the RCA Victor dog, and reexamines the design. "I'm reading this life message, but I keep losing my place."

Her sore throat makes swallowing difficult, and the speech therapist orders her drinks thickened to avoid aspiration. At first, I don't understand the uncharacteristic outrage in my mother's response. On the verge of a tea revolt, she scribbles a bold demand: "Tea for Re." The fiery scroll is mostly unintelligible, but its core message is clear: "No thickener." Words slash the air as she declares her bone of contention.

Rosemary treasured afternoon teas with her grandmother. "When Grossmom was dying, the infirmary refused her final request—a cup of tea. Deathrow inmates are treated with more dignity." Rosemary's voice breaks, as she stifles tears. The thickener revolt is Rosey's tribute to Grossmom. An unthickened cup of tea calms her down.

Mom holds the warm mug while I spoon scant sips into her mouth, one at a time. Some things are more important than breathing.

Rosey and her Grossmom would partake of tea every afternoon in the mid-1930s. Kept home a full school year for her undiagnosed frail health, lonely eight-year-old Rose learned a lot. A strong bond formed between the eldest and youngest in the Martin household. Grossy's wisdom about generosity, history, family, gardening, and cooking nourished the child's insatiable hunger for knowledge.

Crop trees grew in their backyard corner, adjacent to the grade school for special needs children. Fruit-laden branches extended into neighboring trees; Rosey climbed the cherry tree to pick apples and the apple tree for cherries. She dropped fruit into eager hands of kids in the playground below. Grossmom explained to her astute grandchild that scattered fruit trees were once Audubon's orchards on horse farms. Looking out their home's third story windows as they munched on tomato pie (pizza), Rosey and Grossy identified discontiguous patterns of produce trees, once in regimented rows.

We reorganize stacks of greeting cards, scattered in the chaos of care. Respiratory medications work wonders on Rosemary. Relaxed breathing eases her into slumber. Hours later, she awakens, beaming with curiosity.

"I'm hoping some adventure will come along and explain all this. Where am I?"

"What does your call button sign say, Mom?" The mental exercise prompts her to figure things out for herself.

"N-U-R-S-E," Rosey reads with a mischievous grin. "I'm in a nurse's bed."

Bath day at rehab, busy aides load patients into wheelchairs, lined up, awaiting their turn to be bathed. The same goes for Rosemary, despite pneumonia. My husband and I arrive and find her unattended, in the dayroom near the shower. Rosemary's unlocked wheelchair inches across the floor, propelled by her shivering. The locked thermostat reads sixty-six degrees. There's no telling how long she's been waiting, conveyor belt style, uncovered, wearing only a flimsy gown. Robert runs for a blanket while I wrap my warm arms around her. As we bundle Rose, a worker summons me to the nurses' station.

A half-century ago, bathing was a fun luxury. Young mother Rosemary and her siblings took turns hosting weekend get-togethers at their respective homes. The adults often played cards—rummy, poker, and lots of pinochle. We children entertained ourselves on rope swings, crawling through secret passageways, or playing freeze tag, hide-and-seek, huckle buckle beanstalk, and inventive games. A flight of rebuilt steps, still lacking its risers, made an effective skeet ball shoot. Gravity returned the balls.

One autumn afternoon, a renegade ball toppled Aunt Annie's African violet. Uncles shooed us kids outside into the brisk weather where we kept warm in a steamy mound of leaves. The aunts then gathered us from Uncle Homer's compost pile, plunged us all into a bubble bath upstairs, and returned to the dining room below. Bathing children together was expedient and economical. The claw-foot tub's swayed back made a fine waterslide, although our big waves meant we had to refill the tub after each turn. Our frolic was interrupted by an adult stampede, as their card game suddenly required umbrellas.

Rosemary's bath on hold, I answer the urgent summons to the nurses' station. A family acquaintance who offered to stay with Rosemary this morning, instead berates rehab staff. The brash volunteer demands to see my mother's medical records. Attempts to redirect her to Rosemary fall on deaf ears. Sometimes, well-meaning people make matters worse.

"I know patient care," she rants, pushing past occupied wheelchairs at the nurses' station.

Asked to leave, she storms away, tossing insults over her shoulder, leaving a trail of wincing patients in her wake.

Rosemary's well-being matters more than the longstanding relationship. I stay with my mom overnight. A relentless cough won't let her sleep. The nurse orders routine "diaper check and change." Every two hours, an aide comes for Rosemary's diaper needs, but nothing is done to relieve her compromised breathing.

At 5:00 a.m., the night nurse hears Rosemary express a desire to die. Witnessing her respiratory distress, the LPN swears in annoyance over undelivered prescriptions, and improvises, Robin Hood-style. The Zosyn antibiotic she procures helps. Rosemary sleeps an hour before coughing again.

At shift change, I go to thank the departing LPN.

Unaware of my approach, she calls in a sarcastic tone to arriving day shift nurses, "Where do you think you're going? Mrs. Baker needs your undivided attention."

Unprofessional, yes, but the LPN's short fuse is understandable. Understaffed systems force constant compromises. In penny-pinching institutions, patient advocacy is vital. Squeaky-wheel patients get disproportional, yet still-lacking care.

Generally, neither all good nor bad, people possess a mixed bag of virtues and ineptitudes. The most dysfunctional among us sometimes shine, the most capable falter. Knowing this quells the urge to judge, eyes peeled for moments of compassion.

Rosemary's hoarse voice stirs me from my thoughts. "This is a non-traditional hospital. A gas station, maybe?" She croaks, "I'm parked here like a jalopy with occasional visits from non-mechanics. Now I know how a broken-down car feels in a garage." Neglected like an abandoned wreck, still her spirit shines like a Rolls-Royce.

Shifting gears, Rose admires medical personnel's printed smocks. "Hospitals once considered white to be the only sanitary color. I'm glad they got over their monochromatic attitude toward hygiene." On her nightstand, a framed photograph of my dad catches her eye. She returns his smile. "I had excellent taste. Such talent. I loved to watch him shave his dimpled chin."

A contented grin contrasts with her strained breathing. Rosemary treats the nurses to Pez candy from the bear dispenser sent from New Jersey by Marty's friend Rosalba. Rereading the many greeting cards' goodwill messages thrill Rose as if they'd just arrived. "Oh my, a lot of people care. I hope I find a way to deserve it. Please thank everyone for me. People we love are our most valuable treasures."

This afternoon, the rehab administrator phones for an immediate conference concerning my mother. In my writing class at the University of West Florida, I drop everything to attend, hoping for better care, maybe an apology. Nothing could be further from their motive.

The director of nursing and unit manager (RN) begin with the unreported February 13 fall. First the RN insists Rose only imagined falling. Then the woman changes strategy, insisting Rosemary can get to bed herself. On cue, the tag team administrator waves a physical therapy form documenting the patient's ability to get up from the floor unassisted. They dismiss the fact that, after falling, Rosemary was dazed and injured. The administrator insists that due to dementia (BIMS score 9 of 12), Mrs. Baker lacks credibility.

"I trust my staff," the confrontational man concludes.

"I trust my mother," I counter, sitting up straight in opposition. Measuring each face, their fearful expressions tell me this is not a fact-finding meeting, nor an admission of mistakes. It is an ambush. Concern over liability constipates their compassion, trapped in their professional bowels. No one here gives a shit. We reach an impasse on the fall incident.

Next, we discuss yesterday's bath ordeal when Rosemary, ill with pneumonia, was left shivering in a sixty-six-degree room. Unaware it happened in a common area, the administrator deflects blame onto family, asking why we didn't raise her room temperature or provide warmer clothes. In final defense, he insists that being cold cannot cause colds, exposing his ignorance of its compromising effect on patients' immune systems.

I leave the meeting shaken, disheartened by their soulless intent to dodge legal exposure. Embarrassed by my naive trust, I resist the urge to go home and bathe away their filthy waylay. Instead, I go see my mom. A story about her maternal grandmother rejuvenates me.

"Grossmom liked to help with the mending. She once sewed the boys' flies shut."

After the laugh, I mention my upset over some prickly people. No details.

Searching for what advice to offer, she squints and cocks her head. "Maybe I'm ready to turn into an interpreter of the uninterpretable."

My rancor toward the pseudo-professionals fades as my mom's approach to problematic people echoes between my ears: *Hold their heads above water until they surface as human.* She sees the troublesome as drowning in their woeful ways. Rosemary trusts in everyone's potential for decency, even if they lose sight of it themselves. My mom epitomizes what psychologist Carl Rogers called unconditional positive regard, aspiring to love enemies (Matt. 5:44) without exception. Like Mom, my brother also honed that aptitude of valuing everyone's innate worth. We can be contemptuous bombs, or compassionate balms.

Rehab's circumventing responsible care and that disrespectful meeting convince me that my mother's situation is not unique. With all our advocating for Rosemary, if she is unsafe, then no patient is safe in this place of systemic disregard. Some higher authority must intervene. I file an elder neglect report with the Florida Department of Children and Families' abuse registry.

Rosemary's pneumonia intensifies. The facility doctor orders an IV change from normal saline to lactated Ringer's to replenish electrolytes, thereby boosting Rose's ability to ward off infection. However, a communication breakdown ensues between the physician and nurses.

By nightfall, the normal saline IV runs out. Ringer's lactate has not arrived from central supply in Tallahassee. Rather than continue the normal saline, a nurse removes the IV, depriving Rosemary of her only source of fluid. Too sick to drink, she gets nothing.

Robert and I had prepared to bring my mom home to live with us. She was supposed to be discharged but is now too weak. Therapists cancel their home visit, a reality check on what Rosemary pays for negligent mistakes.

Noticeably weakening, Rosemary makes a noise.

"Mom, is that a cough or a laugh?"

A smile lights her gaunt face. "Your father used to sing a fiendish song to me to the tune of 'Carolina in the Morning': 'Nothing could be finer than to have your little heiner in the morning.'"

My dad whistled and tapped his knuckles to songs in his head while working. A lineman for Bell Telephone Company, he would hum a melody and listen to it spread amid other Ma Bell employees. Then he would change tunes and see how long it took everyone to switch.

A framed photo of "my man," as she calls him, inexplicably landed under Rosemary's bed. The Elder Services investigator spots it as she reports success in tracking down the nurse aide on duty when Rosemary fell. I pity the overworked girl's struggle to prioritize the needs of too many patients. I feel worse for my mother. It is tempting to blame the administrator. But the problem goes deeper. Bureaucrats budget to substandard care, set by law.

United States healthcare ranks top in expense and shamefully low in patient care among developed nations.[4] Loving families struggle to fill healthcare voids for patients left in the lurch. As Rosemary's daughter, I bear ultimate responsibility for her well-being. Had she died from a stroke, I could accept it. Had she received adequate care and died, I would understand. But she was improving until the officialdom negligence. Guilt plagues me as I imagine Rosemary on that floor. Cold, hurt, and alone.

Still no Ringer's lactate. Day shift expects Rosemary to die, satisfied that I keep my mother company.

An attentive therapist hears my pleas and comes to check. "Where are you, Rosemary?"

"At the little hospital around the corner from the big hospital."

The semi-accurate geographic description assures the therapist the matter is not dire.

Rosemary withers like an unwatered potted plant. Delicate pinches of arm skin hold peaks like tiny tents. I entice her to sip water, juice, cocoa, and tea, but she cannot swallow. Finally, an afternoon nurse restarts an IV, normal saline only. With Rosemary's dehydration, it takes many pokes.

"I'm fading away," my mother whispers. But bedspread puckers draw her attention. "These covers look like alligators coming up for air." Rosemary envies alligators.

The Martin family moved down the shore near Atlantic City in 1931. Three-year-old Rosey chased after her brothers, who abandoned her in their dust. The marshy inlet of Lyon's Court enticed Rosemary, wandering alone amid tall grasses and meadow-muck perfume.

Neighbors, fearing for the little girl's safety, cautioned her about the shallow water. "Alligators live there."

But young Rosemary misinterpreted their emphatic concern for excitement. She coveted the alligators for their tidal habitat. "When I grow up, I wanna be an alligator in a beautiful bog."

Rosemary escapes from rehab the only way she can, in her mind. Off she retreats, to mossy bogs and other pleasant places, a half-century ago. Staring up at the IV stand, Rosey blurts, "Let's play Change Poles." For

Alligator envy

this inventive 1950s game of tag, clothesline poles provide safety zones from getting caught.

While Mom retreats to safety in her mind, the protective services investigator informs me that each incident, such as the IV fluid fiasco, requires a separate Florida Abuse Hotline call. The woman says her hands are tied, just as a nurse arrives with the lactated Ringer's ordered two days prior. Staff lower the bed back to floor level with mats to cushion falls, absurd measures since Rosemary cannot so much as lift her head. But these added precautions assure me that staff members are on their toes.

Relieved, I head home, confident that my mother is in good hands. On the contrary.

Walking into her room at 7:20 a.m., I cannot believe my eyes. Her bed is elevated to maximum height, rails down. She is unattended, exposed, and shivering. The room is ice cold, the heater off with an outdoor temperature in the 40s. Wet sheets and covers pulled back leave her exposed in a soaked nightgown at the IV site, drenched in Ringer's lactate. The fluid puddles on the floor. Her bed table is across the room.

Rosemary utters three words: "Cold. Wet. Thirsty."

Two efficient day shift aides help me care for my mother. Outraged over the situation, the girls complain that the night shift gave no handover report.

A nurse covertly encourages me to file a formal grievance and confides some grim details. She explains that, since "going corporate," local facilities boost profits by counting office staff in their tally of on-duty aides. I file two grievance reports with the rehab facility and Elder Services in our county, one for neglecting to keep Rosemary hydrated and the other about the IV leak incident.

The rehab center calls another meeting. My husband and I attend, along with the facility director, nursing director, therapy coordinator, and social service manager. Rather than address our concerns, the social service manager tells us Rosemary must move to a skilled nursing facility. *Isn't this supposed to be one?* Another blow comes from the elder services investigator whose only reply is that abuse registry must receive another call. Instead, my attention shifts to finding another facility for my dying mother.

Later, the rehab doctor comes and reiterates that Rosemary's needs exceed the scope of this facility. Seeing my mother's wretched condition, the physician orders her transfer to the ER. Ambulance paramedics cannot get a medical report: the rehab nursing staff refuse to speak to them. Loading Rosemary for transport, the EMS (emergency medical services) crew swears over the rehab's unprofessionalism.

The ER physician shakes his head over Rosemary's deplorable condition. Pneumonia has spread to both lungs. Treated with antibiotics and rehydrated, within an hour of humane care she regains her voice, love of life, and appetite.

"Is that pizza?" she sniffs as someone passes through with their lunch. Scattered comments fly. "It's about time to learn the meaning of traffic 'lifes,'" she says verbatim, then turns her attention upward. "This ceiling is rather high. Let's tile it green and carrot." This revival awakens Rosemary's artistic flair.

Rosemary let loose her aesthetic creativity at our 1950s Runnemede, New Jersey home. She painted a house on the kitchen switch plate and two-toned the living room bookcases earthy green and off-white. Sweet potato vines festooned our living room columns.

My mother further applied her creative talent helping us kids with homework. For my report on Shakespeare at age twelve, Mom showed me how to trace his portrait using stencil paper and freeform sketch the Globe Theatre. Encyclopedia open, side-by-side we each drew our renditions. When finished, I gasped as she tore her beautiful work to shreds. Her aim was not to create a keepsake, only to motivate me. Days later, the teacher showed my A+ report with its lopsided sketch to the entire class. But Mom's art lesson most gratified me.

Lying on the ER gurney, Rosemary requests notepaper and scribbles illegible doodles.

The doctor orders a neck X-ray, fifteen days after the February 13 fall. The radiology tech says he's going to take her picture.

"It'll never sell," Rosemary teases. As he leaves, she notices a resemblance to my brother's lifelong pal.

"I think Glenn has a better relationship with his father now that they're both older. The man finally appreciates his son's attributes."

"Glenn's dad died years ago, Ma."

"Well, that would explain their improved relationship," she quips, and we laugh.

Glenn keeps close contact with "Mrs. B" and roars over her hilarious comments. "Your entire family is a huge part of who I am today." Glenn's mother died when he was a kid. Rosemary took him under her wing. Since Marty's death, each year florist Glenn sends Mrs. B flowers on Marty's birthday.

Although there is no neck fracture, Rosemary's pneumonia earns her hospital admission. My sister Beth expresses support by sending an entire gross of alstroemeria. Flowers spruce up our mom's room and the hospital entryway. The bouquets bring scattered memories of her firstborn.

"My Beth was the prettiest baby, so sick yet good-natured. Radiation treatments the doctor ordered on my tiny baby's throat must have done damage. When she was six, we went to family counseling for assistance with her emotional problems. Their only suggestion was to put her in foster care. Outrageous!"

Lying in bed, weak and frail, Rosemary's voice intensifies to the fierce, protective temper of a grizzly defending her young.

"We sought help for our family, but the counselor's only solution was to split us apart. They didn't think we could handle Beth's special needs. I wasn't about to turn my little girl over to strangers." Rosemary settles down and continues. "Despite her difficulties, Beth grew up to be a decent person."

Back then, my big sister gave me suffocating bear hugs. She sensed things others missed and had a high IQ like our mother. Young Beth scored 99 percent on a national spelling test. As an adult, she received a Camden County Volunteer of the Year award for her work with seniors.

Rosemary rallies once more. Transferred from one room or facility to another, my husband rehangs her cards. The routine grants him a productive chore. Wherever Rosemary lands, he surrounds her with kindhearted wishes of kith and kin. The current room is near the nursing station. Shift change is especially noisy.

Noticing colorful bruises on her arms from IVs, Rose comments, "I should have gotten the artist's signature." A nurse's questions ricochet through Rosemary's mind, and she apologizes for her non sequiturs.

"My communicator is broken. What's on my alleged mind depends on a resonance of who's where and what's actuality."

The mystified nurse stifles a snicker as she documents my mother's responses.

Due to worsened pneumonia, staff move Rosemary to an isolation room. Robert rehangs her cards. This room's double doors give us hope of peaceful quiet. Naïve of us to think she could catch up on sleep in a hospital.

Tai chi instructor Anita visits Rose and sings, "All the Things You Are." My mom joins in, their voices accompanied by hospital clamor, IV alarms, and PA announcements. Yet the duo doesn't miss a beat.

After the final note, someone asks Rose the song title.

"I don't know. I can't listen to myself anymore."

Isolation room acoustics enhance singing voices. Robert tells Rose to imagine an Irish tenor, then launched into a Yeats poem put to music, "Down by the Salley Gardens." His vocal confidence took root as an altar boy, a college glee club member, and barbershop quartet harmonist.

Rosemary tries to account for the many great Irish and Italian tenors. "It must be nutrients in the water," she surmises as a lab tech draws her blood. Finished, the man thanks her. She requests a receipt.

Robert serenades. Rose gets bandaged. And I approach a supervisor in the hall assigning patients to trainees. Knowing the extra care students provide, I ask the woman which eager apprentice will care for Rosemary. She says no one, due to the DNR, isolation, and hospice status. Undaunted, I champion quality end-of-life care for golden-year patients. Until sent home, Rosemary deserves full medical treatment. That settled, student nurse Courtney comes to help.

After providing impeccable care, she prepares to leave. "See you tomorrow, Miss. Rosemary."

"Don't get kidnapped out there," my mom calls to the radiant Nightingale.

"Get better," Courtney laughs and disappears down the hall.

"If you insist," Rose calls after her.

A fall precaution alert triggers whenever Rose attempts to get up. But its incessant beeping defeats the purpose, luring her out of bed. "That's my alarm clock; rise and shine."

The hospitalist confirms that Rosemary is dwindling. Unlikely she'll survive another six months, maybe weeks. He orders a transfusion for anemia before discharge home on hospice. Two stern nurses arrive with equipment and a bag of red blood cells.

"I've become an expert at inertia," Rosemary jokes.

The women ignore her, focused on arm veins. They exchange annoyed looks of dismay. *Reviving an elder destined to die gets their goat*, I surmise. Puncture after puncture misses the frail veins. I lose count after a dozen Voodoo doll stabs. Their irritation mounts. The pump battery dies; its plug is broken. They request another machine "stat." Blood products at room temperature have short lifespans.

One nurse throws the warm covers aside, leaving Rosemary exposed.

"Did someone say we need to suffer in our underwear?" Rose tries to make light of it.

Without a word, the nurse tosses the blanket further, covering the patient's face.

"Not yet, please." Rosemary's polite protest from beneath the shroud fails to penetrate their indifference.

Defeated, the bitter RNs summon an operating room nurse who taps a vein first try.

By morning, Rose has improved.

"You look better," remarks an aide.

"You like this shade of green?" Rosemary replies.

Practiced in chitchat, Robert fills conversation voids. "I balanced the checkbook without fudging, Rose."

"Good, no sirens," she quips.

Continuing the babble, he reports washing laundry, then taking a nap.

"Pounding clothes against a riverside rock is exhausting," Rose empathizes.

A tech enters. "Ms. Rosemary, I'm going to take your vitals."

"You can keep them, for all I care."

Do we read too much into her words—or not enough?

She greets a consulting neurologist. "I don't know you, but I'm glad for such young vigor."

Next her favorite physician, Dr. Michael Neuland, pops in unofficially. His colorful neckties and ever-changing beard designs have amused Rosemary for years. But it's his Fred Rogers kindness, Albert Schweitzer brilliance, and Soupy Sales whimsy she most adores. This rare professional grasps the depth and breadth of her comments.

"See you later, Rosemary," he concludes.

"Is that so?" Rose replies, and they exchange knowing looks.

The transfusion effect is temporary. Her pneumonia worsens. Hands and arms inflate like balloons, making wedding ring removal from an overstuffed sausage finger tricky. Weakening, Rosemary remains talkative. Staff prepares her to come home to die. Her good humor smooths the edges of her gaunt appearance. People see her and look grim but leave laughing.

At last, March 4, my mother comes home to live with us. She is elated.

"I can't visualize where I am, but I definitely am."

Sipping a cup of tea, she bursts into an uplifting Depression-era ditty, "Let's Have Another Cup of Coffee."

Rosemary's jovial spirit conceals her rough physical condition. Minimal oral hygiene in the facilities left her teeth discolored like tombstones in an abandoned cemetery. Her wavy hair has turned to cotton candy fuzz. A hospice nurse enters the sunny bedroom. For a split second, she looks aghast. After a deep breath, she regains her professional composure and speculates Rosemary only has weeks left. The RN orders equipment—wheelchair, commode, bedrails.

"My breathing sounds like beginner bagpipe lessons," Rosemary wheezes.

It's all okay. At home in her own bed, she can die in loving comfort. Our death doula pats Rose's hand and suggests, in lieu of an after-the-fact funeral, we open our door to well-wishers now, for a "living wake."

"What a sensible idea," chimes Rosemary as she dozes off.

Phone trees have many branches these days with Facebook, Twitter, and social media communication beyond our know-how. Friends spread word that it's time to pay last respects to Rosemary.

Throughout March, nieces, nephews, cousins, grandkids, great-grands, friends, and neighbors shower Rose with affection. Church friend Aaron brings his little dog, a pleasant surprise. People bring uplifting conversation, homemade flan, Eudora Welty-style prose, and lots of laughter. Doula Deborah makes sure my mother is comfortable, encircled with love . . . and flowers galore.

Alstroemeria by the gross

The Garden State cultivated Rosemary's reverence for trees and anything in nature—except mosquitoes. The Martin family nested back in Audubon around 1933 when her pop secured a job with "Ma Bell," the one-and-only telephone company. Their kindergartener's fascination with seagulls and sandpipers broadened with inland songbird acquaintances—robins, cardinals, mockingbirds . . . . For decades to follow, wildlife ventures and birdwatching with the fledgling National Audubon Society filled Rosemary's world.

German grandmother Grossy and Rosey formed a strong bond. In contrast, unruly grandsons exhausted the matriarch, who chortled in her native tongue, "Du bischt furchterlich, meine kinder" (You are outrageous, my children).

Anything the green-thumbed grandma put in the ground thrived. Fragrant rainbow gardens encircled the burgundy abode. Five-foot-tall hollyhocks towered over Rosey's head. And the rich Jersey soil's victory garden fed the neighborhood. Nature's bounty thrilled Rosey to no end. In springtime, she snickered at "birds behaving unabashedly in public."

Rosemary lacked Grossy's finesse and gave up gardening, convinced her own thumbs were brown. But Rosey absorbed common flora names and characteristics. She could identify sassafras, bergamot, and bay leaf by scent. At child's eye view, Rose smiled back at pansy faces. "Green is good for the eyes," she often quoted from *The Ugly Duckling*. Fond memories formed over chatter-mouth snapdragons, maple seed noses, plantain shooters, lion's teeth, sycamore buttonballs, and moments of anticipation holding buttercup blossoms under chins.

"Grossy once cut a maple sprig and shoved it in the ground to protect her hollyhocks from my brothers, who would jump over the garden. The boys named the protective stake 'the goosey stick.' Years later, they returned from the war and found the stick was a full-grown tree."

Although Rosemary resembles a war survivor, her wit heroes on. A hospice nurse asks bedridden Rosemary if she can swing her legs around.

"Why, of course. Nobody swings their legs a-square."

Hoisting my mother, I notice I'm still wearing her wedding rings for safekeeping. Our role reversal reflects in our hands. Mine keep busy; hers seek support. Swelling subsided, I offer the nuptial charms back to their rightful owner. She declines, settles into bed, and gives my hand a tender double pat.

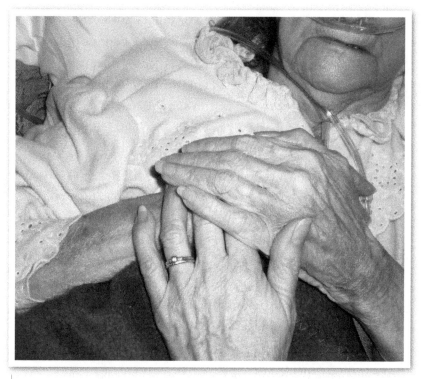

Nuptial charms and tender hand pats

Supplemental oxygen dries Rosemary's sinuses and her nose bleeds. Hospice adds a humidifier with breathing medication. We take turns positioning the mask as Rose removes it, the purpose forgotten.

"What's this?" Abandoned on the bed, the dejected thing hisses until we put it back on her again and again. Rose's charm outshines her panting for air. But a degree of surrender comes across. "If I could do jumping jacks, it wouldn't do much good."

Respiratory distress worsens. By morning, she is unresponsive. Pulse rapid and faint, blood pressure plunges. Sat upright, her head flops forward. The nurse asks if we made final arrangements. I dial a mortuary and tell Robert the situation.

He enters her bedroom to say goodbye, grappling for words. At a loss, Robert resorts to his own mode of comfort.

"Hey, Rose, you want a piece of pizza?"

Wide-eyed, the RN and I gawk at him in disbelief. But his offer diverts my mother's attention from her struggle to breathe. Lifting her chin, she pulls off the oxygen mask and takes a deep breath.

"Pizza sounds good," Rosemary smiles.

Such are the blessings and curses of short-term memory loss. Thoughts of pizza distracted her from dying. Hereafter, we refer to this as "the pizza resuscitation."

A few hours later, trouble comes knocking. A relative arrives, intoxicated (overmedicated?) and reeking of cigarette smoke. She rushes into my mother's bedroom and throws herself on top of Rose.

Struggling to breathe under the weight, Rosemary smiles, happy to have company.

The inebriated guest announces she's staying "for the duration." Besides my mom's care, we must also deal with a well-intentioned interloper. I call her adult son who comes and retrieves his clueless mother, so I can focus on my own mother, saddened that ties to a valued branch of family may be forever broken.

The next day, disappointment dawns on Rosemary. The pizza resuscitation sidestepped her anticipated exit. Death failed her once again.

"We got gypped. The third floor of this building is supposed to have two papers with chemical agents that, when wrapped together, do the trick. Yet, here I am."

She wilts like the Sahara Forest. Amused by her raspy wheeze, young Rosey remarks, "Glad to hear we've got that tuned." Then adult Rosemary resumes composure and greets a pastor sent by hospice.

What the heck? I ask myself, whiplashed by her sudden shifts in personality. While the minister ministers, I collect my thoughts. *How many lost brain cells before I lose her forever? Where sets the line between life and death? And where has adorable Rosey been all my life?* Reengaged by my mother's raised eyebrows, I realize the man has lost his way, perhaps more so than my demented mom.

Rosemary listed her religious preference as Unitarian Universalism, the one she finds most inclusive regardless of people's spiritual paths. This preacher of another ilk seizes the opportunity to proselytize his pious bias. Pokerfaced, he offers prayer.

She responds with honesty. "It won't bother me or make me jump over the moon. But if it makes you feel better, go ahead." The minister stiffens, recites a rote prayer void of compassion, and departs.

Religious only in the purest sense, Rose adopted moral convictions without succumbing to any official dogma. No exclusive Christian immersion, still she walked Jesus's teachings, going the extra mile, turning her other cheek, and loving neighbors without exception. Not Buddhist, she sauntered a Zen path of mindfulness, perceiving inner beauty like a Bodhisattva. Not Jewish, she climbed the Tree of Life, grasping divinity along its branches. Unfamiliar with Islam, her struggle within for loving understanding reflected jihad's deepest meaning. Only acquainted with Druid and Indigenous beliefs through reading, Rosemary identified with nature with a capital N. The antithesis of absolutisms that brandish sacred texts as weapons, her piety was that of a true mystic, rooted in love.

Walks in the woods with Rosemary in the 1950s were downright devotional. Behind our Runnemede, New Jersey home, sunlight filtered through old-growth canopies far above my child's eye view. Mom's beaming face illuminated the forest from below. She introduced us kids to sycamores, oaks, and hickories like ancestors who set our lives in motion long before our conception. My breath deepened hearing her explain photosynthesis. While we hopped over logs, across creeks, forest balance engaged our senses. "Earthworm perfume" I named the divine fragrance of soil-quenched petrichor. Our noses detected skunk cabbage before we spotted its broad leaves and primordial flowers. Tithing took several forms. We removed litter left by ignorant people and snipped dead twigs as if scratching trees' itches. And we festooned garlands of popcorn, Cheerios, walnuts, and cranberries as gifts for forest wildlife.

One bedtime storybook passage raised our mother's hackles. *The Incredible Journey* mentioned treacherous, encroaching forest kept in "subjection."[5] Quite the contrary, exploitive people and stray pets invade the wilderness, not the other way around. Our wooded paradise was a place we escaped *to*, not *from*. "In the company of trees, you're never alone" was Mom's benediction.

The chaplain departs our Florida home and Rosemary's mind follows suit.

"I'm better off horizontal than vertical, but why are we in Central America?"

Around the corner at her house, I find things for her new bedroom. Eureka! A *National Geographic* world atlas. Hung in her bedroom, we can mark wherever her mind teleports.

A nurse thumps Rosemary's distended belly, checking for a possible GI bleed.

"If anybody answers, I'm leaving," Rose tells her.

"I'm going to listen to your lungs, okay?"

"Feel free. They still speak the same language."

The RN advises, "Discontinue the Phenergan. Use Compazine and Senna-S for constipation."

Rosemary chimes in. "And I'd appreciate potatoes too." Down to 111 pounds, her appetite returns. She devours a hearty lunch, morsel by morsel.

Next day, Rosemary beams with promise. "I feel strangely normal." She recalls enough to realize her improvement. Up with her walker, Rose bears full weight for the first time since her initial rehab fall. Wincing, she grabs her hip. But a crossword puzzle diverts her attention. Seated, she picks up a pencil. "I'm returning to the land of the living."

A short time later, she loses her grounding again. "I'm in Europe?"

"No, Ma, this is Shalimar, Florida."

"I'm everywhere except where I'm expected to be." She sings about Shalimar, an old ditty called "Kashmiri Song."

Progress notwithstanding, she still requires constant reassurance to counter tricks her mind plays. We cram the hospital bed beside the other one where I'll sleep, in case she needs help.

As expected, at 3:00 a.m. she sits up and looks around as if lost. "Whatcha doin', Ma?"

"I'm not sure what I'm *supposed* to be doing in such limited visibility."

"It's dark because it's nighttime. You're supposed to sleep."

"Oh, okay." She lies down. "I wish somebody had told me."

"O day and night, but this is wondrous strange!"[6] Death doula Deborah predicted days like this to come. Sunrise jimmies open an other-worldly window. Rosemary hovers between dreaming and wakefulness, time and space, present and post-life. The ethereal fog fascinates her to no end. She literally takes leave of her senses on a marvelous cerebral adventure:

> *This can't be real, this in-betweenness. I'm going to have to lie down and go back in the blanket cocoon to be reborn. This is a curious world. We're every age at once. I'm twenty right now, the age of discovery. I'm here but semi-detached. It's funny, this semi-being and coming to . . . to this material world. I think I came from an egg, like a baby chick fully formed but slightly liquid. There's no terminology for the before—the fluid existence. Uncoagulated. The world I half remember, of half being . . . half-jelled. I'm here but not quite formed. We're sure we're real when we arrive but become less certain . . . I'm like a birdish being . . . not human . . . fully formed, not waiting to grow up, but wet and uncomposed. I could be hairy or smooth, round or birdlike.*

As usual, she waves her left hand but, for now, understands its diminished sensation. Missing aspects exist on another plane, waiting for the rest of her to catch up. Fascinated, she explains:

> *I need to keep moving this like a hand, so that is what it continues to be. It's such a convenient feature. My right hand is all here, fully formed, more hand-like. The left feels rounded, slightly liquid. This is a whole different world than where I left it. Still formative . . . like in a jar of liquid and not quite settled on what it wants to be. Hairy or smooth? I think I'll give up the hairy—another thing to maintain.*

Only one foot in this world, Rosemary roams an atemporal realm, like that described by brain scientist and stroke survivor Dr. Jill Bolte Taylor.[7] Whether the mystical scene is transcendent, macrocosmic, or misfiring cerebral circuitry is irrelevant. This is my mother's beguiling journey. Her voice trails off, leaving me yearning for more. But until my time comes, I am but a spectator.

A serious look melts her smile. "I have to ask a truth: Blackie, Beth,

Chris, Mart (nicknames for her husband and children)? Do they exist? Did they ever exist?"

To reassure her, I call Beth in New Jersey and put Mom on the phone. Conversation complete, her fretting continues. Tag team, Robert intervenes, trying to understand his discombobulated mother-in-law.

"What's on your mind, Rose?"

"Less than there used to be. I'm working with one-eighth of a brain, and you're asking three-fourth questions." She brightens as they exchange jokes and jabs.

Enchanted guests jot Rosemary's remarks on scraps of paper. Lots of them. Gathered handfuls mount on household surfaces, preserving my mother's eloquence, lest we forget.

Dark clouds descend today as my brother's birthday approaches. Fragmented memories of his death from brain cancer haunt our mother. Her wailing intensifies as barbed recollections resurface: a colander-like apparatus screwed into Martin's skull for Gamma Knife radiosurgery, the bleak prognosis of mere months, his stifled moans. White-knuckled, she manned his unwieldy van, driving him over Newport Bridge for a doctor's appointment; Mart retched with nausea and fear. Fond memories bring heartache too: her Little Leaguer running for home, her little drummer boy's uncanny sense of rhythm, attic walls lined with egg cartons to muffle his practice sessions . . .

Memory gaps leave Rosemary howling in self-reproach, "A mother should remember her son's death. I can't even remember his life." Curled into fetal position on a chair, she recalls only enough to realize what she has lost. A nearby shelf contains the photo album of his life, if only I had thought to grab it and ease her cries with beautiful memories beyond what photos preserve.

Our jubilant parents rejoiced over the March 13, 1956 birth of their third and final offspring, a flawless son. They named the wee redhead Martin, Mom's maiden name. Introduced to us as a precious gift, sister Beth and I adored him. From then on, we were "Marty and the girls." Dad expanded the house to accommodate our family. The additional bedroom gave Mom a forest view, and baby Marty his own room.

The photo album of Martin always brings Rosemary's joy. Turning the page to his toddler years, she'd laugh as usual at Marty's antics. A genuine smile would have dried her tears.

"There goes Marty, crawling through the magazine rack. He always fell asleep in his highchair at supper time. That's his christening; you girls wore dresses I made for you, remember?"

Yes, Mom. I remember in vivid detail. Hypermnesia allows me to recall virtually everything. Since I could speak, I've been the keeper of family history. Mom stirred spaghetti sauce with Marty on her hip, his foot resting inside her apron pocket. Marty drummed on his overturned trash can. His drum rolled as our father opened the front door to our weekday five o'clock choruses of "Dad's home! Black and white photos don't do Marty's crimson hair justice. And prints cannot capture his gracious disposition.

If only that had happened. Instead, my brother's album remained on its shelf.

Taser-stunned by revived shock over Marty's death, I sit motionless. Mom's screaming bears witness to our shared agony. Brutal brainwaves shipwreck her on the salt-stained chair beside me.

Our death doula suggests we use "compassionate deception" if she asks about Martin. No point putting her through his cancer each time she recalls her wonderful son. For the sake of empathy, "Marty lives in Newport, Rhode Island," his last home.

For the first time since Marty was born, Rosemary forgets it's his birthday. Her body acknowledges his absence with nausea. She scowls at her breakfast.

"I'm looking at this hot chocolate, and I don't like the way it looks back."

Marty's birthday boosts my determination to handle an issue I've put off for too long. I leave our mother in the care of Robert and a hospice aide. It's time to confront an assailant, lest others fall prey to his abuse.

One of Rosemary's visitors repeatedly jeopardized her well-being while she lay helpless. But I could only spare enough energy to deflect his unwelcomed advances. Confronting the man had to wait until she was in safe hands.

The first sign of trouble happened before my mother's fourth stroke. She told me an elderly minister had made "suggestive, naughty little boy remarks." Back then, she possessed the wherewithal to dismiss the man's lewdness. However, as she lost the capacity to fend for herself, his deviant sexual misconduct worsened at the rehab and hospital. A band of friends coordinated shifts to watch over Rosemary. During one rehab visit, our death doula was repulsed by the pastor's introduction.

Pointing at Rosemary he said: "I'm her secret lover. She has many because she's so foxy." An uncouth innuendo, but no big deal.

Another sitter caught the creepy guy lying beside Rose as she pushed him away. The caregiver ran in and redirected the cleric to a chair.

The minister's misconduct escalated to blatant sexual battery in February, the day Rosemary struggled for her life at the hospital. Seeing my distraught exhaustion, the pastor feigned an offer of comfort. "You need a big Gospel hug." His arms around me, trembling with a surge of hormones, he grabbed my buttocks, pulled me into his crotch, and gyrated his pelvis against my groin.

"Stop that." I recoiled. Years of childhood sexual abuse by grown men replayed, and my knees buckled. Just as fast, I braced myself with mature revulsion that the once-dignified cleric would stoop to such reprehensible behavior.

With a smirk and deranged glint in his eyes, he released me.

Fretting over what action to take sapped energy from my mother's care. I contacted Lutheran church officials at the national level to determine how to file a formal complaint. I confided in a Catholic priest and Unitarian Universalist minister we knew. My husband agreed with me that the depraved pastor showed signs of senility. But, at that time, Rosemary's care took priority.

After my mother moved in with us, the man showed up once. A parishioner from his church came to visit Rosemary, and the crude minister tagged along. My mom flinched in recognition. People noticed her recoil. I took her aside and asked what bothered her.

"He makes my skin crawl," was all she said, unable to remember specifics.

Marty's birthday infuses me with strength to address the matter. I make an appointment with the minister during church business hours. Printed, documented incident reports in hand, I head for the church. Feeling vulnerable, I stop at a friend's house for moral support, but nobody is home. I collect myself for the encounter, imagining my brother by my side. The cleric targets vulnerable women. *If I'm alone, he'll be less defensive.* Outrage fuels my determination.

Upon my arrival, we exchange salutations, and I present the printed complaint. He reads aloud with pride rather than regret. He admits to everything, pleased someone noticed his perverse sexual prowess. Reading on, he struts the church library like a rooster, oblivious to me jotting down his comments.

"That sounds right. That's me. Yep, I said that." Eventually, he notices my revulsion and promises never to touch Rosemary *again*, implying that he already made sexual advances toward her. He then addresses his blatant offense against me.

"Why didn't you clobber me?"

This is how civilized people "clobber" assailants, with assertive confrontation, neither complacent nor violent, I think. "Consider yourself clobbered. We never want to see you again," I say aloud and leave.

Police involvement would be too taxing along with my mom's care. But his current church addresses the situation, and others he abused come forward. One victim was too humiliated by his "big Gospel hug" to speak sooner. A mentally-challenged woman felt flattered by his attention. At a public park, someone caught him groping a gullible lady. Unreported until now, the man had continued his lewd behavior.

The minister claimed to be a member in good standing of the American Association of Lutheran Churches and a life member of the Unitarian Universalist Ministers Association. Various church officials handle the matter. Relieved, I turn my attention back to my mom.

Rosemary greets the morning, from somewhere in the frigid north. "It's an adventure sleeping in one place and waking up in another. Why is Carol shivering near the Arctic Circle?" she asks about her niece, who is not here and lives in California. Rose shuffles to the bathroom. Toothbrush in hand, she stares into the mirror.

"Why are we brushing our teeth in Alaska?"

Robert bids Rosemary good morning and mentions flying squirrels in our backyard last night.

"I'm sorry, I don't speak Aleutian," she replies with polite sincerity as if addressing a foreign stranger.

A Post-it marks Alaska on the atlas. The map grows colorful with out-of-body travel notes. She wanders the planet unhinged; we map her whereabouts to keep ourselves grounded.

Today, dressed in green, we honor St. Patrick. Perky, half-Irish Rosemary helps make her bed. Instead of hot chocolate, this morning I make strawberry milk for variety.

She smacks her lips. "This drink is similar but with a judicious change."

Her differentiation signifies improvement. I imagine my mom fully recovered. But that Pollyanna fantasy wavers with her next comments.

"I look forward to liberation from uncertainty." She clarifies: "I've had a good life. I think there must be some further realm. Humans are persistent in everything else. Why not persist in existence?" Cheerful anticipation outflanks the past's pleasantries.

Like everyone, Rosemary needs a sense of purpose. Household responsibilities assure her that she belongs. Regardless of circumstance, this is no less true for retirees, foster children, caged prisoners, the terribly affluent, than for those with dementia.

We compile a list of easy chores. Rosemary sharpens pencils, pairs socks, and dusts nearby surfaces. Longing to cook, she contents herself peeling carrots or potatoes. We supervise, then redo everything once she's out of sight. If she gets confused, no worry. Dementia comes to her rescue, and she forgets her bewilderment. Surrounded by carrot skins, peeler abandoned, she reads the produce bag.

Child Rosey keeps close company with adult Rosemary. This morning, she springs up with a chipper song, "How Much is that Doggie in the Window?" and mentions ululation. I'm clueless.

"A woooo," she howls, neck stretched upward in wolf fashion.

Regardless of age, dying seldom concludes with "that's that." The dead leave unfinished matters. Lifelong potential dies with children. For elders like Rosemary, death severs bonds cultivated over decades. Young or old, postmortem closure does not exist. Life is insatiable. We want more.

The neediness of my mother during her slow demise imparts a blessing. Exhaustion does not allow time to lament. As we watch her trickle away, duty stifles grief. I miss my mom but keep busy caring for her shadow.

Months turn to years since her strokes began, and we must recharge our batteries periodically. Medicare allows five days of respite per month in a skilled nursing home for hospice patients in family care. It's economical. If families collapse, then the state foots the bill for full-time institutionalization. And people like my mom lose loving attention.

It's a grueling decision. No facility can handle Rosemary well. Medications changed to facility protocol force her body to adapt. Negligence is inevitable with insufficient staff. She always returns to us worse off—with infections, impactions, bruises, knots on her head, and diminished mental function. The best facilities available charge five-digit monthly fees for full-time residency.

Rosemary is neither rich nor poor. Our country only affords top quality care to the wealthy; the indigent are at the mercy of whatever their state provides. As a middle-class elder with senility, Rose faces major defects in the system as well. All her life, she dutifully squirreled away for retirement. But institutional memory care would eat savings like chicken feed and leave her no better off than the poorest of the poor. Long-term care insurance would not have helped with arbitrary definitions of "facility," price hikes, and exclusions. Rosemary has supportive family; others are at the mercy of an understaffed healthcare industry.

Needed improvements in elder care require legislative action. This rarely happens unless brought by successful lawsuits. But attorneys' bread-and-butter monetary settlements hinge on future wage-earning potential, inapplicable to retired seniors.

Rosemary has sensible savings, Social Security, my dad's pension, his VA benefits, Medicare, and secondary health insurance. Yet the sum is nowhere near adequate for around-the-clock care. Thank God for family, sitters, and supportive community.

People wealthy in heart, not pocket, learn what money cannot buy. My brother's death taught me what he needed most was loving devotion. In shock over his fate, I focused on his medical care, something I understood. Detached, I lost sight of what matters most and let my brother down. Marty deserved more from me.

Automatic pilot desensitizes people to bleak duties. Foot soldiers develop this deadening effect; with each combat kill, they dissociate with greater ease. Likewise, drudgeries done in thoughtless routine callous caregivers. Answering endless questions, walking in tiny steps, cleaning poop from fingernails . . . unpleasantries deaden emotions. Unchecked detachment hampers the humane care Rosemary deserves.

In my teens, I discovered a babysitting trick. When changing dirty diapers, focus on the child, not the mess. Applied to paramedic runs, I focused on patients, not just bloodshed. One-on-one connection eclipses foul tasks with impressionable infants, injured patients, troubled foster children, and now with Rosemary. Revived compassion comes in momentary revelations, those tender instances when we catch each other's eyes.

Traces of Rosemary, the way she was, punctuate her existence. They surface with Rosey, in song bursts, outlandish one-liners, and her trumpet nose blows. Her Jersey dialect unfurls as do welcoming arms and fiddles on a fern. Decades in Florida, she still drinks "wooder"—watch out for those splinters. Dessert is "schleck." Horrible is "harrible." She savors northern cuisine's scrapple, pork roll, and hoagies, but no dippy eggs, please.

Opportunities arise unexpectedly. Rosemary drops the box of freshly sharpened pencils on the kitchen floor. She bends down to gather the ungainly heap. Instead, we park ourselves feet-to-feet on either side of the pile and play a makeshift game of pick-up sticks.

Along with nostalgic hindsight, Rosemary develops spiritual antennae attuned to what awaits. She foretells renewed relationships with people long passed, horseback adventures, and pending tea parties. These perks of her predicament relax our caregiving toil. Right now, she sings about dear, dead days. Aha! The lyrics lead into "Love's Old Sweet Song."

Rosemary remains a walking, talking encyclopedia. She cannot button, cut food on her plate, or pull blankets over herself. Yet she recites Shakespeare and does *New York Times* crosswords. Faster than a dictionary or computer, she spells and defines with impeccable accuracy as I call to her.

"Ma, how do you spell an-TEN-I? Pre-DIK-uh-mint? Em-PECK-a bul?"

Lessons learned in childhood stick like glue. Rosemary rises from nested couch covers. Heading for the john, she swipes renegade hair strands from her face, a good sign that the hip no longer hurts. Teetering along, she grabs anything handy for stability. The walker serves little purpose; she trips over the device. The wheelchair works no better. Mistaking it for a walker, she bends over, clutches the seat support, and hobbles forward, unable to see where she is going. Mostly, she clings to furniture and wobbly doorknobs. Even so, she seldom falls. An accomplished tree climber in her youth, Rosemary knows to keep three of her four extremities secure as she lurches along, adept if not graceful.

"ME JANE"

Growing up in the Tarzan era and true to her middle name, Rosemary Jane Martin took to the trees. High in a weeping willow canopy, she knew Audubon, New Jersey from a bird's eye view. She coursed through the air bursting forth cringe-worthy yodels. The cousins marveled at Rose's agility. She taught those kids to select trees with strong lateral branches. And always stay three-fourths secure to avoid breaking limbs–tree or otherwise.

Rejecting conventional gender biases, Rosemary knew that girls could do darn near anything boys could, and vice versa. She preferred slacks over housedresses and spoke her mind, albeit in a low-key manner. Her arboreal knowledge surpassed that of peers. Rose recognized trees as homes to wildlife, providers of shade, and givers of the air we breathe.

No more tree climbing for Rosemary in this lifetime. She longs for some productive task.

"I'm a step above a wall ornament," she says, staring into space.

In an effort to boost her spirit above wall ornament, I devise a task. My mom and I sort get-well cards into same-size piles. Sewing each stack together at the folds creates free-standing loops. Not only better organized, in theory, this will keep her reading in circles. But after a few notes, she forgets what she is doing. It's fine. The circular greetings compile heaps of loving messages into decorative displays.

Rosemary JANE Martin

Nieces Ginny and Rita visit from New Jersey to bid their dear aunt a final farewell. Besides offering moral support, they clean her house. Aunt Rosie serenades with, "Work for the Night is Coming."

Lung damage from pneumonia could explain Rosemary's chronic respiratory distress. Struggling for air, she remembers a similar sensation at high elevations. "My body has become regionally disloyal. I'm in mountainous terrain, a different locale than the last time I breathed. When in doubt, lie down." With that, she flops onto the couch.

A metaphysical shuffle disrupts her 3-D grounding for several days. Temporal and spatial acuity shift in and out of awareness. Discombobulated Rosemary weirds out.

"Where am I? What am I? What time am I?"

Robert diverts her existential angst. His rendition of a Persian Sanskrit proverb reroutes his fretful mother-in-law into laughter:

He who knows not and knows not that he knows not is a fool—avoid him.
He who knows not and knows that he knows not is a student—teach him.
He who knows and knows not that he knows is asleep—wake him.
He who knows and knows that he knows is wise—follow him.

"Sounds like a bunch of knotty noses," Rosemary teases. Sorting the lines into meaningful snippets, fascination nudges out my mother's frustration.

Following a peaceful night's sleep, we function better. My mom's dementia subdues as well. The upside of sundowner syndrome, I call the phenomenon "sunup syndrome." Vital to mental health, the importance of sleep is an ancient Earth wisdom. My Anishinaabe Ojibwe friend Hwana Quense's name means "filled with early morning awareness." Rest cleanses the brain; clearer thought prevails.

"I feel like a real person." Rosemary sings, "Happy Days are Here Again," shoving her arms into the sleeves I hold. Feet wiggle into their respective socks in time to the tune.

Late March, Rosemary aims for the bathroom and misses. Robert and I hear the minor fall and gallop to her aid. She has already forgotten how she got on the floor. Perplexed and hurting, she looks at us.

"Did I just give birth?" she asks with troubled sincerity. Hip, elbow, and finger impact points demand attention. The fall soon forgotten, the pain persists.

"Oh, ouch. What happened here?" echoes off the walls all day long.

Outside, waking birds greet the morning in twittering conversation. Indoors, Rosemary considers her options.

"Mom, what would you like to do today?"

"Well, it's not going to be anything athletic. Where's the vacuum cleaner?"

"It's around the corner at your house, Ma."

"If you bring this house around the corner, I'll get these floors done."

Robert reads aloud to Rose about the physics standard model of quantum mechanics. Another animated discussion ensues. Intrigued, they consider the hypothesis that elementary particles jump in and out of existence.

"If that is true, Rose, then what are we?"

"Apparently, we're space savers," the sage matriarch responds.

Therapy brings blessings and curses. An occupational therapist provides crossword puzzles for mental stimulation. After twenty minutes, Rosemary fixates on them. Recent memories refuse to congeal but repetitive activities logjam. Crossword-headed, she enters the bathroom. Perched on the toilet, she forgets what to do.

"What are the rules here? I don't know what letter I need to start."

With considerable coaxing, she urinates. At the sink, she washes her hands but forgets how to dry them, across or down. Holding the walker's arms she hesitates, unsure how it works.

"What are the restrictions on the operation of this? Does it have to start or end with a certain number of letters?"

A jigsaw puzzle breaks the crossword spell. While I cook supper, she sorts pieces and a new fixation seizes her brain. During dinner, she forgets how to eat, arranging spaghetti, broccoli, and pills together on her plate.

Robert asks what she's doing.

"Edible jigsaw, if I can just figure out the pattern."

The big picture surpasses her comprehension. I stop eating and feed my mom.

April Fool's Day, Rose awakens in contemplation. "I need to ask a serious question: Have your father and your brother died? We need to plan their memorial service. At a designated time, say 2:00 p.m. on Sunday, everyone go to their front doors, wave goodbye, and blow them kisses."

This new tradition will serve well whenever she pines for them. We show her photographs: the live band at Marty's Rhode Island memorial and the second service for New Jersey friends at Knight's Park in Collingswood. A decade prior, my father's Florida VFW funeral ended at Crowder Chapel cemetery near Shoal Sanctuary Nature Preserve. Photos bring awful memories. Guests gasped as she sprinkled my father's ashes. Whole, unpulverized bones and teeth fell from the crematorium container onto the gravesite. Rose remembers with gratitude how Robert buried my dad's bones. Suddenly, she forgets the hour-long conversation and concludes with one final question:

"Tell me something, Chris. Are Marty and your father dead?"

At the front door, we wave goodbye and blow them kisses.

Strolling the street out front, my mother looks anxious. Sunlight filters through the leaves. A gust of wind stirs. She shudders like a frightened child.

"I'd just as soon go airborne on a breeze. It's scary. Everything is going away."

I let go of her hand and put my arm snug around her shoulders. "I gotcha, Mom."

I sing Nat King Cole's "Nature Boy" to comfort her, replacing "boy" with "mom."

Back inside, she examines her half-finished 100-piece jigsaw. Attention shifts from the mound to the segment between her fingers. "This is a challenge but not as puzzling as what's going on in my brain."

At a Zumba Gold musical exercise class for seniors, Rose watches from her wheelchair and sways to the beat. Heading home, we run errands.

At Kohl's department store, the elevator is safer, but Rosey wants to ride the escalator.

"If you're worried about falling, install a sliding board." She frolics over and grabs the moving handrail.

As the amusement ride ascends, I clutch her waistband. Exiting, she notices my security grip and follows my arm to my face. Pleasant familiarity dawns.

"I've known you since you were born." She pats my cheek.

Heading home, we first stop to visit her friend Lois who resides nearby Hawthorn House, an assisted living facility. The tough old birds wisecrack over mortality.

Rose reiterates her death motto to Lois. "My mouth will be the last thing to go."

"After we die," agrees Lois, "they'll have to kill our still-yapping traps."

Rosemary notices that dramatic weight loss has left Lois flabby.

"You don't have as many groceries, but you still have the empty shopping bags."

A day later, Rose awakens in her bedroom, yet somewhere else.

"I like it here with these Icelandic people—very civil."

Another map Post-it affixed, her colorful atlas outshines today's outfit as I dress her. She asks if plain slacks and shirt are customary Nordic attire. Thinking the geological reference means she's cold, I bundle on more layers. She thanks me with the polite demeanor of a patron at a haberdashery.

Sometimes she mistakes me and Robert for my reclusive sister Beth and her husband Frank. Generations superimpose, and she confuses her son Martin and grandson Adam. But Rosemary could never be mistaken for anyone else. Our "RoseMom" is one of a kind.

At nightfall, Robert and I try blocking her in with the bedside commode. In theory, she'll find it, use it, and get back into bed. In reality, she climbs over and makes her way to the toilet. Awakened by the ruckus, I stumble down the hall and flip on the light. Sorrowful Rosemary gropes around the bathroom, searching for the pot.

"Why has everyone left me? Am I a bad person?" Her eyes well with tears.

Situated on the seat, she takes care of business while I list people who adore her. Poof, Rosey's voice chimes. She recalls her eldest sibling, nicknamed Dolly because she was a premature infant. Rosemary remembers Dolly alive, married, and with children—lots of children.

"My sister has a one-bedroom house with an outhouse and fifteen kids. I think it's the only way she and her husband know how to communicate."

Greeting cards brighten Rosemary's eighty-ninth birthday. From her house, I add cards she kept over the years. Thanks to lost brain cells, old greetings bring joy anew. Rosemary's world is timeless.

Reading the cards holds her attention longer this birthday. She most treasures the signatures. If she struggles to remember someone, I pencil a reminder for the next time around.

A keepsake since my father died two decades ago, I give Mom my dad's pajamas.

Robert kept a pair of his father's too. Sometimes we wear them and reminisce about our dads, Herman and Oscar. Rosemary dons the brown checkered, way-too-big-for-her sleepwear and waltzes in place.

"It's like being in my darling's embrace."

Another day older, my mother accompanies me to tai chi. She watches the synchronized exercise like a sports fan, mesmerized by the slow-motion dance as if seeing it for the first time. She applauds the group's sixty-four-position ballet.

"Beautiful, like reeds blowing in the breeze."

In closing, class members form a circle, Rosemary included. Hands together, we bow in mutual respect and say, "Namaste," Sanskrit for "The image of God within me honors the image of God within you." Rosemary and instructor Anita launch into song. Today, it's "By the

Light of the Silvery Moon." Those who know the lyrics join in. Bodies sway. Smiles beam. Then members share gifts from their hearts.

"Rosemary's presence warms my soul," says Anita.

"Those Rosemaryisms, so pithy, timeless, and universal," adds Marilyn.

Classmate Robin remarks, "Her distinct ways make me appreciate my own beauties and foibles."

Back home, Rose twiddles her thumbs. "I feel like I should be doing something productive. Maybe licking stamps for letters."

"Postage comes with peel-off backing now, Ma."

"There goes my career," she shrugs. Unable to summon a memory, her eyes narrow. "I have no history."

To jog her mind, I mention climbing trees, hosting gatherings, cooking, mothering, filing, writing . . . her New Jersey past, concealed by dusty dementia cobwebs.

She interrupts, "I'm not in the right place zone or time zone."

"It's the strokes, Mom. Parts of you have been spirited away by dementia. But don't worry. The rest of you will catch up eventually."

Outside, fluffy clouds broaden her disposition. She points skyward.

"Looks like somebody baked them in the kitchen."

Another beautiful spring day, tai chi meets outdoors at Shoal Sanctuary Nature Preserve. Rosemary watches from a rocking chair, shooing mosquitoes with a small stick. Bundled in a blanket, she waves her scepter like an orchestra conductor. After our concluding "namaste," Robert escorts her to the farmhouse along leafy trails. Others follow. I'm the caboose.

Arm in arm, the in-laws exchange playful insults followed by apologetic back scratches. It's a pact they made after my father Herman Baker died. Robert had read that loss of touch worsens grief for surviving spouses. He remembered Rose's wish that her wedding vows had been "love, honor, and scratch each other's backs." An acceptable form of physical contact for in-laws, the feisty pair permits one another's smart-aleck remarks if followed by conciliatory back scratches.

Scanning *Physics Today*, he bellows to overcome her tinnitus. His boisterous recitation is clear to me from the kitchen where I cook. My heart sings with their uproarious laughter as Rosemary summarizes a quantum query about the nature of being.

"Apparently, we're confused by design."

"Loved ones are our greatest treasures." That's how Rosemary justified astronomical long-distance telephone bills over the years. Now, she wants to call her people, many long gone. To help prepare her for death, I superimpose her past-tense loved ones on a future-tense collage. Those who once peopled her world go toward the light of Doré's "Paradiso." The poster looks forward to a reunion-ever-after in the great wherever-we-go.

Newspaper headlines about shameful injustices raise Rosemary's ire. Dangerous white supremacist incivilities get her goat. "Racism is ridiculous. This country owes its richness to our diversity."

During a trip to the bathroom, she startles at the mirror's reflection. "Oh my, how old am I?"

"You're 89, Mumz."

"I'd better get busy and register to vote."

Today's nurse notices Rose's twitchy toes. "How are your feet, Rosemary?"

The question baffles her. Staring down at them she replies, "One on the end of each leg."

The woman asks about my mother's bladder habits. Rose answers from decades ago, oblivious to what now transpires each night.

"I usually get up once at night in the wee hours, if you'll excuse the expression."

Rose longs to hear the voices of Jeanette MacDonald and Nelson Eddy. Old clips on YouTube play as we eat popcorn. The operatic duo inspires her to sing along to "Indian Love Call," "Maytime," and "Sweethearts."

Waving her permanently numb appendage, she gripes, "I can't hear with this left hand."

"Neither can anyone else, Ma."

"I'm philosophical, not frustrated. I wonder what this hand is thinking." Left wrist grasped in her right hand, she flaps the floppy thing as if trying to awaken a rag doll.

Something on the carpet catches her eye. She abandons her left hand, stoops over, and grabs a bell that fell off her anklet. Mistaken for hard candy, she pops the colorful thing in her mouth.

I lunge my open hand under her chin. "Spit it out in Mommy's hand," I quote what she said when we were little. We restitch the bell onto the ankle band and jingle to the car for errands with Robert.

"In you go," he says, holding the door open for her in gentlemanly fashion.

"Dark blue," she replies.

The two of us pause, exchange deciphering looks, then raise our eyebrows in unison.

"Ah, indigo," we chime. That one took a second.

During the ride, Rosemary self-reflects with uncanny anatomical accuracy. "Fragmented memories are merciful. I don't know how much I've lost because the connections are missing." Losing white matter cells that bind gray matter thoughts, her mind abandons memories like broken promises.

A thunderstorm blows a drenched hospice gal through our front door. Already soaked, she showers Rosemary. Afterward, at my mother's insistence, the soggy aide joins us for hot tea. A civilizing tradition—from Ireland to China, Morocco to England, Russia to Japan—teatime warms the bones.

Jersey brevity is in full swing this morning.

"M'ere (Come here). Lu-ka-dis (Look at this)." She gestures at nothing visible.

"S'up (What is up), Ma?"

"Jeet (Did you eat)?"

"Na, j'u (No, did you)?" I fry scrapple and peel an arange (orange).

She recites relatives' names, anticipating birthdays. "Where d'we keep greeting cards?"

Shorthand Jersey speech sounds like Rosemary is fit as a fiddle. But hugging her, my arms embrace a skin-and-bones relic.

The Paradiso poster jigsaw arrives, customized online via Portrait Puzzles. Pieces held in Rosemary's palm connect past and future. Images of people from her past roll out a red carpet to her mortal future. With tempered excitement, my mother scrutinizes segmented features.

> *Let's see, this is your father's dimpled chin. Here's Marty's crimson hair. Why is Nanny Muller's leg bandaged? Homer's waving. Grosspop's wearing the vest Grossy made; that's his pocket watch chain. There's Dona beside the chief. Uncle Tom keeps loose change beneath his sweater. Sweet Jane's looking at something. Here's our dogs Wolfie and Charlie and Splash. Ha, Mag's up in the clouds.*

Delicious dreams awaken Rosemary this morning. "I'm making spaghetti sauce. Wanna taste?"

"Mmm, yummy thought, Ma." Once she's dressed, we stagger to the living room.

"If I could walk straight instead of wavering, I'd cover more territory."

Until the strokes, Rosemary was a meat-and-potatoes gal. A throwback to Irish ancestry, spuds still top her favorite foods list. Mashed, baked, scalloped, riced, or rissoled, they make her life complete. And her German genes crave sauerkraut at least monthly. Leftovers become superb Reuben sandwiches. Cheese melted on the bread is Mom's secret to seal out sauerkraut moisture. Heredities merge with warm German potato salad.

Preparing dinner, she asks what we're making.

Recipes only consulted for inspiration, modified ingredients and improvised instructions create original meals. Tonight's rice concoction contains sautéed onions, fresh ginger, roasted pecans, anise, and orange peels, simmered in coconut rice.

Pre-stroke Rosemary disparaged my cooking, leery of unfamiliar foods. She'd have scoffed at this menu, thumbs down. "Where're the meat and potatoes?" Instead, she savors every bite. In some ways, our altered relationship is an honest-to-God pleasure.

Accustomed to Rosemary's proclivity, Robert offers potato chips.

"Sure," she perks. "I'd gladly be in the company of the lowly potato." After a handful, she exalts the vegetable further.

"If there was a potato political party, I'd join."

The three of us lounge in the living room. "Oof," says Robert falling into his chair.

"What's that?" Rose asks with concern.

"Woof, woof," he revises.

"Arf, arf," she responds in kind.

Their unpredictable exchanges sparkle my world.

Tinnitus hounds her like a Baskerville plague. "I wish my ears would howl a different tune," Rose gripes. "I don't know why they call it a handicap. It sure feels like an unhandy cap."

The visiting nurse announces that Rosemary's blood pressure, pulse, O_2 saturation, and temperature are all textbook perfect.

"Were they okay yesterday?" she asks.

"Yes, Ms. Rose. Good vitals yesterday too.

"Guess I'm getting the hang of it."

5-B, STROKE-FREE

INTERMISSION: R.I.P. POSTPONED

*Although the weather has made little mention of spring,
the maples are making a determined effort
to convince the world of its approach.
Promising nodes protrude pinkly
from skeleton fingers like a hopeful sort of arthritis.*
– ROSEMARY, 1966

ROSEMARY FEELS FINE AND DANDY. Her condition no longer meets Medicare criteria for hospice. Her death march has detoured. Back on home healthcare, therapy resumes. Hospice picks up their O2, wheelchair, and hospital bed. Her room regains its homey appeal.

The program shift means new helpers. The intake nurse forgets something in her car.

"I'll be right back."

"We've been threatened," Rosemary orients the woman to her tongue-in-cheek humor.

Near the front door, a Potter's wasp takes up residence. Rose names it Jiminy Bee and says it's the buzzing conscience of people past. Hovering in midair, Jiminy keeps a civil distance.

"Jim, for short." The buzz triggers a mental excursion to Rosey's childhood.

"Grapevines attract bees," she announces. "People with an outhouse plant grape arbors," for privacy along the well-worn path from their house.

The Martins prized their two indoor bathrooms at their Audubon, New Jersey home. The muddy dirt road of Atlantic Avenue rutted with activity from countless get-togethers. On sunny day gatherings, everyone congregated in the backyard. During stormy weather, only ten could cram into the dining room, elbow to elbow. Living room overflow held another ten, packed like sardines. A year of determination converted the cellar into a rumpus room. Stoop-shouldered, neighbors formed bucket brigades, bantering as they shoveled out the dirt floor. That basement became a local hot spot.

Reunions, birthdays, wedding receptions, christenings, Sweet Adelines practice, formative Toastmasters talks, Artisans Cooperative Insurance meetings, and Bell Telephone pioneers converged in the Martins' cellar-turned-basement. Rosemary believed the draw was her parents' kindness. Although not rich, the family was resourceful and coordinated feasts during Depression years. Like parables of stone soup, loaves and fishes, and water turned to wine, people shared whatever food they had. Their World War II victory garden yielded kohlrabi, carrots, potatoes, lettuce, cabbage, beans, corn, eggplant, and, of course, Jersey tomatoes. Mothers made pies, cakes, and irresistible red cabbage. The popular Martin home earned the affectionate abbreviation, "240."

Rosemary likes her flip phone with its 240 prefix that reminds her of New Jersey gatherings. This morning, she recites the names of her thirty-three nieces and nephews but interrupts herself. "We are overdue for a get-together at 240."

Hmm? I try to decipher why she's reciting addresses. *Oh, it's the places she lived in New Jersey and Florida.*

"Genoa Avenue north of the Black Horse Pike, Lions Court inland from Atlantic City, Kendal Boulevard in Oaklyn, "240" in Audubon, Sheppard Avenue in Runnemede, Newton Avenue back in Oaklyn, Osborne Drive in Fort Walton Beach." Her past eight years in Shalimar have all but erased.

Diagnosed with postural hypotension, it's official: Rosemary is a dizzy broad. "How is it possible that a house this big can spin?" she asks. "I'm glad no one else can hear the ringing in my ears," she remarks, plagued by the constant barrage of tinnitus. Aware of her mental deficit, Rose ponders legal aspects. "Let's see, *non compos mentis.* Which one am I still missing, the *non,* the *compos,* or the *mentis?*"

Assured that she handled legal formalities before needed, she summarizes her state of affairs: "Sufficeth to say, I'm a bona fide nincompoop."

Memorial Day arrives and, like Mother's Day, we honor its original intent. Founded post-Civil War by freed slaves who decorated graves of fallen liberators, Decoration Day commemorates freedom from oppression. In celebration of Rosemary's reprieve, I design a T-shirt that reads, *I survived hospice, R.I.P. postponed,* and a tombstone pronouncing, *Not Yet.*

Donning her liberation shirt, we take a stroll. She leans over to pet Louise, a Chihuahua-mix pup on the lower end of a leash. Rosemary follows the tether to the other end and arches her eyebrows at the neighbor she calls Thelma. "Would you like your ears scratched too?"

Black-and-white movies on YouTube keep Rosemary entertained. Her attention span is too limited to follow plots, but she recognizes actors.

"This was Dorothy Lamour's first hit. She plays a Polynesian woman, with Jon Hall as the guy. I always wanted hair long enough to sit on."

I interject some Rapunzel reality. Long hair closes in car windows, snags in zippers, and must be wrapped around the neck before sitting, especially on toilets. My braid tucked inside my jacket dangles below. The tail end leaves her in stitches.

An occupational therapist takes Rosemary for a walk around the corner to her old home to trigger memories. She spots the low Magnolia limb she used to climb with her toddler great-granddaughter, Kayla. Flowerbeds planted by like-a-son Glenn rekindle his visits. Recognitions revive seeing the kitchen pass-through, oak floors, Dad's John D. Edwards model ship, and his azalea we transplanted when she moved here. Memory to memory she hops as if on stepping stones to her past.

After returning, the OT gal leaves . . . and my mother disappears. We search the house in vain. Neighbors join the hunt. Eventually, we discover Rosemary sitting on her porch around the corner.

"I did *not* wander off," she protests. "I was finished and it was time to come home." She points to the sign above the front door: "Herman & Rosemary Baker."

Relieved, search party members hug her. She returns each embrace.

"Hugs are great because they're reciprocal," says Rose.

Back around the corner in bed, she forgets the incident. However, thoughts linger of yesterday's storm. "What a beautiful day this is. The sun's dappling the carpet with 'Sure, I can do it' rays. Nature is apologizing for yesterday." Her rainfall recollection signals some reengaged short-term memory.

Rose pitches in with chores. Robert follows behind, refolding her laundry attempts. After lunch, she washes dishes. Then I mop the floor, change her wet clothes, and rewash the dishes. It's worth it. She is pleased to be functional.

"I'm beginning to do minor chores. Hope for a promotion to vacuuming soon."

Never a dull moment, Mom sees me zoom through the living room and recalls the pleasure of driving, on a whim, wherever her heart desired. We are happy to chauffeur her, but that's not the point. What she misses is the freedom, not the destination. She forgets why she stopped driving and shifts gears to a childhood poem from primary school:

"I'm sure that I can drive a car. I know that I could travel far.

For this is all you need to know, that red means stop and green means go."

Rosemary had a flawless driving record until her late seventies. First there were a few fender benders. Then an alarming incident convinced her to stop driving forever. At a stop sign, she halted and looked both ways, three times. On the second glance, she saw a couple on bicycles approaching. Rose looked again and pulled out right in front of them. If not for the cyclists' quick reflexes, she would have bowled them over. Rosemary confided in horror that her mind hadn't registered what she'd seen. She never drove again, for fear of hurting someone—a commendable insight on when to quit.

Cognitive wherewithal outpaces Rosemary's physical coordination. Doing New York Times-level crosswords, eraser debris mounts from sloppy penmanship, not mistakes. Fanning a handful of cards, she fumbles. Fifty-Two Pickup replaces Rummy. Language retains its appeal to her, not math, not dexterity. Playing Scrabble, words she makes dance on my tongue—lollygag, chutzpah, iambic, crinoline—but she cannot count seven tiles or place them on the stand.

Neighbor Don engages her in jigsaw puzzles as they did for years at her house. She drops pieces on the floor; he patiently gathers them up. Although she loses herself in the puzzle, Rosemary is pleased with his good-natured company.

Jigsaw puzzling in good-natured company

Out of the blue, Rose describes her rehab fall months ago. She paints a semi-accurate picture, tinted in nonsensical hues. Instead of a hospital bed, she talks about getting out of a carriage.

"Sitting on that cold floor, waiting for someone to come, I wondered where the horses were stabled."

For exercise, Robert and I take Rose with us to the athletics complex on Northwest Florida State College campus where Robert taught for thirty years. The fitness center abuts my tai chi classroom with a windowed partition between. Mom stays with me while Robert lifts weights in the next room. Through the glass, we seniors imagine absorbing the invigorating energy ("chi" in Mandarin Chinese) of spry athletes next door. The more able-bodied huff and puff while we navigate through the slow-motion movements. Rose spots Robert and shuffles over to the window. Standing by the glass partition, she mimics his weightlifting and gets a little exercise herself.

Back at home, Rosemary scrutinizes her lunch. "I don't eat cottage cheese." Using her fork like a snowplow, she pushes the white curds aside. The voiced distaste brims with significance. She has regained preferences. Since her stroke four months ago, she would eat anything, wear anything, and go anywhere. Declining cottage cheese shows persnickety discernment. Selective choice requires self-awareness. Rosemary's renewed individuality sheds light on cantankerous youthful stages. Rite-of-passage "terrible twos" and "rebellious teens" steer us toward mature humanhood.

Yesterday's predilection was short-lived. Today Rosemary eats cottage cheese without notice. Her personal preferences disappear again. Life is a phase of existence marked by distinctions, undetermined near birth, unimportant near death.

Another spurt of independent thought occurs at our family forest, Shoal Sanctuary. Rosemary takes part in nurturing Florida Torreya yews. An assisted migration program, these are the most endangered North American tree and most endangered conifer on Earth. Torreyas cannot survive climate change without human help. Paleoecologist and lead authority on Torreya taxifolia Connie Barlow entrusted forty seeds of this ancient species to us. With Smithsonian Institute input, we guided forty children to name and plant each seed.

Rosemary applauded the novel idea of an eight-year-old participant. Kyle modeled his concept after Disney World's Hall of Presidents where guests stand in the footprints of Abraham Lincoln to hear the animatron speak. Kyle and his grandma Kitty fashioned a set of cardboard footprints where volunteers stand and speak on the trees' behalf. For my mom's turn, we try to make it easy, suggesting she simply say, "I'm a Torreya, happy to be alive."

Instead, she improvises. Hands overhead, fingertips peaked like a treetop, she sways in the breeze. "I am a Torreya tree. I don't talk much, but the wind and I sing together." Never underestimate Rosemary.

The woodland purchase was made possible from a settlement for my fractured neck, broken in the line of duty as a paramedic. A truck driver—arrested for driving intoxicated—totaled the ambulance as I tended to a critical patient. The patient fared okay. I was left lucky to be breathing on my own, let alone walking.

Acquainting ourselves with the land, we removed 100 years of human debris, then planted thousands of trees to reintroduce the natural longleaf forest. Generations to come inherit fresher air from our family forest. And every dawn, visions for Shoal Sanctuary ease my griping neck.

Our necks behaving, we visit friends and take a dip in their pool, Rosemary's first swim in twelve years. The eighty-nine-year-old paddles effortlessly from one end to the other. She only needs help with overcoming gravity as she gets out. I snap her photo, sun drying by the poolside. Later, I find a similar photo of her at age twenty-one, beside the Avalon meadow.

Swimmer at ages 21 and 89

At Zumba class during one particular song, my mother scrunches her face as if in pain. Before the next tune begins, I ask what's troubling her.

"That's the Russian tune, 'Field and Forest,' but played with a Latin rhythm."

After the session, I put the car radio on a station I assume she prefers. It plays 1940s music with big band sounds of Tommy Dorsey, Duke Ellington, and Benny Goodman.

She smiles. "This is the kind of music my brother Bill liked."

I ask what music she likes best.

Without hesitation, she answers. "Classical: 'Rhapsody in Blue,' 'Fields and Forest,' 'Warsaw Concerto' . . ."

I turn to a classical station and her demeanor transforms. Big-band style fills her with sibling nostalgia. Familiar songs with lyrics animate her. And classical music instills Rosemary with a far-off tranquility.

Back home, her cell phone rings. She reels it in from her pocket. It's my Aunt Pat making her weekly check-in call. Rose loves chats with Pat. Her forever-friend needs no introduction. Other callers must remind her who they are and how she knows them. Younger relatives start the conversation from generations ago and work forward. Some folks send selfies that I show my mother so she knows who is talking. After Pat, another call comes. Her niece's name appears on caller ID and I show my cousin's photo to my mom as I put the phone to her ear.

"Hi, Aunt Rosie. I'm your sister Jean's, daughter Judy's, daughter Mary's, daughter Bridget. Remember?"

Although Rosemary requires 24/7 dementia care, her body is mending. This is the first known time in her life that she is not anemic. Discharged from hospice last month and from home healthcare now, the three of us are on our own.

Our friend Sonia comes to visit, and we gals head to the Gulf Coast for a summer swim. Cool saltwater beckons us to leave the sultry shore. Holding my mom's hands, we make our way across the white quartz beach, admire a child's sandcastle, and wade in. Pelicans fly over the turquoise water. Sandpipers scurry along the retreating shoreline.

"Awk, awk," Rosemary calls to the seagulls. Ankle deep, she wiggles her toes in the sand and turns her face toward the sun like a potted plant set free in fertile soil. But the shallow surf proves too much. Splash! Down she flops and cannot get up from the puddle-deep water. Her legs are too weak. My grasp cannot hold her slippery arms. After many tries, she crawls to shore on her hands and knees. With dry land for friction, we succeed in raising her upright.

Proud parents celebrate milestones: a baby's first tooth, first step, first word. If only we knew what would be our last tree climb, last cartwheel, last meal. These momentous occasions deserve comparable reflection. This will be Rosemary's last ocean dip.

At home, Robert and I feel isolated, castaway caregivers adrift in a sea teeming with social activity. Yearning for time to ourselves, we offer free room and board to anyone able to help for a few days. Understandably, people are busy with their own lives. But relativity comes to our rescue. Small thrills put an exciting spin on mundane chores. Filling the bird feeder, fetching the mail, and taking out the trash become mini retreats.

To break the monotony, my mother and I bake cinnamon buns. As we work, a stream of disjointed comments bursts from her in rapid succession. My dough-covered hands hinder jotting down her words. By the time I clean up, pencil ready, only a few phrases remain salvageable. Like picked flowers forgotten on a forest boulder, I gather her word bouquet.

"Fay Wray was the actress who played opposite King Kong, but all I noticed was the ape." Sprinkling cinnamon, she rambled about assorted fairy tales by the Brothers Grimm and Hans Christian Anderson: "The Shoemaker and the Elves," "Seven in One Blow," and "The Emperor's New Clothes." Rolling the dough, she mentioned the original "Glass Slipper" story, then jumped to the spunky film version, *Ever After*,[8] in which heroic Cinderella hoisted the prince over her shoulder to save him. "That's *my* kind of gal," says Rosemary, placing buns into heart-shaped pans.

The three of us attend our friend Jack's ninetieth-birthday luau. Rose nestles on the couch, applauding the parade of women in floral dresses and guys in Hawaiian shirts. Bubble wands appear, and the air dances with orbs. In a nearby chair, the birthday boy belts out the first line of "I'm Forever Blowing Bubbles." Rosemary joins in and continues through every verse. Guests gather to listen. Lyrics of fleeting joy highlight the daily gumption of antique elders. When time comes to head home, it's hard to part with such good company.

The sun sinks behind the horizon as if in need of rest. Moonlight through bedroom windows backdrops Rosemary's frequent excursions to the bathroom. I tag along for safety. Perched on the pot, she asks me if she's finished.

"Sure thing," I say having heard her stream of success. "It's midnight, and your bed awaits."

She sings, "Celery Stalks at Midnight" as back to bed we toddle.

Snuggled beside her, I recall snacks of celery sticks stuffed with Cheez Whiz. Mom wrapped them in wax paper. My school lunch pail's red plaid pattern curtains the inside of my eyelids as I dose off, my arm around her.

She awakens at dawn with vegetables on her mind. "A song keeps sprouting in my head: 'Celery Stalks at Midnight.'"

Another day unwinds into a pleasant summer evening. The three of us watch a meteor shower. We take turns cupping each other's tilted heads in our palms like makeshift pillows. Blazes of light streak across the sky, their trails fading like lost memories.

Tuesday, neighbor Don invites us for dinner at his house two blocks away. Mom and I make her apple pie. None better on the planet, her recipe brims with TLC. Freshly baked, the fragrance fills the car on the short drive. This evening outing is a virtual holiday for us. We chat and catch up on the news—world, local, and personal. Rosemary dozes in Don's guest room for a couple of hours. Tuesday evenings with Don become a weekly event. Like Christmas Eve, we anticipate the amicable break in routine. The change of pace in good fellowship eases caregiving fatigue.

Gramma Rose writes to forty-three-year-old grandson Adam in

San Francisco. Florida humidity smears her words. But an indignity she conveys alerts us to upgrade our approach.

"It's hard to keep myself useful. But my mouth goes right on flapping," she writes. "I see myself as a household pet. The least I can do is wag my tail occasionally."

Rosemary ends the correspondence reminiscing about how toddler Adam used to bathe in her enamel soup pot. "Betcha couldn't do that now. But my lap will still hold you."

In September this 2017 hurricane season, Hurricane Irma is threatening the entire Florida peninsula. Evacuees flock north toward the panhandle. Rosemary hears a weather report of wind gusts already 90 mph.

"That's nothing to sneeze about," she declares, then endeavors to lighten the tension. "Uh-oh, here comes a hurricane. Nobody sneeze!"

We open her house via Airbnb to Irma evacuees in hasty retreat. Ten strangers come to wait out the approaching storm. Appreciative and respectful, the "visiting firemen" rest on every cushioned surface: beds, sofas, and recliners.

"Hello, fellow humans," Rosemary chimes to arriving travelers. "It's gratifying milling our way through each day."

Her unpredictable words entertain the houseguests; her neediness distracts them from pressing concerns about their homes under Irma's rampage.

Poking fun at her own addled brain, Rosemary quotes her whimsical mother. "If I had six more wits, I'd be a half-wit." Like court jesters' jibes during oppressive reigns, her wisecracks ease the fierce weather tension. She cuts jokes. Sudden silence hits the room as people pause to comprehend. Then blurts of laughter vent Hurricane Irma anxiety.

Robert overhears her mental self-evaluation and adds his own take. "We try to keep our wits about us, but our wits just go along without us." The looming hurricane does its thing as hilarity reigns indoors.

✲

Mid-September, Rosemary has a series of ministrokes. Her feet kick, then relax. She cannot speak, then regains control of her tongue. After one episode, she crawls from her bedroom to the living room on all fours. Fretfulness gives way to determination.

"My legs don't want to hold me. But my knees still work, and I have places to go." Aimless thoughts mosey from her mouth. She tries to stand but body parts vie for attention, knees shaking. "My legs feel like laundry on a clothesline, blowing in the breeze."

Following the string of ministrokes, her primary care physician orders home healthcare to resume. Rosemary decides to donate her body to science once she's done with it. A physical therapist asks if he can check her balance.

"I already checked it at the door," Rose tells the fellow.

Uneasy whenever I'm out of sight, Rosey asks Robert, "Where's Chris?"

"Outside taking pictures of turtles."

"My best speed is slow motion too, and I'm willing to pose." Neck outstretched, she mimics the reptile.

Hearing my hearty laugh as I enter, a bona fide smile lights her eyes. Rosemary is incapable of faking happiness. Asked to say cheese for a camera, a very un-Mona Lisa glower appears. Bared teeth reveal a sneer-imbedded glare that could send shivers all the way up a giraffe's spine. Genuine Rosemary smiles burst straight from her soul, even imitating a turtle.

A few minutes pass. "Ha ha," blurts jubilant, jack-in-the-box Rose. "I love these vagrant thoughts. I was making an orange chiffon cake, up to my elbows in batter, when your father walked in and proposed. He wanted to put an engagement ring on my sticky finger. I'm rich with memories. Life without joy is just 'oy,'" she quotes in Yiddish.

Robert and I adore the anecdotes that pop into her noggin and out her mouth. Accustomed to the odd workings of Rosemary's mind, her surprises still boost our adrenaline and keep us energized.

Awaking from a snooze, out comes another zinger. "Expensive bicycles cost dozens of moneys."

Today's doctor orders an ankle brace for her lameness from bone degeneration. In her young teens, she fell down cement steps and twisted that ankle. Rosemary used crutches and then a cane. Bodies hold lifelong grudges for every insult.

Reminiscing about her fall, Rosemary's mind migrates to Merchant Street in Audubon, New Jersey. "A truck hit your cousin Laural at age five, fractured her skull. The corner bakery had superb kaiser rolls. That same block, Hattie's Beauty Parlor had a bookie. Aunt Jenny used to frequent the place . . . not for her looks."

Rosemary awakens reciting lists. After naming all thirty-three nieces and nephews, she tries to recall her three children's birth weights, her siblings' birthdays, and distant people on family tree branches. Etymology is another mental muscle she flexes. She inventories the months of the year with detailed origins of each name. "January: Janus, the double-faced Roman god of doorways, coming and going, beginnings and endings; February: Latin for purification; March: from Mars . . .

Eighty-two-year-old Gramma Rose thought out loud, "I know the name origins for six days of the week, but what is 'Tuesday' named after?"

Helpful four-year-old great-granddaughter Kayla chimed in, "Tuesday is named after Monday, Gram."

Dementia imposes no discernible effect on Rosemary's way with words. After a pleasant phone conversation with her now twelve-year-old great-granddaughter, my mother hands me back the phone.

Kayla requests interpretation. "What's Gram mean by 'circuitous,' 'unpretentious,' and 'penmanship?'"

Gramma Rose lounges in bed staring at the ceiling. "I'm trying to think of a word that makes sense no matter what vowel is inserted. Here's one: blander, blender, blinder, blonder, blunder. I'm a great source of useless information."

Growing up in South Jersey, Rose knew the worst insult was to be called "ignorant." The pervasive social slam extended to improper manners. Anyone who dared to swipe an ear of Silver Queen from the dinner tray before everybody was seated received a swift admonishment: "Don't be ignorant."

By all accounts, Rosemary was a well-behaved child and an excellent student. No rule-breaker's dunce cap ever topped her head. Super smart, she inhaled academic subjects like fresh air. High school was another matter. Foisted into secretarial courses that went against her grain, she felt bored and annoyed. Audubon High offered Rose only three lifelines: English class, geography, and Miss Louise Housel's ancient history. At age sixteen, Rosemary had enough of typing, steno, decorum, and other compulsory lessons; she dropped out. A few years later, the GED test became available to civilians and she obtained a diploma, but always regretted her limited education.

After Rosemary's kids were grown, she took classes at the local vocational school. Daytime, she filed at her Philadelphia job. Evenings, she absorbed knowledge like a refugee rescued from starvation. Lacking a stapler, she sewed corners of homework assignments together on her mother's old Singer. Rosemary thoroughly enjoyed night school, earning her high school diploma at age forty-eight.

Had she been offered college prep rather than forced down the secretarial path, there's no telling what additional contributions she might have made to the world. Only forty-seven miles from Princeton, she could have studied under Einstein. So many seeds of human potential fall on barren ground. But autodidact Rosemary never stopped developing depth and breadth of thought.

Often asked how she is doing, Rose replies with the same retort she's used for decades: "Another day older, just like the rest of us." Most of her thoughts arise from bygone days. "My Aunt Regina's arduous youth left her with an aversion to motherhood. It's a shame she remained blind to her own success, raising truly fine children."

Simple pleasures invigorate Rosemary. She munches breakfast celery with satisfaction.

"Starting the morning with a stalk of celery makes the day fresh and crisp."

Matters complicate this week. Hearing-impaired Rosemary realizes her caregiving duo, Robert and I, are under the weather. Both with laryngitis, comical communication efforts exhaust us further. She wants to make us tea. I supervise boiling water while she fetches cups and mugs from the cupboard. But she forgets why and continues until the shelf is empty. Rosey sees the dozen beverage containers on the counter and gets excited.

"Hurray, a tea party."

She brings up a phrase. "What's the source of 'never hide your light under a bushel'?" We find answers, encyclopedic and biblical (Matt 5:15-16). She paraphrases aloud: "A bushel container, used to measure dry goods. A wooden eight-gallon bucket. Upside-down over a lit candle, the flame goes out for lack of oxygen. Put practical skills to use," she interprets, "share your wealth."

Why this particular metaphor, I wonder. Drat, she's short of breath again. The slightest exertion threatens to snuff her candle. The visiting nurse considers supplemental oxygen, but it's impossible to keep Rosemary from pulling it off.

Attempting to dress for another day, Rose looks out the window. "Wow, a fresh-minted sunshine." She puzzles over the sleeve I hold for her. "Is it morning or night? Should I put my arm in or pull it out?"

Layered with clothes, still she shivers. I add her full-length down coat. It resembles a turquoise comforter with pockets. Aiming her arm into the sleeve, she misses. And misses again as I chase after her in tight circles. Laughing on a whirling dervish merry-go-round, Rosey forgets what she's doing and comes to an abrupt halt at her sewing cabinet. I almost plow her over. Coat half-on, she grabs a pencil and starts a crossword puzzle.

I escort her to the car and we drive to a doctor's appointment. Along the way, Mom gazes out the window, entranced by the impressionistic contrast of foliage greens and deep orange clay along the roadway. "Look at the sunlight hitting that embankment. It's like somebody swashed it on with a paintbrush."

Red-letter moments like this fleet by fast. I pull off the road to capture her Renoir depiction. My mother's description is a colorful foreground to the scenery we take in together.

Evening arrives, along with an opossum walking by our windows. My mom follows the wiry creature, paraphrasing the iconic song, "The Impossible Dream."

"To dream the oppossumable dream."

In keeping with our holiday tradition, Rosemary wants to welcome people over who otherwise would be alone for Thanksgiving.

But this year is different. *We* are the strays. Neighbors welcome us to their feast. As usual, we prepare crowd-pleasing Florida sweet potatoes, consisting of more citrus than mashed spuds. My mom helps with the oranges and cranberries.

Upon our arrival, two small pups—a rat terrier and a Chihuahua—greet her. Rosemary mistakes them for a single pooch. Astonished when the canines depart in separate directions, she exclaims, "Good grief, the little dog just broke in half."

While decorating for the December holidays, she admires a wrinkle-faced fairy godmother ornament and dubs it "the ghost of Christmas *present.*" In the words of Rilke,[9] childhood and future are equally present for Rosemary.

Shopping for gifts at an estate sale, Rose rests in a cushioned chair and greets customers. "Anybody want to buy an antique lady?"

"Hang on to my arm, Rose," Robert tells her as we make our way to the car.

"Okay, I won't let you fall. At this age, we end up addlepated. I'm wading through life with an I've-forgotten-something feeling."

A few days before Christmas, Rosemary goes bananas with holiday panic. "This is December? I need to buy ninety-five Christmas cards. And stamps. And send Beth's birthday card." (My sister was born fifty-one minutes after Christmas.)

Rather than explain the vast volume of emails sent to loved ones on her behalf, I simply assure her that she mailed the whole kit and kaboodle of cards, including Beth's not-to-open-until-the-26th. Wrapped gifts await beneath the little ceramic tree her friend Gloria made. No dying conifer corpse for us. I show Mom our stockings hung on a sculpture with care. Robert's "Piano Peace" serves as a makeshift fireplace for the peculiar gift-laden-socks custom.

Rose is contented until nightfall. Christmas lights outside her bedroom window confuse her.

"I can see it's morning, Chris. I'm not blind."

No point arguing. We shut off all Christmas lights, inside and out, so she can sleep. At midnight, she flips on her bedroom light. Thumbing through her address book, she struggles to understand her circumstances. "We need to get to the post office right away with holiday cards. Is your father alive? Why wasn't I notified of his death?" After an hour of reassurance, she relaxes . . . and happy-go-lucky three-year-old Rosey surfaces.

"On Christmas Eve, my parents decorated the tree as I fell asleep on the couch. I awoke to dreamy blue lights." Her voice glistens like the cerulean sparkle she describes.

I ask what she likes best about the holidays now.

"I can't remember what now means. Is this 240?"

It will upset my mother if she has no gift for Robert and me. We wrap a candy box, on hand for when family arrives. Labeled with an old Yuletide tag she wrote years before, we place it under the colorful fake tree.

Christmas morning, Rose is pleased to see she remembered us. After opening gifts, we return the box to the kitchen. Our four grown offspring appear with spirits bright from San Francisco, Maryland, and New Jersey.

Gramma Rose sings a Christmas song from her mother, "Over the land and the sea far away, over the woods and the hollow, Santa will come in his jingling sleigh, swifter than flight of a swallow . . . ." At the dinner table, Rosemary proposes a toast.

"Raise your glass to harmonious relationships."

A few smart alecks raise their eyeglasses. Gram sips grape juice from her last surviving wedding glass, brought out on special occasions like this. Keeping the holiday merry, everyone is on best behavior. Such peace on earth for the memorable moment boosts aspirations to do so year-round.

"Raise your glasses to good relationships."

Weather permitting, every few years we coordinate a prescribed burn at our family forest, Shoal Sanctuary Nature Preserve. Coaxed in the right direction, fire reduces rapid-growing invasives—wisteria, Chinese tallow, cane, cogongrass—and discourages secondary growth such as laurel oaks and yaupon. This makes way for native wildlife (no more caged pets) and slower, primary growth including the 17,000 longleaf pines we planted to reestablish the natural forest.

Before the burn, local merchants donate empty containers. Rose helps fill jugs with water and covers irrigation heads with old soup cans. We mark protected flora—Torreya yews, sourwoods, black gums, magnolias, hollies, maples, live oaks, hawthorns, palms, and delicate berries. On burn day, firefighters divert flames from flagged vegetation. Cleared fire breaks make walking easier, especially for Rosemary.

For this prescribed burn, three fire departments and two dozen volunteers come to help rejuvenate the land. Participants determine their own level of ability. Our lunch crew coordinates food and water for the field crew. Rosemary is on kitchen duty.

During our past dozen burns, she coordinated the meals. This year, she contents herself as a willing worker bee. They make fresh lemonade and hot cocoa, and then fill biodegradable wax paper bags with fruit, pinwheel sandwiches, vegetables, nuts, and raisins. Each firefighter and field crew volunteer gets a brown lunch bag containing nutritious goodies.

Kitchen crew makes lunch

Shoal Sanctuary prescribed burns offer firefighters a chance for training and certification hours. They teach techniques to novices, develop leadership skills, and get to interact with other departments. Inexperienced workers learn about fire from professionals. Spotters equipped with binoculars keep watch from a safer distance upwind. Flagged flora get extra care. Volunteers rake leaves back beyond canopy drip lines and douse trees with water.

13th Shoal Sanctuary burn>

Once the field crew finishes eating, they toss wrappers into the flames. No litter. Back at the farmhouse, the kitchen crew cleans up and joins the outdoor workers. Rosemary and six escorts peruse the burn, and a Peregrine falcon flies off.

The following day, we do post-burn cleanup. Rose removes markers from protected trees. Others gather jugs and cans. We store cleaned tools back in the barn. And diehard volunteers graze on yesterday's leftovers. Mom calls it encore food. She adopted that expression in rebuttal to my father who called repeat meals "the remains."

Removing markers from protected trees

Back in her bedroom, Rose finds scraps of paper to jot down happy memories before they fade. She tears snippets of Christmas cards to write about yesterday's prescribed burn. But the pen fails to catch her thoughts in time. Her mind travels to grandson James who got his favorite cinnamon toothpaste for Christmas, then to interfaith stockings she made—Kwanzaa for foster children of African heritage and a Hanukkah menorah one, much appreciated by a Jewish friend who joined us for holiday festivities. Mom punctuates her thoughts with a serenade of "Auld Lang Syne."

Spry Rosemary, raising children, upheld a year-end tradition dating back generations. Everyone raided the kitchen cabinets for pots, pans, and large spoons. At the stroke of midnight, we paraded out the back door to usher away the old year. Banging the pots and pans, we marched through the yard and entered the front door, welcoming the New Year. That family custom faded as dented, wobbly pots became unstable for cooking.

The New Year of 2018 shrugs an indifferent portent. Robert and I run fevers with the flu. Dazed, I make Mom her morning hot chocolate. Removing the wooden clothespin used to secure the marshmallow bag, I take one out, and drop it into her warm drink. Fumbling to reseal the plastic bag with a marshmallow, I look into the mug and see a clothespin bobbing in the cocoa. Thus, 2018 starts off with weird foreboding.

The influenza bug bypasses Rosemary, but she gets an ear infection. The cause is hard to explain and harder to avoid but, for the sake of others with dementia, I'll try. Sitting on the toilet, my fastidious, hygienic mother forgets what she is doing and shoves unwashed dirty fingers in her itchy ears. From now on, when she's on the throne I shield her hands with socks—like infant mittens that keep babies' fingernails from gouging their delicate faces.

Various doctors order antibiotics for her ears. That makes way for fungal growth. The earache, fever, and prescription side effects combine with dementia. Rosemary becomes delirious and paranoid. I discover her packing a bag with her belongings.

"I'm heading for 240," she announces, determined to return to her New Jersey girlhood home.

Inescapable pangs of pain terrify her. Pitiful and wary, Rosemary's voice lures us to her aid. But she glares with uncharacteristic suspicion. Unable to understand what is happening, she recoils and looks at us with dread. I know not to take paranoid accusations personally, but it's difficult to dismiss their cuts of incrimination.

"I know what you two are doing. You're giving me strokes so I can't think straight."

Erect and unyielding as a straight-back chair, she accuses us of confiscating her pocketbook. I find her old handbag, stuff in a wallet of money, and hang it by her bed . . . where it remains, untouched, for the rest of her life.

The neurologist ignores the underlying ear infection and diagnoses paranoid delirium, a regretful aspect of dementia. The prescribed antipsychotic proves useless since she is too distrustful to take any pills. The only thing helpful is rest. She dozes off disgruntled and awakens her sweet self, until the throbbing drums up another call of the wild.

"I refuse to be consoled. I'm just going to sit here and pout."

At wit's end, I telephone my mom's old friend. Pat to the rescue. "See if this helps your ear feel better, Mom." I put the phone gently to her cheek.

Her tone softens. Tension in her face dissolves. Childhood memories ease her back to civility.

In her teens, Rosemary formed enduring bonds with six girl-friends—Pat (Annette), Maggie (Anna), Lenny (Lenore), Bennie (Benita), Bubbles (Muriel), and Margie (Margaret). Rose was the linchpin around whom lifelong friendships revolved. The gals would gather at each other's houses to read, play rummy, discuss family matters or world affairs, and do homework. Arm in arm, they roamed through town memorizing school assignments: the preamble to the US Constitution, Lincoln's "Gettysburg Address," Whitman's "O' Captain, My Captain," Poe's "The Raven," and the prelude to Longfellow's lyrical eulogy, "Evangeline."

Lifelong friends

Movies at the New Century Theater on the White Horse Pike provided entertainment. Mothers paid their daughters' twenty-five cents admission in exchange for the theater's promotional offer of free dishes to patrons. Many movies later, Rosemary's mom had a complete set of tableware to use as a wedding gift. Besides receiving the plates and seeing films, the theater held another appeal on hot, summer days: it boasted of air conditioning.

The1940s version of AC consisted of large ice blocks near the stage with huge fans blowing over the melting slabs. The noisy motors were the only audible sound, but the girls didn't care, busy enjoying each other's company. Free-dish matinees only showed low-budget movies. The loud drone of fans mercifully drowned out feeble dialogue in B-rated talkies, as sweltering days cooled to tolerable temperatures.

The big screen welcomed them into other worlds. The most memorable A-rated films cost fifty cents to see. When a film ended and applause ceased, the girls shared their impressions while walking home. Entertaining fluff—*Dumbo, Bambi, Curly Top, Stowaway,* and *Yankee Doodle Dandy*—were popular. But Rose preferred thoughtful plots: *Fantasia* for its elaborate animation to classical accompaniment, *Little Women's* depiction of females with backbones, *The Great Dictator's* comic take on grave, international strife, and the Christmas classic, *It's a Wonderful Life*, for showing how subtle personal efforts blow away the tumbleweeds of mere existence.

Across the railroad tracks from 240 West Atlantic, Rosie lived literally a hop, skip, and a jump from her friend Lenny on East Atlantic. Frequent visits formed a zigzag path up and down either side of the steep railway embankment, ribboned evidence of their bond.

Nothing pleased the girls more than horseback riding at the Nicholson Road farm (later to become Audubon Shopping Center). But it was cost-prohibitive at "two bits" (a quarter). Fortunately, Lenny's father's friend had horses. Rosemary and Lenny tackled daily equestrian chores in exchange for free, unsupervised canters.

In their teens, the seven girls caught a bus to the Philadelphia Museum of Art and strolled for hours, walking the soles off their patent leather shoes. Sometimes the young ladies took the passenger train east from Audubon's Orston Station to Atlantic City, where they "walked the boards" sightseeing. Rosemary denounced exploitive entertainment: rolling chairs powered by Black men, animals forced to perform, and "freak shows" of human anomalies. While her friends rode the Ferris wheel and rollercoaster, Rose held their coats. The only ride she enjoyed was the soothing carousel.

Over the years, as motherhood commenced, the women kept in close contact. Rosemary devised an economical way to communicate despite being apart. Round-robin letters were hardcopy precursors to blogs, Instagram, and Facebook. To save on postage without repetition, a single envelope held seven news updates, one from each friend. As the bundle circulated in the established sequence, each gal replaced her old journal tick-tock with an updated account on what was happening in her world.

The last of the troop, Pat and Rose, hold fast to each other. Close friends for eighty-three years, weekly phone conversations sweep away the decades. Plugged into each other's wavelength, their voices revitalize each other. Listening to Pat reprioritizes Rosemary attention from her earache. Following the call, we head to an otolaryngologist appointment.

I never thought I'd be carrying a diaper bag again after four children and 145 foster children. The satchel holds Mom's diapers, wipes, extra clothes, medications, snacks, and books in case no reading material is available. I also cart a chair cushion under one arm to protect her skeletal tush from hard surfaces.

"I like this chair. It's nice and soft on my boney butt." She sits comfortably in the doctor's waiting room until it's her turn.

The physician looks in her ear and Rosemary makes a request. "Answer that phone while you're in there, please." His questions about symptoms may as well be in Greek.

She looks at him wide-eyed. "Ask Chris. I just float around, only touching down now and then." She sees him scrutinize the drainage from her infected ear. "That's my brains oozing out because I'm so open-minded."

The doctor prescribes an elaborate concoction of antifungals and antibiotics in warm oil.

A few days later, Mom shows signs of recovery—no more pain or paranoia. She awakens thinking we are in Alaska. Reminded that we are in Florida, she becomes baffled.

"What's Florida doing in Alaska?"

Incessantly, Rosemary questions life with the insatiable craving of a child asking, "Why?" On the bright side, her loopy mind replays nostalgic family lore. After a year of this, son-in-law Robert knows every story by heart. In unison, Rosemary and Robert recite anecdotes of Schwab, Martin, and Baker family histories. My husband's favorite tale took place when I was seven:

Our neighbor electrician, Phil, needed his work truck taken for its official annual safety inspection. In those days, suburban families were lucky to have one vehicle, and seatbelts were not yet standard. That day, Phil hitched a ride to work with a colleague, leaving his wife Dona to handle the required assessment of their green 1956 Ford panel van. To make the tedious errand more enjoyable, Dona invited Rosemary. The two women loaded their broods, along with their children's friends, into the truck. The moms rode on the front seat bench with baby Gary on Rose's lap while Dona drove. The rest of us kids hopped in back, perched on the spare tire and assorted electrical equipment. Better than any amusement park ride, coils of wire served as cushions. We gripped cloth-covered cables as handles. Dips and curves in the road livened the trip with unpredictable bumps into each other, and heads knocked on the ceiling, coming back to rest on coils, tires, and each other.

At the station, the inspector needed all passengers to vacate the vehicle so he could jack it up to check the brakes, tire wear, suspension, muffler, and such. First out were the mothers and little Gary. Then Dona opened the back door.

In the waiting room, bored car owners took notice as the rest of us kids exited in single file—Beth, Philip, Chrissy, Debbie, Billy, Stevie, and Marty. The parade of children emerging created a spectacle. Peals of laughter from spectators cheered each emerging child. No sidewalk, we lined up on tiptoes along the narrow curbing. Barefoot, my toes curled around the curb rim to keep balance. I still feel us holding hands, wiggling and giggling amid automotive clutter. After the mechanic's rushed stamp of approval for the truck, we piled back in for the ride home.

Rosemary's stories enchant listeners the first few dozen times. Incessant retellings threaten to drive Robert and me batty. Her sensible neurologist suggests we divert my mother's attention to the present. Give her something to do. It works.

Put a cleaning cloth in Rose's hand, and she gets busy dusting. Give her a stack of laundered socks, she folds them into sorted pairs. But we dare not look away. Rose's attention turns on a dime. She pairs the dust cloth neatly with a similar-colored sock and uses its sparkling clean mate to dust furniture. Rosemary sings while we work, making chores pleasurable. We join in as we redo whatever job she's done. Mom sets the table with socks; I simmer oatmeal. Watching the bubbling brew, she serenades my stirring with "Cement Mixer Put-ti Put-ti."

A truly fortunate upside of my mom's dementia is that she has forgotten regrets and harbors no grudges. Memories of discontent and discomfort vaporize as if they never happened. The terrible earache is lost to the past. An inner vitality keeps her laughing over the antics of lost mental marbles. A grueling labor of love, caregiving Rosemary is equally joyful.

Getting acquainted with her sweet-natured child self is an indescribable pleasure. Rosey arises from Rosemary's deepest sanctum, the place theologian Origen of Alexandria described as the individual soul that reveals divine mystery in its own unique ways.[10] Beaming with the curiosity of an infant, her senses awaken to life's minute details. Quizzical fascination overpowers unpleasantries. Pain and dementia cannot divert Rosey's passion. Her inquisitive voice rises in pitch as glorious epiphanies unfold that only her twinkling eyes can see.

On the last day of January, my mother is well enough for a fun outing. Gaining confidence as her health improves, we become a capable threesome rather than a pair of caregivers and a patient. Out we venture to Okaloosa Island and park beside palms at the entrance to Gulf Islands National Seashore Park. We sing "I'll Be Seeing You" and my mom dances a little jig as the full blood moon rises over Choctawhatchee Bay. She calls the lunar spectacle an "auspicious tangerine" and "impressive pumpkin."

After the marvelous moonrise, we go to our favorite local restaurant, named Sealand after the boat that rescued the proprietor during the Vietnam War. Rosemary orders a baked potato. Robert and I add bites of grouper and salad to her plate. We finish dining, and Rose cracks jokes as we pay the bill. Then she closes her eyes as if asleep, drops her head to her chest, stops breathing, and turns blue.

STROKE 6

BREATHTAKING,
WE HATH A THOLE

Time anesthetizes old hurts.

– ROSEMARY, 1980s

NO SOCIAL PROTOCOL HAS YET been devised that allows people to die peacefully in public. "Mom?" I hold her head to open her airway. Restaurant patrons call 9-1-1. A few minutes without oxygenated blood, more gray matter in Rosemary's brain ceases function. She begins breathing again but remains cyanotic and unresponsive as an ambulance arrives to transport her to the hospital. Despite her DNR, which is with her at all times, en route the paramedic administers oxygen, starts an IV, and otherwise jostles her back from wherever she was heading.

The ER doc orders tests and suspects another stroke. He also notes that she now has congestive heart failure. In essence, her heart cannot keep pace with her accustomed enthusiasm. The physician and paramedic clarify current finer points of do-not-resuscitate orders. Do Not Resuscitate orders only apply to resuscitation from death, not pre-death treatment. Had her heart stopped before they arrived, Rosemary would now be gone. But if paramedics arrive before the patient dies, they are required to treat. We thank them and let the doctor know she prefers to be at home. Several hours after the respiratory arrest, she becomes responsive. The physician tells her she is in the ER and explains that she stopped breathing after watching the moon rise.

Rosemary blames the moon: "Well, what do you expect? It was breathtaking."

Home again and back on hospice care, any exertion, even getting out of bed, causes shortness of breath. Her lips turn bluish for a minute. Operating at about a two-year-old level, she can no longer be trusted with hot food. She burns her mouth several times before we realize that she forgets to blow with every single bite. Holding her napkin, toothbrush, or folded pajamas in hand, she stares at them and cannot recall their use. Seated in front of a jigsaw puzzle, a piece hangs from her fingers, suspended in midair until I ease her release, and it tumbles back into the mound.

Some cultures honor seniors as national treasures–Native Americans, Greeks, and Japanese, for example.[11]In blatant contrast, others target elders as easy prey, gleaning family savings, milking health insurance, and indulging the worst side of human nature. A phone scammer once called Rosemary allegedly from jail and posed as her grandson. I intervened just as she was writing him a check.

Intense, 24/7 caregiving requires scheduling my own needs around those of my mom. It takes flexibility and constant reprioritizing to get myself dressed, fed, showered, or absolutely anything. All must wait until Rose is either asleep or with someone else. Unfinished chores mount. She must be tended to every minute. While my mother naps, I walk out the front door to check our curbside mailbox. Fortunately, I notice a delay in the door slam behind me and swing around to see her chasing after. I run back just in time to catch her as she tumbles.

Distant family members express concern over Rosemary's ER episode. She reassures them by video, singing the chorus of the Bee Gee's "Stayin' Alive."

Flipping through a calendar, Rosemary doubts its accuracy. Months appear scrambled. Dates fail to affirm any order despite their numerical sequence. Clocks incomprehensible, she sings, "Till the End of Time."

"'Polonaise' with lyrics," she comments.

"Now" and "then" are convincing illusions. Einstein said the flow of time is relative, based on where we are and how fast we travel . . . whatever that means. Dementia alters Rosemary's perception of where and when. Maps hold no sway over her as brain gaps open to other eras and realms. Parts of her mind, already promoted, beckon from afar. Off she goes, no ticket necessary. Her spirit soars. Rational, full-function analytics just don't get it.

She notices a missing button on her owl pajama top. "Where on earth is Grossy's button box, the dented Liberty Bell tin?"

I find a replacement button in our converted cookie can and hand her a threaded needle. She attempts to sew but moves on to something else. I snip the gnarled mess and reattach the button. My mental note to find Grossmom's Liberty Bell tin gets lost with Aunt Jenny's dress and never happens.

For continuity, we request the same hospice company as before. However, an unfamiliar young nurse arrives who does not know my mother. The inexperienced woman views Rosemary's erudite vocabulary and effervescence as incongruous with her malady. Despite the patient's blue lips, the novice RN fails to confirm that Rose meets insurance coverage criteria. No sooner had she arrived, the woman was gone. Questions hover like stirred dust and settle over my ailing mother, unanswered. A different hospice agency sends a more seasoned palliative care provider who sees the whole picture and has no problem qualifying my mom for hospice. She asks Rosemary if her feet are cold.

"Not as cold as they will be if I allow them to get any colder."

I interpret this as "yes." An additional set of warm-from-the-dryer socks suffices.

She exhales a satisfied sigh and sings "Popsicle Toes" as we fold the remaining laundry. While pairing socks, an enchanted look on her face announces the arrival of a whimsical soul. In no uncertain terms, Rosemary poses a rhetorical, Buddhist-style question:

"What is the sound of a single sock laughing out loud?"

Joy and toil pull us in constant circles, like saltwater taffy mixers on Wildwood, New Jersey's boardwalk drawing infinity signs. Whirls of elation create sugar-high cravings for who Rosemary once was. Her words make less sense with each stroke, but her sweet voice soothes regardless.

For gatherings, our dad added both table extensions, leaving barely enough space to scoot sideways around the dining room. Marty and I slid off Mom's lap onto the floor under the tabletop canopy. Surrounded by knees in the womb-like comfort of muffled voices, we exchanged grins. Seated Indian-style (Uncle John said we were part Blackfeet), blanketed by overlapping conversations, outbursts of laughter sent startled thrills up our spines. And Mom's voice wove reassurance amid the vibrant cacophony.

Caring for a fading family treasure is inconceivably rough and deeply moving. Like the Chinese word for crisis, perils and opportunities combine. Caregiver dangers grow from detachment and sleep deprivation. But focused on what truly matters, wonders arise.

Neighbor Nancy takes Rose on an excursion for burgers and fries. They know I disapprove of nutrition-weak fast food. But sneaking a forbidden meal is part of their fun, way more important than occasional empty calories.

My mom and husband accompany me to a college campus writing group. Rosemary hangs onto Robert for stability. As we approach the door, he asks her if it's the correct room.

"Don't ask me. I don't know where I've been either."

They listen as I read a poem, written for the group's benefit.

IN THEIR SHOES

by Rosemary's daughter, Christina

FEBRUARY 2018

Awkward, interfering, rather endearing,
they shuffle into class,
like uneasy skaters on slippery glass.
A Siamese duo, daughter/mother,
one goes nowhere without the other.
Hands intertwine, arms overlap,
with diaper bag and a school backpack.
One will fall, the other not, and
love forever not forgotten.

Exiting the classroom, Rose focuses on balancing upright and comments on her unsteady gait. "Barely able to wobble around on my own two feet feels kinda like a pleasant drunk. I don't know why only little kids are called toddlers. It occurs at either end of life's spectrum."

Holding her arm, Robert remarks that she's a little more stable. "Long as I don't smell a little more like a stable."

Growing up just after the transition from horse-drawn carriages to cars, Rosey assimilated her father's longing for well-paved roads. She deplored muddy potholes. By the 1950s, her transportation peeves switched gears to traffic congestion, inept drivers, traffic circles, and billboards. Mostly, she loathed deforestation for roadways.

Young mother Rosemary opened the Golden Book Encyclopedia's "H" volume and showed her brood an aerial highway view of a cloverleaf interchange. To us, it resembled a Philadelphia soft pretzel. We kids drove Marty's toy cars around the illustrated underpasses and overpasses. Stale pretzels extended our roadways off the page, onto the living room floor. Mom's approving looks boosted our inventiveness.

Rosemary's mind travels to destinations hard to locate. She tenderly touches the bedrail and the toilet paper roll affixed to the commode as if exotic antiquities. "I can't tell whether we're in Africa or Asia. This seems to be where they meet on the calendar."

I label another Post-it verbatim and try to figure out where to place it on her world map. The Arabian Sea seems as suitable a spot as any.

"I don't know which end is up, but I guess as long as I'm not underwater, it doesn't matter," Rose tells no one in particular. "I'm pretty much out of touch with everything, so I just go with the flow and hope it doesn't flow over me." Thumbing through the newspaper, she notices a photograph of a martial arts demonstration. "Karate seems like a good skill to have if you're ever attacked by a stack of boards. Hoy!" she chops the air, mimicking a karate shout she heard years ago in Jersey.

Community spirit flourished on our block. After the VFW karate demonstration, neighbor kids adopted "hoy!" for a burst of energy. When situations arose beyond the norm, people turned to Rosemary for aid. She rescued Marty and Stevie from a wasp attack. She handled unwelcome snakes, rashes, and ailments. Rose plucked cactus barbs from Philp, buried dead pets, assisted Minnie after her pressure cooker exploded, and determined ambulances were needed for a badly injured bicyclist, a three-year-old attacked by a dog, and a convulsing child.

Our home was the site of seasonal festivities. Halloween 1957, Herman and Rose hosted a block party. One spring, Rosemary organized a parade of local kids followed by a talent show; sheets draped over clotheslines became curtains. Sweltering summer days, Rose coordinated kiddie pool parties. Whichever mom finished her chores first would welcome neighbors who brought their wading pools to inflate wherever they congregated. A dozen kids splashed about, overseen by the moms. On weekends, the dads joined in with construction projects, barbeques, and quoit games.

Christmas Eves, after the kids were asleep, Herman and Rose gathered parents outside to make snowmen and snow angels, toss snowballs, and sled down Sheppard Avenue. "Hoy!"

A 1956 Pool Party

Spring arrives, by and by, and we attend the marriage ceremony of Rosemary's great-granddaughter Kelsey beneath Spanish-moss garlanded Live Oaks in Central Florida. Gramma Rose looks baffled, trying to decipher the purpose of the festive outdoor gathering.

"Aha, we're here for a wedding perception."

Decked out in her weddings-and-funerals dress, Gram galivants through the venue in baby steps. People pitch in, happy to assist Rosemary. Grandson Adam escorts her to a comfortable sofa by the barn. Its overstuffed folds engulf her small frame as she relaxes.

"This couch is a friendly alligator who hasn't swallowed yet, risen from the mud with quaking of the earth."

On the drive home, Rose loses track of where we've been. "Is this Pennsylvania? No matter where I go, I remain in the state of confusion."

Although scattered across the planet, our four kids made it to Florida for Kelsy's wedding. Later, we gather at Shoal Sanctuary. The tranquil setting is fragrant with Ashe magnolia blossoms. Clear, sweet spring water "like Grandma used to drink" quenches thirsts. A dozen of us amble the sculpture trails, hoping for encounters with rejuvenating flora and fauna. Gopher tortoises, Florida chipmunks, pine snakes, and fox squirrels forage among heartleaf, coontie palms, clethra, mountain laurel, and pine-barren tridens grass. Gramma Rose punctuates the serenity.

"Listen to the quiet. Did you ever hear so much silence?"

What Hath a Thole?

Leaving the nature preserve with seven of us snuggled into one car, Rosemary gets repetitive. Great-granddaughter Kayla opens her phone to a *Word Cookies!* game to redirect Gram's attention.[12] The game offers assorted letters from which to make words, and everyone chimes their suggestions. But Rosemary outsmarts the gadget when she comes up with "THOLE." No one knows what it means, not even the machine.

"Of course, it's a word," Gram insists.

Regardless of her dementia, we know Gramma Rose well enough not to doubt her. Robert suggests a definition.

"I'm not thure, but I think it'th thomething like the thpirit."

Gram informs us that a thole supports an oar. Granddaughter Mary searches the Internet and, to no one's surprise, Rose is correct. Despite a scrambled brain, Rosemary remains one smart cookie.

A rowboat's thole secures the oar to steer in the desired direction with enough flexibility to keep the journey interesting. Gram remembers that Emile Renouf's painting *Helping Hands* has a thole. This reminds us of the reprint that hung over grandson Adam's bed.

During a childhood fever, Adam stared at the depiction of a grandfather/ granddaughter duo rowing a small fishing skiff. "They're going in circles," he remarked with red-hot cheeks. I assured him it was a delusion from his illness. "No," he insisted. "With only one oar, the boaters must have kept circling around for the sake of the painter."

Car rides with Gramma Rose always elicit fabulous conversations. Morning dawns and my mother arises, mouth first.

"A full day ahead? Somebody better measure and be sure it's got all twenty-four hours."

At senior exercise class, Zumba dancers bedecked in colorful regalia greet Rosemary as if she is an adored mascot. She looks them over with reciprocal admiration.

"Your festive outfits look like you just stepped out of a crayon box."

After watching class from the sidelines, Rose greets dancers. One holds the door for her wheelchair as we leave. The woman jokingly asks for a tip.

"Don't bet on the horses," Rosemary replies.

Tuesday evening arrives, and we scoot over to neighbor Don's for dinner. Rose settles into his recliner chair. He lays it back for her, and she folds her hands, corpse-like across her chest.

"Don't I look natural?"

A few hours later, she wakes up and we head for the car to go home.

"Hmm, foggy weather," Rose observes, half-asleep. "It matches my outlook."

The next morning, we run late for a doctor's appointment. With Mom and her wheelchair aboard, I pull out of the driveway to the tune of a nagging signal. The trunk is not fully latched. No time to spare, I drive on. The obnoxious beeper announces the problem every minute. Surprised each time, Rosemary echoes the alert with her own version of alarm. It reminds me of community emergency sirens designed to announce approaching danger—a tornado, tsunami, air raid, nuclear fallout. During pending doom, people need their wits sharp. Loud, nerve-racking alarms impinge on our ability to keep cool, calm, and collected. Between the car's loose-latch alerts and my startled mother's, "What's that?" I cannot focus safely on driving. I pull over and secure the trunk. Our fate sealed, we arrive late. No matter, the doctor, too, is running late.

One nippy morning, we bundle into warm coats for a neighborhood stroll. Passing under a shade tree, Rosemary's voice takes the lead.

"I need to walk in the sunlight before I shiver so hard it cracks the sidewalk."

Back home, wrapped in a blanket, I settle her into a chair by the door. Just outside, a turtle awaits a snack. As I head out, my mom beckons.

I call back, "I'll be in in a sec."

"You'll be an insect?"

She cracks me up. Hardships make work, and efforts exercise our potential. Caring for my mother teaches me how beautiful, glimmering moments outshine agony. Mom's humor lightens my load. Emerging from the creases of my elderly mother's face, bright-eyed Rosey overcomes unimaginable horrors. When needed, she pops to the surface.

The morning sky blushes red with foreboding. Rosemary lies in bed trying to make sense of things. In a blink, perplexity turns to childlike wonder. Spying me in the doorway, Rosey erupts with questions.

"What is this place? How have I come to be here?"

Untroubled, eager for answers, fairy dust glitters her words with astonishment. Fascination over where she *is*, reroutes to where she's *been*.

"I've been playing softball all morning. Not good at it. I never get to run around the bases. But it's sure fun. And that's the object of any game."

Robert bids her good morning and says she looks alert.

"I never make false claims," she replies.

Peering out a window, Rose watches thirst-quenched trees dance in a rowdy breeze. "How nice. Earth is getting her face washed."

After a bath, Rosemary sighs. "I feel like I've had my passport stamped to associate with civilized people." But her words logjam into redundant circles. My mother's personhood fragments like tossed puzzle pieces. No point in answering her wheres, whens, whos, and whys regarding places, time, and people. She'll ask again. Our eyes meet in mutual realization; we are both terribly lost. *No worry, Mom. Your bewilderment will pass in a moment.* I console myself by imagining Rosey as my daughter, a little girl . . . who bears a striking resemblance to my mother.

For her ninetieth birthday, we give Rosemary a soft blanket imprinted with family photographs. Customized online, the spread turned out beyond my greatest hope. She peers into each framed picture as if through open windows to her past.

"Here's Uncle Joe with his sisters." "Look, all six of us together with Mom." "My weeping willow!" "Marty's a baby, trying to catch your father's tongue." Rose turns to the birthday cards sent from across the globe. She opens each envelope with joyful anticipation. "Oh, look. My niece sent me three exclamation points!!!"

We drive to tai chi. Rosemary sits astute in the classroom, hands on her lap with interlaced fingers. After the balancing spiritual practice, classmates surprise her with candles and a birthday song. Artist Mary gives my mother hand-painted floral note cards. Astonished to be ninety, Rosemary sings every verse of "My Grandfather's Clock" for the appreciative class. Everyone joins in the "tick, tock, tick, tock" chorus.

Exhausted when we arrive home, my dear old mom drags herself to the bedroom. An hour-long outing is all she can handle.

"My knees are shaking so hard, it's a shame we don't have any butter to churn." Flopped on the bed, she wraps herself in the new photo blanket. "It's like being embraced by everyone." With that, Rosemary dozes off with a deep sigh from her surrendering soul.

Her life seconds numbering

STROKE 7

AHA! HA-HA, AND AHHHH

The sea endlessly tats her lace of bubbly veils
and spreads their tiers across the beach.
– ROSEMARY, 1983

ANOTHER EPISODE PUTS MORE BRAIN cells to rest in April 2018. Lips blue, extremities ice-cold white, but her core temperature remains a normal 98.6. Blood pressure and pulse are high at 164/82 and 84. Panting, her respirations race to 26. Rosemary feels dizzy, shaky, and chilly even under four comforters. My mother assures us that she is not anxious.

"Death is calling to me."

Weakly, she whispers a song of appreciation to people present and long gone: "Thanks for the Memories." A hospice nurse offers to come, but Rose is not suffering, just trying to die. Marty's death taught me that what she needs at this point is the compassionate company of family.

"We appreciate the offer," I tell the RN, "but if Rosemary survives this one, down the road we might need you more. For now, other patients take priority." Trusting the system and an unpredictable future, how little I know of what's to come.

Several hours pass and her shaking subsides. She then sleeps as if hibernating. The ensuing day, she's only awake three hours. Semiconscious, she muttered one-sided conversations. I overheard her mention "Philly curbing," "the mills," and "Uncle Joe."

It's a wonder how the Martins kept their gumption. Rosemary's hardworking grandfather William Senior suffered a heatstroke while installing Philadelphia street curbs. Subsequent brain damage, seizures, and unemployability led to alcohol abuse. That left Rosemary's grandmother Elizabeth (née McGlynn), to raise their six children, working as a washwoman. The oldest at age eight, William Jr. (Rosemary's father), had to quit school and work in a Kensington lace mill to supplement their meager income. Family said they were too poor to give him a middle name. Six years later, their mother died, and the children were dispersed. The second oldest, Francis, became a Philadelphia country club caddy. The McGlynn grandparents took in eldest daughter, Regina, as their nursemaid. And the three youngest—Margaret, Catherine, and six-year-old Joseph—were placed in "orphan asylums" for the rest of their childhoods.

Rosemary's consciousness returns from visits with long-gone relatives in uncharted territory. She spies the iconic family photograph of my brother Marty, a babe in the arms, held by Dad. She'd kept this favorite image on her dresser for the past decade. Today however, Rose mistakes the baby for her grandson Adam and cannot be convinced otherwise.

Iconic photo of Marty and dear old dad

The connective embroidery of short-term memories weaves lives together. Without it, Rosemary lives in jumbled swatches. Every minute is a new patch of disconnected time. But bewilderment passes with the blink of her eyes. Looking out the open window, Rosey catches the breeze in her hair and marvels at the "sparkly sunlight."

Full-time care of my mother would be impossible without the community spirit that thrives in our Florida panhandle suburb. Neighbors Tim, Cara, and Joe greet her as we shuffle along the roadside. Mike climbs a ladder and fills Robert's bear-proofed bird feeders for Rose's avian enjoyment. An anonymous neighbor mows her lawn. Ann and Dick drop off their old newspapers for her to read. Unaware of the date, it's all news to Rose.

The hospice nurse arrives and asks if she gets cyanotic when short of breath. My mom breaks into song. "Am I Blue?"

Her body temperature regulator is on the fritz. An aide warms her with a hot shower while I heat towels and clothes in the dryer. With each pampering layer, Rose reacts as if it is a new experience, thrilled by the luxurious heat.

The following day, she keeps shivering, regardless how many blankets I pile on her—the photo-adorned spread, the blue-onion-patterned comforter, the poofy pastel cover she made for me as a teen, Granny's handsewn quilt. Worried she'll smother under the mound, I run her a hot bath instead. That does the trick.

"Ahhh," she sighs immersed in warmth, and bursts into song. "Little Ducky Duddle."

I haven't heard that tune since age three. Enchanted, I join in the finale: "Quack, quack." What fascinated me as a tyke with its word reversal. "Said he . . ." Its meaning held. I gained appreciation for the fluidity of language, despite my undiagnosed dyslexia.

Ninety-year-old Rosemary relaxes in the tub. Looking down, she makes a carefree observation. "My breasts are very buoyant. In fact, more *boyant* than *girlant*."

A real looker, Rosemary never knew it. In her budding prime, she had a classic build—23" waist and generous bosoms. The 5'4" gal retained a trim figure, topping the scale at 136 pounds by middle-age. Entering her senior years, she joked about the spent breasts that rested on her belly and kept a cartoon in her "Ha-Ha Humor" file.

The two-framed comic depicted a burly male sporting a T-shirt that read, "Show me your tits." In the next frame, an elderly woman hoisted her skirt to expose her breasts dangling at knee level.

Although photographs attest to the contrary, Rosemary always considered herself unattractive. First came an early sense of rejection from her siblings. In her pubescent years, adolescent tormenters reinforced her bleak self-image. They mistook her for Italian or Jewish and amused themselves by casting ethnic insults. From then on, mirrors falsely accused dark-haired Rosemary of a nose too large and ears too big. Nothing ever convinced her of the natural beauty with which she was graced.

But self-perceived homeliness and societal pressures to conform could not grind Rosemary down. Witnessing vicious anti-Semitism, hatred toward immigrants, and unjust poverty of slave descendants strengthened her resolve to champion underdogs. She sought the humanity in everyone, bullies included. She consoled hooligans, bandaged skinned knees of brats, and offered hankies to sniffling neighborhood ogres.

Male supremacy was no match for Rosemary either. She cast off submissive femininity. With precision cuts into mocking male conversation, she halted rude banter in an instant. Although always pleasant, Rose never fell blindly agreeable. Reasonably ladylike, yes, but coy conduct was not in her repertoire. Teenage ballet lessons failed to impart graceful poise. By the 1950s, Rose was equally comfortable in a homemade sundress to appease her husband or a pair of trousers for climbing trees, shoveling snow, or teaching her daughters skin-the-cat calisthenics. Although polite, she confronted antagonism and indifference head on.

Unlike her sister Anna Mae who liked to get "dolled up," Rosemary scoffed at the cosmetic industry for its marketing tactic to make women feel unsightly without their products. She found it best to make do with whatever Mother Nature bestows.

"True beauty comes from a genuine smile, not lipstick. Makeup merely conceals. Blush is for mannequins. Rosy cheeks come from healthy vigor."

The only exception to her clean-face rule was on formal occasions, such as conventions she enjoyed where my Grand Commander father presided over the Military Order of the Cooties (a fun-loving, honorary branch of the VFW). Rose would dab on a modest shade of lipstick, then blot most of it off. Sometimes she patted each cheek with just the right amount of rouge to avoid looking anemic. Two prized quotes from her mother bolstered Rose's confidence: "My face, I don't mind it because I'm behind it," and "Be it ever so humble, there's no face like your own." But Rosemary failed to recognize her vivacious charm. From ugly-duckling self-loathing emerged a gorgeous matriarchal swan with joie de vivre invisible to its bearer.

Cooties: Rosemary and
Grand Commander Herman

Rosemary's angelic expression turns puckish as she lies in bed staring upward.

"Ordinarily, people look at the ceiling and watch the fan go around. At this stage, I look at the fan, and the ceiling goes around." Reminded that the nurse is coming after lunch, she acknowledges, "Okay, I'll cancel my plans for the grand ball."

Her eyes fidget, seeking to establish their bearings. Picture a child exiting a rapid merry-go-round. Brows alternate, one up, one down, accentuating her bemused expression. Her nonconformist eyebrows curl this way and that, an eccentric departure from their youthful norm. Her adorable forehead caterpillars spurn the cosmetic industry definition of feminine attractiveness. Classic Rosemary.

Off to the bathroom, perched on the pot for her morning pee, Rosemary hearkens back to her equestrian years.

"Sitting here so dizzy feels like riding the toilet around the bathroom."

Afterward, Robert and I escort her to the couch, and the three of us watch *Star Trek*, the one television show she still enjoys. The Gene Roddenberry masterpiece debuted in the late 1980s. Old, intact memories help Rose follow the plot. New observations beam into her consciousness.

"The *Starship Enterprise* resembles a cake pan."

"Or an inverted wok," I suggest. We watch the spaceship get caught in a time warp and career out of control, as does my mother's mind.

"At least there aren't any telephone poles to sideswipe." Robert's ludicrous practicality tells us he is absorbed in the plot, rather than the vehicle design.

After morning tai chi at the college, we mosey arm-in-arm to the parking lot. Mom spots a man on the roof of the emergency operations shed. He is stringing a huge coil of lightning cable.

"Look!" Rose exclaims, "he's lassoed that building."

My mom's old driver's license has expired, so I take her to get an identification card. She notices the crumbling state of her birth certificate.

"It's a race to see which decomposes first. It would be nice if the paper expires before me . . . depending on your definition of 'nice.'"

Awaiting our turn at the county bureau, Rosemary tries to communicate another point. Half-spoken, a non sequitur dangles in the office air. With the absurdity of playwright Samuel Beckett, an incomplete thought flounders, destined to meaninglessness.

"My brain is full of gaps, but . . . what was I saying?" She gives up speaking and sings an old tune I had never heard about dwindling time as life progresses. Packed in the waiting area like herded cattle, people grow quiet, listening to Rosemary's peaceful song. We go through the ropes, get her ID, and head home. Secure in our adobe, I search the Internet and find the 1938 Kurt Weill tune she sang: "September Song."

Sundowner evenings, Rosemary makes memory soup, mixing dribs and drabs of this and that into whatever her remaining mind cooks up. We savor the wacky word salad she concocts. Flashes of momentary frustrations flicker through her stunning vocabulary and insight.

"Far as I recall, I used to have a pretty good brain. Now it's full of moth holes." She looks around with satisfaction. "Whose house is this? I'd like to thank the hosts."

You're welcome, Mom.

On Mother's Day, Rosemary's mind expands beyond motherhood and planetary limitations. Aha moments of discernment surprise her, like the friendly lick of a shy puppy. Her excitement rises to a fevered pitch. Quietly I listen, fascinated. *Don't distract her; don't break the spell.* Knowing it will soon dissipate into fog, I preserve what I can, noted in snippets for posterity.

She sits in the chair next to my desk, gazing out the window. Steepled fingers like a rocket ship rest in her lap, ready for blast off. Beyond the glass, a towhee stuffs mealworms into the open beak of her flapping chick. A handsome skink whips under a rock followed by its cobalt blue tail. Box turtles mate under Japonica azaleas.

I try to film my mom, but the camera light's reflection in the glass distracts her attention. *Dagnabbit.* Instead, I take dictation on my computer keyboard. At first in whispers, her voice tiptoes over delicate moss. Then she launches into existential, eco-philosophical orbit. Her mind and mouth zoom faster than my arthritic fingers can keep pace:

> *The way life has evolved on other planets must be different than on Earth. Although, with all the variety out of the same basic elements, this one of ours is pretty satisfactory. Logic tells me there must be a God. This world isn't just a delightful accident. The purpose of it all is to marvel. Look at the trees; what a miracle! I suppose other planets have their own menageries. But I never wonder what they are like. I'm too busy enjoying what we've got here. Humankind thinks this was all created for our benefit. Maybe we're supposed to be the appreciators.*

Her diction sounds pre-stroke sharp. She talks nonstop for an hour. My mom reminds me of naturalists Richard Powers describes in his forest novel *Overstory*,[13] the precious few attuned to nature, thereby "immune to consensual reality." Furious keyboard tap-tap-taps race to keep up with her lucid voyage. Blue jays, cardinals, and mourning doves flutter through the fern garden. She startles with delight, as a rabbit hops over the amorous turtles.

> *If turtles talk, I wonder how they describe us to other turtles. If not for birds and airborne bugs, would man have thought to fly? The whole interactive pattern of nature is wonderful. Dancing sunrays filtering through the pines catch her eye. Look at that beautiful sunshine, so volatile and dangerous up close but life-sustaining from this distance. We Earthlings have it good.*

Her voice trails off, ending her pastoral soliloquy with a comment worthy of an Earth Day bumper sticker: "I'm glad for chlorophyll, and that we evolved to appreciate it."

I hear the dryer stop. Time to fold laundry, to the tune of Mom's serenade. Our same-size clothes are interchangeable. Living under one roof, wardrobes mesh. All she cares about is warmth and pockets. I dress her in my nice outfits, an outward expression of love.

Sunday afternoon, Robert and I take my mother to the community chorus spring concert. Making our way into the auditorium, people notice Rosemary's instability; the dense crowd parts. Rose thanks them and chuckles under her breath, mentioning bowling alley pins.

"Probably afraid I'll tumble and bowl them over."

We find our well-cushioned seats and settle in, but her mind continues bowling. She talks about my dad's league, his dust-collecting trophies, and the time he bowled 300. Looking around the theater, astounded by the assortment of attire, Rosemary reflects on past norms.

"Everyone used to wear their Sunday best to theater performances. My romantic Pop always got Mom a corsage for outings and pinned the posy near her heart. Most fellows wore fedoras. Your father, in uniform, wore his navy cap. Along Jersey boardwalks, we gals wore white gloves, ironed skirts, seamed stockings, and well-polished shoes. Eventually, the salty breeze would undo fastidious hair curls and relax starched posturing into carefree conversation."

On this warm spring day in Florida, the municipal auditorium is bustling. The eclectic array of outfits deemed appropriate for the occasion spans the gamut from churchgoers in stiff Sunday suits to beachgoers, blown in fresh off the Gulf in flip-flops and cut-offs. The variety of garb under one roof is a vibrant sign of the times. Ninety-year-old Rosemary prefers comfort over classy. I dressed her in my attractive pantsuit over thermal underwear. But before the program begins, she shivers. My warm shawl conceals her outfit, but the mismatched layer accentuates the loving intent and blends with divergent audience wear.

Lights dim, curtains open, and the stage comes alive with an audience participation compilation of old, familiar songs. Rosemary merrily sings along to "Meet Me in St. Louis," "And the Band Played On," and "In the Good Old Summertime." When the chorus concludes each song, Rose continues belting out another verse. I redirect her to the playlist for what's to come. Synchronized lighting effects, costumes, and choreography enhance the festivity. Rose gives her hands a workout with applause for the beaming chorus. After the grand finale, we wait for the crowd to dissipate before we exit. The director instructs performers to line up for a photograph.

"Time for pictures, people."

"And a happy New Year," a jubilant Rose bellows back, for reasons all her own.

At home, Great-Gramma Rose asks the whereabouts of her descendants. We discuss their distant homes. Scattered to the wind, they presently reside in San Francisco, Australia, New Zealand, and China.

"What a restless country this is. It just keeps percolating people, moving from one place to another as the ground shifts. Well, at least they're all in English-speaking Arabian nations."

My mother's awareness of Earth's plate tectonics holds firm. But she has lost interest in manmade boundaries. And occasional comments materialize as if from some dimensionless nebulae.

"I'm glad no one in my ringing ears asks me to dance. Maybe last week I'll remember."

She attempts a jigsaw puzzle. Robert looks over her shoulder, wondering aloud.

"Does that picture theme concern the chain of being or the tree of life?"

"A can of beans or the change of life," Rose reiterates, viewing the grand scheme.

Evening descends, and Rosemary contemplates the quiet household.

"The night is so still . . . like it's waiting for something to happen."

We mention that her great-granddaughter Kayla did well in her improvisation course with a portrayal of melting ice cream.

"I can't imagine anyone in this family not being mouthy," replies Gramma Rose. "Half of our ancestors kissed the Blarney Stone, giving us the 'gift of gab.' What melting ice cream says, I suspect, depends on the flavor."

With that, Rosemary's mind wanders to an ice cream parlor in Stone Harbor, New Jersey. "Blueberry's my favorite Springer's flavor; you always order almond bisque." She proceeds to rattle off everybody's preferences.

After a hard rain, a break in the weather allows Rose a brief step outside to inhale deep breaths of freshened air. With meteorological scrutiny, she looks skyward and speculates, "Hmm, sunshine and gray clouds. I guess that makes us half-baked."

A loud news broadcast lures her attention to the television. Insolent, unpresidential comments spew and Rosemary calls for a higher authority.

"Sic his mother on him." She elaborates, contemplating the source of the President's misconduct. "Some people are hard to follow. It's like they need to keep themselves on an even keel by throwing everyone else off balance."

In Jersey, such misbehavior is called ignorant. In the south, it's just plain sorry.

This summer day we make lemonade, using her mother's old juicer. Rose repeats the story of how Granny received the gadget as a gift from a vacuum cleaner salesman after watching his demonstration. Following Rosemary's recipe, we drop the rinds into boiling water to extract essential oils and then give each segment a final squeeze.

We refrigerate the lemonade and relax at the table for dinner. But the repetitive lemon-squeezing activity tangles her thoughts. She takes her pills and flusters. "Damn, I meant to squeeze them again before I swallowed."

After dinner, we watch *The Medium*, a TV series about a clairvoyant who worked for the Phoenix District Attorney's office.

"I believe that. Some of my best friends are ghosts," says Rosemary.

Using the remote, I mute and fast-forward through prerecorded news. The footage passes a photo op, meet-and-greet in North Korea. Donald Trump and Kim Jong Un stand shoulder to shoulder in silence.

Hearing nothing, Rose observes the stilted body language of the posturing dignitaries.

"Would you say they're having a vacuous conversation?"

Her blissful, unruffled disposition came with the dementia.

Pre-stroke Rose was not always Rosy. Civil, yes, but no laugh lines radiated from the corners of her eyes. Such testaments of joy take decades to form. At the crux of adulthood, she flaunted her dislikes. These were a few of her *least* favorite things: parades ("too noisy"), circuses ("too hectic"), pep rallies ("forced glee"), drinking water ("makes me choke"), cities ("corrupt rat races"), fresh air and smelly flowers ("they make me sneeze"), red licorice ("nauseating"), cold weather ("I shiver at the thought"), mangos ("taste rotten"), blue jays ("once pecked my head"), and right-side-out underwear ("seams are too rough").

Rosemary had a nervous breakdown at age nineteen. That same year, she met her future husband. His support emboldened her against debilitating gloom. And writing vented the plague of insurmountable injustices that weighed her down. Forty-two years later, widowhood confined her to misery beyond grief. Mourning tapped into something festering, a never-acknowledged anguish from her past. Nine years later, my brother died, and Rosemary clicked away the next decade with the television remote or buried herself in books, only surfacing, duty-bound, to make meals and do volunteer work to divert her sorrow.

Cheer plastered on her face in public, she wore expressionless melancholy in the privacy of her home. Asked to smile, she bared her teeth. During that bleak decade of dreary indifference, she found nothing to sing about. Rosemary confessed to trusted allies, "I'm serving a life sentence." Then along came the strokes.

Dementia exchanges her sadness for sublime tranquility. Whatever darkness lurked in the shadows of her character vanquished. Granted, she's no saint. But as sharp edges soften, genuine smiles appear, and I envision her aura complemented by wings and a halo. Unencumbered, she discovers hints of bliss, once mistaken for trivia. Her list of favorite things multiplies.

Rosemary raises a small, cobalt blue glass to the sunlight and marvels; it has remained her favorite color since a childhood Christmas tree twinkled with brilliant blue lights. Queen Anne's lace flowers with purple-dotted centers remind her of her "240" home's backyard field (now the site of the Audubon Library). She adores cornflowers, "the truest bluest." She collects blue onion (lotus) dinnerware, matching homemade curtains, bedspread, pillow covers, and a two-piece outfit. Her favorite birds are female cardinals, not to be overshadowed by their flamboyant, male counterparts. Seafood-wise, she likes "ha-ha fish": halibut and haddock. Her treasured pastime is reading and the clever mechanics of pop-up books. Each page turn holds suspense, followed by elation at the 3-D artistry . . . unveiled as if for the first time. Shuffling on walks outside, she admires the sand, the light, the neighbors, and—ahhh—the trees.

In utter contrast, on this sunny day she awakens in fretful, existential brooding.

"I'm so confused. I wonder if I exist."

"Who wants to know?" asks philosophical Robert.

"Ha-ha," they erupt with laughter. *Je doute, donc je suis:* I doubt, therefore I am. Descartes cartwheels in his grave.

An ominous radio broadcast predicts the sun will engulf Earth in 4½ billion years. The three of us respond in celebration: "Hooray, we're alive. This is fun, for now."

Getting undressed, she bumps a framed photograph of my father. It topples to the floor. "Aah!" she startles. Then in two shakes, she shrugs. "Oh, well, my darling was always athletic."

A few of my parents' wedding gifts survived the passing decades—the cake topper, a pair of ceramic deer, and an amber wine glass. Rosemary donated keepsakes and fragments of her past for installation in the *Memory Walls* of Shoal Sanctuary's farmhouse. Interspersed between stones, they join Marty's model train, Granny's tin mug, a rotary phone dial, Dad's pencil sharpener, a Czechoslovakian toy of universal harmony . . . and shards of broken dinnerware that still hold thoughts of lovingly prepared meals.

One reason Rosemary cherishes her role of cooking for everyone is the famine that forced our Irish ancestors to resettle in England where the children were used as slave labor. That history of hunger stuck to our bones. The least I can do for my mother, and in tribute to my predecessors, is make meals interesting.

A school cafeteria tray comes in handy. One section holds fruit, another pills. Two beverages keep her hydrated. A stalk of celery fits well in the space designed for utensils. A food plate occupies the largest space. A "chow hound," in tiny bites she savors whatever is served.

Special touches add sustenance for the soul—her name spelled out in alphabet soup or in Scrabble tile-shaped crackers, a quartz centerpiece, tiny bouquets of flowers, fruit arranged into silly smiles, flavorful dabs of cardamom in cocoa. Compassion penetrates into prepared food and passes into its consumers, a lesson from the award-winning 1992 movie *Like Water for Chocolate* and in the Beatles' George Harrison's "Savoy Truffle." Each delectable morsel on Rosemary's tray is a thank you for the meals she made everyone else over the years.

Meals to pamper a deserving Mom

Mom's pleasure in making meals inspired us kids. When not in use, the kitchen became our full-scale chemistry set. She granted us free reign to cook whatever we wanted so long as we obeyed one imperative rule. No, it was not to clean up; that went without saying. And our mother did not demand we eat what we made; taste determined if our creations were for people or pets. Rosemary's rule was a vote of confidence. We had to write down experimental recipes, in case they turned out delicious. From the kitchen came noteworthy flops of peanut butter and bologna sandwiches, orange juice with rainbow sprinkles, and chocolate chip cream of mushroom soup. Although none of our concoctions proved cookbook-worthy, Mom bestowed a priceless gift: faith in our creative abilities.

Under Rosemary's tutelage, we learned to lick beaters, to show respect for yeast, and how to prevent garbage from growing maggots. Carrot tops waded in water on window sill saucers to grow filigree leaves for rabbits, hamsters, and guinea pigs. Potato eyes sprouted forth greenery. And a majestic sweet potato vine twined around our living room bookcases.

Mom suggested, Rorschach-style, that everyone's approach to eating corn on the cob divulged personality traits. Dad's rolling pin method, circling the cob in vertical fashion, meant an adventurous Ferris-wheel-ride character. Marty's focus on the rhythmic chewing sound foretold his music aptitude. Big sister Beth varied her technique to keep us guessing. We regarded Mom's typewriter flair—horizontal bites from left to right—as a sign of efficiency. When she reached the cob's end, we'd yell, "Ding!" imitating the manual typewriter return noise, and she'd move to the next row. The hit-or-miss technique typified rights of passage for dental-challenged elders and children passing from baby to adult teeth. I remained a hit-or-misser for six years, my two front teeth knocked out at age one.

Mom often retold the story of how I toddled through the house with my glass baby bottle nipple tight between my teeth to free both hands. A tumble knocked those baby teeth into my nostrils. I sneezed blood all the way to the doctor's office and Beth fainted at the sight. It was not until age seven that I could eat corn with any accuracy.

Rose's ears perk, overhearing talk about the International House of Pancakes. Someone uses the abbreviation IHOP and she adds her two cents.

"I'm more inclined to crawl."

Today, the church gymnasium where Zumba class meets is cluttered with athletic equipment. I position Rose's wheelchair out of harm's way in a corner. She observes the painted basketball lines on the floor. "Guess I'm third base."

On the drive home, she watches the world go by outside her window. "Look, a Red Cross blood bank. Can I make a withdrawal?" The witticism makes me wonder if she's feeling anemic.

Disjointed exchanges keep life lively. Rather than answer the same questions over and over, I provide my mom paper to jot down my answers in her own writing. Thereafter, each time she asks, I offer the bulging folder. Beside the tree lamp, she thumbs through the stack of her handwritten responses. The method does not stop her questions, but it allows pauses while she reads. Most notes involve where she lives, who she lives with, how she got from New Jersey to Florida, the location of loved ones, and—no matter the month—reassurance that she already sent Christmas cards.

Keeping track of Rosemary's bowel movements is crucial to avoid constipation. Her peripheral neuropathy makes it a serious challenge. She cannot remember . . . Correction: she remembers but has no sense of time. Her last success may have been yesterday or a week ago. We unhook the flusher on her toilet, so evidence doesn't disappear down the drain before documented. Her diet adjusts daily with prune juice and medications.

For a bit of exercise to help keep her regular, we take more walks. My mother points to an azalea bush sporting new growth.

"Here's a tiny leaf. If we find another, won't that be a re-leaf."

After strolling a few yards, she gets winded. Pausing, she rests her head on my chest. Looking upward into the branches overhead, she grins.

"I used to swing in the trees . . . many yesterdays ago. Now they swing and sway without me."

Back home at a pace that would please turtles, she conks out exhausted. A brief nap later, Rosemary lies in bed reacquainting herself with the world.

"It's a trick, trying to navigate the future from inside a dream."

With no sitter available and Robert busy, Rose accompanies me to *my* doctor's appointment. Like mother, like daughter, I seem to be catching what she's got with confusion, memory loss, weakness, and severe joint pain. The physician knows Rosemary well and is aware of our situation but has not seen her for quite a while. He greets my mom with an energetic hug.

"Rosemary, I missed you."

"Why? Are you a bad aim?" she retorts pokerfaced.

The good doctor diagnoses me with "caregiver fatigue." He's still laughing over Rosemary's remarks as Mom and I depart for lunch. We head for a diner. Robert and our youngest son Adam who's in town for a visit, escort Gramma Rose in for a pleasant lunch.

Driving home, an engorged cloud does what clouds do, releasing its contents in a downpour. Rose notes, "Nice to have a traveling roof along as an umbrella." She serenades with "April Showers." No point telling her it's July. After the outing, my mom gets lightheaded. "The world's going 'round and 'round. May as well enjoy the ride."

Rosemary now sleeps for long stretches of time, fourteen to sixteen hours. After one marathon sleep, she awakens alarmed, saying she cannot breathe. I check her pulse and respirations. Normal. Reassured, my mom relaxes, distracted by the sound of a prancing squirrel on the roof. Here comment seems unrelated: "I'd like to let my parents know how much I appreciate them. Such a loving couple."

A pretty nurse in her twenties comes to check on my mom. The RN mentions that she misplaced her pen. I offer her mine, and Rosemary offers the young woman cautionary advice.

"Always carry a pen, so if you are accosted by a molester, you can write insulting words on him."

An urgent matter arises in August. Our daughter-in-law Melissa has developed a brain tumor. She and our middle son, James--who goes by David--need moral support while Melissa undergoes surgery at Shands Hospital in Gainesville, five hours away. With no other family able to care for Rosemary, I arrange for her to stay at a nursing home until Robert and I return. We dread entrusting her to a nursing home. Each time we take a brief hospice respite break, she comes home looking like a war survivor. But we're caught between a rock and a hard place, forced to sacrifice one generation for another.

A Crestview nursing facility agrees to provide temporary quarters for Rosemary. (A few years from now, the parent company of this shabby place will file for bankruptcy.) For now, the kindness of nursing staff convinces me she is in good hands. I label drawers and doors in large print and memorize the layout. Briefing the staff of her needs proves futile. Rose's charm and wit fool them into thinking she's fully functional. Aides refill her untouched water pitcher daily, but no one tells Rosemary to drink. They simply mark it with the date. From Gainesville, I call several times a day and coach my mother.

"Fill your cup with water, Mom. Drink it. Drink it all. Is it empty yet? Have some more."

I keep daily track of her status by phone. "What color is your outfit, Ma?" Her response tells me she slept in yesterday's clothes. She requires guidance through every step. "Go to the television. Open the drawer below. Take out a clean shirt. What color is it? Put it on your bed. Sit down. Take off your shirt. Hold the phone in your other hand . . ." If she puts down the phone, she forgets to pick it back up. Then I must call the understaffed facility to have someone go to her room and find her phone among her sheets. In the unfamiliar setting, out of her routine, Rosemary's confusion worsens, and she falls.

Torn between the needs of my mother and our son and his wife, we split the difference. After several days, we return to north Florida and go straight to pick up Rosemary. Her deterioration is alarming. She smells overripe, has severe dehydration, and black, tarry stools—evidence of a high gastrointestinal bleed. Her blood pressure is low, under 100 systolic, and drops when she exerts.

She is far safer with loving family than in such state-licensed places. Arriving home, she faints in the driveway. Our fire chief neighbor Larry stops mowing and runs over. Scooping Rosemary into his arms, he carries her indoors. Halfway there, she regains consciousness.

"Thanks for the lift. Having a stroke feels like someone slipped me a Mickey." Then Rosemary sings an unknown song to the laughing firefighter. "Cuckoo, I'm going cuckoo, no one can coo like you coo." She offers to make him iced tea and cinnamon buns. After he declines and bids farewell, she waves goodbye, determined to send the man a thank-you card.

Robert and Rosemary chat about Dick Tracy comic characters, named for their dispositions. After careful consideration, he dubs his mother-in-law "Dense Fog Dame." She graciously accepts the befitting nickname. I kiss my scrawny mother's cheek.

"Ah oh ah, that's nice," she smiles and dozes off.

The rigmarole of our absence leaves her resigned to her pending demise. "When I die, give your brother and sister a hug from me." Reminded that Beth lives in New Jersey and Marty is dead, she laughs in acknowledgment and agrees to embrace him for the both of us when the time comes.

We explain to my mother that we were away due to Melissa's brain surgery.

Rosemary replies with conciliatory empathy. "She deserves to be called 'Militia' and given a medal for bravery after enduring such a harrowing experience. Once she gets out of the hospital, I'll make her a special dessert, anything she wants."

Nephew Bill sends his "Aunt Re" fresh tomatoes from New Jersey. Her mason jars and huge canning pot sit dormant, collecting dust. But the fresh produce thrill Rosemary to no end.

"What a wonderful way to die, with the taste of Jersey tomatoes in my mouth. I'd rather have Jerseys than diamonds."

Jersey tomatoes, better than diamonds

Rosemary reads the local newspaper front to back, scrutinizing every article and ad. The familiar crumple of printed pages soothes her. Although her level of comprehension is unclear, she always finds typos and grammatical errors.

Rose skips a headline about guns. "Too noisy, in every way." Paper pushed aside, she delves into the dictionary. "I can't remember the distinction of articulation—joint and speech." On the bookshelf, a vintage copy of Emerson's essays seizes her attention. With the dexterity of a three-year-old, Rose tears the fragile pages apart as she reads. Fortunately, she remains clueless about her *faux pas*. With her love of literature, had she the capacity to realize her klutzy blunder, it would mortify her.

A hospice aide arrives to shower Rosemary. Afterward, I fetch a heated towel and nightgown, warm from the dryer. Snuggled into bed, my mother expresses contentment.

"Ahhh, almost as good as being cremated."

Could there be a sweeter smell than that of a fresh-bathed infant, or mom?

"Sunup Syndrome" reboots known reality

From lucid to semi-sleep, Rosemary gallops away on horseback. "I'm driving a herd of cattle down the Black Horse Pike with my sisters, Annie and Jean. Don't know if it's real, but it's sure a fond memory."

Dozing in and out, she announces with a squeal, "My cousin Eva has joined us, riding bareback along the Delaware River's eastern shoreline. We're driving cattle up an inland waterway near Paulsboro. Don't think I've ever been here before."

Enough with the cows; it's time for yard work at Mom's house around the corner, where we rent out the bedrooms. I take her to the Florida Room with its outdoor view. About to sit, she spies a speck of biscuit on the cushion, left by a careless renter.

"There's a crumb on the seat. Oh, well, maybe I can hatch it into a cracker."

In her well-organized, fully stocked kitchen, I prepare lunch. While Mom and I eat, we watch the yard guy tend her garden. Fig and chaste trees look raring to grow. Clematis clings. Hostas brighten shady nooks. Daylilies outshine the sun. Feathery yarrow and muhly grass soften her yard's edges.

Tasting the soup, Rosemary superimposes gardening with eating. "Nature's nourishment, such refreshing flavors and colors—salad is poetry of the soil."

After eating, she burps with Amish-style contentment.

"That's my kind of dinner music."

Directed toward her grandmother's 1936 *Garden Encyclopedia* on the coffee table, she examines the book with an expression of undetermined familiarity. Peering inside the front jacket, Rosey beams with recognition at the green and white nature illustration.

"Oh, Grossmom's garden book," my little girl mom sings. She thumbs through the massive volume as if reacquainting herself with a long-lost friend.

Two hours vertical, Rosemary must rest.

"I need to get horizontal. It's a lot of work carrying around a head."

"You can watch the action, Mom."

"I didn't know there were oxen in this region." Her raised eyebrows relax as she nods off.

Stepping outside, I leave the door ajar while tending to her angel trumpets on the other side of the window. Some dead limbs need trimming off Dad's dwarf red azalea we transplanted her from her previous home. A half-hour later Rosemary stirs, and we call it quits.

The yardman turns to leave, and my mom offers him a parting gesture, reminiscent of her Irish great-grand Aunt Sarah. Rosemary forms fists, knuckles together at her waist, and bows to the fellow.

"I bid ye goodnight . . . ," although it's midday.

The two of us mosey back from her old home to ours. Along the way, a brown thrasher belts out an articulate song. If only we understood the language.

STROKE 8
UNDRESSED REHEARSAL: HANGING ON FOR DEAR LIFE

Dusk, a calm and secret time when the world is muffled in the lessened light,
Yet darkness has not yet hidden all from our inadequate eyes.
– ROSEMARY, 1960S

L ATE AT NIGHT, ROSEMARY'S SCUFFLES in the bathroom sound worrisome. Rushing to her aid, the odor hits before I round the corner. White-knuckled, she clings to the sink. Heaps of toilet paper litter the floor along with organic waste. *At least she's not constipated*, I think. But her rigid posture indicates trouble.

"I'm fainting," she whispers.

Her words sound alarm in me. Like the EMS red phone ring before the 9-1-1 system was installed, she summons my paramedic instinct.

"Let me help you, Mom," I assure. And, "Robert!" I bellow.

He leaps up from sleep and charges down the hall. We lock our arms under hers and try to walk her to bed. Big mistake. Rosemary is thin, but her knees buckle and we cannot support her. We are also seniors. Robert's torn rotator cuff and my arthritic joints fail the task. She collapses onto the carpet. Robert tosses us pillows, then dials non-emergency EMS to request "manpower assist." I check her vitals. Her racing pulse weakens. Once again, she appears to be dying—ashen and unresponsive. I lay beside her on the floor, awaiting help, singing lullabies: "All Aboard for Blanket Bay" and "When Poppies Close Their Crimson Eyes." First responder firefighters arrive and graciously put her to bed. She regains only enough consciousness to grunt in response to questions.

At dawn, we evaluate damages incurred last night. Robert's reinjured shoulder won't lift his arm. My arthritic hands refuse to so much as hold a pencil. But the worst injury is to Rosemary. Our feeble grasp tore the frail skin under her arms. A hospice nurse dresses the large, open wounds. Her skin will heal. My guilt, never.

Rosemary can only puff one-word responses. She cannot see well or feed herself. This stroke has taken away her greatest pleasure—reading. Offered a book, she examines it like a box, unable to open it or turn pages. She utters an indifferent noise, "ih."

My exhausted mind spells her resignation in Scrabble tiles, "I" and "H." It's the inverse of the "HI" she found under my brother's table after he died. Books now useless, I show her family photos. She cannot focus or recognize anyone.

The day progresses. She regains her voice and notices me fumbling around her bedroom.

"I hear you, but I can't see you." It's her first complete sentence since this stroke.

Waving my arms in front of her, we zero in on each other, nose-to-nose.

"Oh, it's you, Chris. Hello." Her voice chimes with recognition, the criteria she set for life worth living. But evening adds sundowner syndrome to Rosemary's befuddled brain.

"What's happened here? The whole system is corrupted." Her eyes flit side to side like frightened prey dodging a predator.

"What is corrupted, Mom?"

"My spot in nature and this apparatus." Her index finger points, trying to light on something within visual range. The accusative digit indicates gnarled sheets, the bedside commode, and, perhaps, thin air.

Rosemary conveys exasperation. "Everything is sprinky-dinky."

Robert and I console her with hugs and explain the stroke. We offer half-hearted assurance. Things could be worse. Sprinky-dinky is just below hunky-dory, a stone's throw from okey dokey.

This episode destroys Rosemary's right field of vision. Further modifications are necessary. Furniture, food, toilet paper . . . everything must be positioned on her left. She tries to walk, veers sideways, and falls—precisely what happened decades ago to our sixteen-year-old dog, Charlie, after a stroke.

Rose grasps for balance, eyes searching aimlessly until she dozes off. We head for the living room. Almost seated, we hear her call. Running back, we locate her in the far-left corner of her room, unable to find her way out. Trapped.

It was unusual for our dog, Charlie, not to greet us kids when we arrived home from high school. That fateful day, she struggled to her feet, tail wagging, and attempted to welcome us. Instead, our pooch staggered in circles, veering left. Alerted by our concerned call, Mom returned from work early. She recognized the stroke and said it would be cruel to keep poor Charlie alive in such a sorrowful state.

Our lifelong companion did not die of natural causes. Rosemary took Charlie to the vet and came home with a limp, sheet-wrapped furry bundle. The three of us kids were so saddened by the loss and upset over our mother's decision to euthanize, that—I am ashamed to admit—we failed to help our crying mother bury Charlie beneath the ancient oak tree out back.

Here in the twenty-first century, beloved pets often fare better than people as death approaches. Starving animals is illegal but common practice on terminal human beings.

> *Marty wanted grape juice; without explanation, hospice advised us to let him dwindle away. All we had available was apple juice; he choked on it. I turned to his doctor, who ordered an IV to ease Marty's thirst. His lungs filled with fluid and he began to drown. Marty in one room, our mother in the next, both voiced identical pleas, with opposite meanings.*
>
> *"Can't you do something, Chris?" That's when I went numb.*

Death with Dignity advocates promote the right to a tranquil, painless departure. Across the aisle, people with disabilities fear that legalized euthanasia could be broadened to violate their right to live. People want to decide for themselves, neither forced to live in agony nor "put down" against their will . . . like a dog.

Following her eighth stroke, Rosemary hangs on for dear life. She knows who she is and recognizes me, her criteria worthwhile living. But the sparkle has left her eyes.

A sleep deprivation triathlon commences with endurance tests in walking, eating, and communicating. Her dull eyeballs dart in their sockets, unable to focus. She's literally lost sight of her whereabouts. We remove household signs; she cannot read.

"Dizzy. I can't see anything on my right," she repeats every few minutes. Explanations cannot adhere to her remaining brain matter. Yet, her wit prevails.

"That doesn't give me the right to be lazy, but how 'bout what's left to be lazy?"

A modicum of her philosophical optimism also persists. "If death were nothingness, at least it would be painless. But I anticipate a cast of pleasant characters joining together."

She wears only pajamas and remains in bed except for escorted trips to the bathroom. Bells on her ankles seldom chime. Attempts to be vertical leave her short of breath. Rising to sit up, she rests her head on me "until the room stops spinning." She slumps onto the rollator walker for breaks along the nine steps from bed to bathroom. Her knees often give out. Unassisted, she veers left. The bedside commode becomes a necessity.

"I'd like to get out of here."

This could mean out of bed, outdoors, or out of her ailing body. Low blood pressure forces her to recline, and she clarifies.

"I think my mission is accomplished, and it's time for me to leave this parking lot."

"Where do you want to go, Mom?" The leading question coaxes her to contemplate death.

"Time to get on the road and head for someplace, anyplace besides the toilet."

A nurse notes Rosemary's inability to find the food on the tray. It contains a banana, orange segments, blueberries, blackberries, oatmeal, juice, cocoa, and a tiny bouquet. As I feed her, the RN questions why I persist in presenting elaborate meals. "What's the point?"

The notion that this modest meal was excessive, let alone futile, had not occurred to me. Under these circumstances, does sustenance constitute cruelty? The Earth shifts beneath my feet. Her body's struggle to let go opposes her cling to life. My thoughts tangle in contradictions. Caregiver duty asks what I can do; my paramedic training keeps her viable. Both resist daughterly practicality for what *not* to do. The time has come when meals only feed mindless survival, hanging on for dear life.

Rosemary's face acquires Picasso cubist irregularity as she tries to eat. *Another stroke*, I wonder. Stifling dread, I pose a blasé question. "What's that look mean, Mumz?"

"This is my mystery squint," Rose assures with a smirk. Attempting to locate food, all she does is tap-tap-tap the bowl.

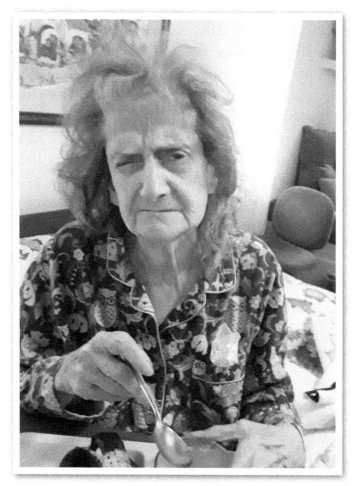

"My mystery squint"

I spoon morsels into her baby bird mouth. Rosemary snickers, but stares through dead fisheyes. Nothing makes sense. An impossible predicament, the options for caring devotion shift.

Dementia voids fill with song. Lyrics replace missing words. Rosemary can scarcely carry a tune. But her full-throated, off-key deliveries make listening a pleasure. Lying in bed, she sings "Get Out of Town." Sorrowful Hungarian "Gloomy Sunday" she pairs with "Over the Rainbow." Her mysterious musical messages sound joyous.

A nurse introduces herself as Penny; Rose serenades her with "Pennies from Heaven." When my mother gets frustrated, I begin a melody. Joining in, her mood transforms. Rosemary knows every verse, including obscure introductions like those of "Accentuate the Positive" and "Love's Old Sweet Song." She never misses a beat and fills any forgotten words with "la ti da."

I start to ask a question. "Ma, a long time ago . . ."

This sends her into a prelude. Once again, it's "Pennies from Heaven." Listening closer, the lyrics describe relativity, like the 1965 musical *Zulu and the Zayda* song, "River of Tears." It's another yin and yang tale of nature's ever-evolving balance. The contrast of conflict makes joy that much sweeter.

Reluctantly, I disconnect Rosemary's phone line. Farewell to the 240 prefix that reminded her of home in New Jersey. We rotate her custom bedspread 180°, so the friendly faces peer in her direction. Back and forth to the bedside commode, the unit is right beside her, but she cannot find it. After use, she leans on me while I pull up her drawers. Then she crawls onto the mattress and cannot figure out how to lie down without guidance.

Rose flops diagonally, shivering atop the covers. Her eyes aim toward the sewing machine—repurposed as a nightstand, piled with medications.

"What's happening, Ma?"

"I'm trying to figure out how to stitch a seam on the bias." Attempting to find her way into bed, the old Singer distracted her attention. Thoughts of sewing tangle with the task of getting under the warm covers.

Tucked in, her head on the pillow, she expresses contentment. "Finally, the mending is done."

A long, disjointed night of ups and downs to the commode ends with morning. Trying to get her arm into the sleeve, Rose walks in circles like a canine about to settle. I chase after.

"Is this an historical outfit? Didn't someone die wearing this attire?"

Nights of uninterrupted sleep no longer exist. I doze off beside my

mother, my fingers clutching her pajamas for security. Her slightest
movement springs me to full alert. Rosemary tosses and turns. She
explains that something must be done but she cannot say what it
is. I learn to distinguish her fidgeting from attempts to get up. This
happens at least twice an hour.

Lullabies don't help anymore. I suggest she picture pastoral fields and count sheep hopping a fence. She reports their progress.

"Does it count if one goes under? Some needs help." She rolls onto her hands and knees, so they can use her back as a step, but forgets why. Scrambling to get up or lie down, she cannot recall how to do either.

Sleep deprivation sends me literally running into walls. Most crashes occur the far side of midnight. Needing help from hospice, I race to get my phone from its charger at the opposite end of the house. Not wanting to leave her unattended, my mind plays "Flight of the Bumble Bee." Rounding a corner like a deranged insect, Bam! Full tilt, my face slams into the bookcase. Bruises, white hairs, arthritic joints . . . these are the purple hearts of caregiving.

Desperate for sleep, Robert and I reluctantly agree to put her in a skilled nursing home for a few days of respite. During such stays, hospice assumes responsibility for her care.

Checking in at this Fort Walton Beach facility, I suggest they use a bed alarm.

The admission clerk looks me square in the eye. "It's against Florida law to violate a patient's right to fall." The woman's unblinking, straight-faced stare begs between-the-lines interpretation. I suspect the administration told her to recite this for liability purposes.

Knowing Florida's reputation for cockamamie statutes, I research bed alarms. Sure enough, FL law 400.0222-5(0) gives patients the right to be free from restraints . . . *except* when authorized in writing by a physician for a resident's safety. A doctor's note is needed to protect Rose against "her right to fall."

Between naps, Robert and I visit my mother and call her on the facility phone. Getting some sleep rejuvenates us. In contrast to constant vigilance, the household atmosphere calms. Thoughts clear, temperaments relax, but anxiety over Rosemary's well-being rises. We miss her.

At first, we are pleasantly surprised. Staff members at the facility are attentive, taken in by Rosemary's charm. They roll her to the dining room to socialize. Either she has improved, or we were too exhausted to provide adequate care.

But the staff cannot reconcile Rosemary's effervescent character with her limitations. Patients with moderately severe dementia typically lack her communication skills. Rose's ability to hold up her end of a conversation leaves nurses unprepared for her sundowner outlandishness. An exasperated RN calls and hands my mother the phone.

"I'm stuck in an intersection. My bed is in heavy traffic, and it isn't safe here." Her troubled plea alarms me. But knowing how hard hospice worked to procure respite and how much a full night's sleep has cleared our heads, I resist the urge to bring her home right away.

Rosemary is a paradox, which is to say, she is at once agile and in danger of falling, articulate and incoherent, monumental and nonchalant, humorous and tormented, wise and meek. The facility hasn't had her for twenty-four hours when the charge nurse confesses that they are struggling to cope. With Rose so active and so lost, no one can imagine how we manage her care at home. We visit twice a day and call often. Nurses hand my mother the phone, confident that I can reassure her.

Warning signs of constipation arise, and we take her fresh fruits and vegetables. Produce pleases Rose. A stalk of celery in hand, she munches.

"My ears ring louder than the chew of celery."

Before leaving, I memorize the layout of her groceries. Each time I call, I remind her how to eat. Otherwise, she does not know to put it in her mouth, chew, and swallow.

On the second day, heading toward my mother's room, an unexpected sight catches my eye. A wheelchair rolls down the hallway with a patient wearing Rosemary's distinctive sweater, the one that disappeared from her closet two years ago. Still missing a button, it is worn by a sweet, skinny resident. The frail woman wears otherwise tattered clothes, her hair unkempt, fingernails filthy. My heart warms to see the garment on a needy patient. She is welcome to it. Rosemary would agree.

The last day of respite, I arrive to bring my mother home. A nurse avoids eye contact and reports that Rosemary had "an episode" a few minutes earlier. Rose is in a wheelchair, parked in a row of other patients who require constant observation. Some are agitated. Some wail. A few slouch, parts of their bodies touching the floor. No one is tending to any of them. Rosemary wears one skimpy layer and no blanket in the cold hallway. She slumps, barely responsive. Extremities ice cold, lips and fingernail beds blue, she has a seven-centimeter knot on her head that no one mentions. I wheel her to her assigned room for warmth and await help from hospice.

Warmed up and more responsive, my mother informs me and the hospice nurse that she needs to pee. The bathroom and commode are caked with hardened feces. We clean it thoroughly so Rose can relieve herself. Then we get my mother to my car. Nurse Penny follows us home.

In our driveway, Penny hops out and readies the wheelchair. "Upsy-daisy, Rosemary."

"Feel free to put my daisy anywhere you'd like," says Rose. Seated in the wheelchair, my mom closes her eyes, head back and chin up, basking in the sunlight. While Penny rolls her in, I get an ice pack for the head bump.

In the wee hours long before daybreak, sleepless Rosemary goes into show business.

"Is this a stage? What are we doing here? Why is the bed a theater?"

My drowsy, hour-long reorientation and lullaby endurance contest finally elicits her telltale rhythmic breathing. I relax, snuggle down, and doze off beside her. A whispered exhale parts my lips. A moment later . . .

"What are we doing on stage?" Her siren voice pierces the night.

On a hunch, I flip the light on and ask if she knows who she is. For the first time, Rosemary wavers.

"I, I . . .?" She looks at me with beseeching little-girl eyes, like a sole survivor lost on rough seas, clinging to the bottom of a capsized lifeboat.

Quick to the rescue, I cut her quandary with a cheerful memory cue. "Who am I, Mom?"

"Well, I call you 'Mom,' so you must be my mother."

Her words sting like a Jersey snowball caught in the face. Wide awake, I consider what she wrote years ago about recognizing herself and me as a way to gauge her quality of life. After a personal plate tectonic shift, I regain my balance with a rationalization. Greater than dementia, a head injury, and mental pandemonium, Rosemary appreciates the power of maternal love. She just cannot figure out who's who at this stage of life.

Rosey nestles against me, her childlike frame smaller every day. It's an honor that she calls me "Mom." With this role flip, arms around each other, the burden of caregiving evaporates. She falls to sleep and so do I . . . until a minute later.

Rosemary blurts to the world, "Blah, I feel odd. Have I had a stroke?"

Professional sitter Cari stays with my mother while I shop for comfortable pajamas, hoping they'll help her sleep better. I find two soft rayon sets, a paisley print in soothing blues and one with sheep jumping over a scenic pasture fence. Perfect.

Back home, I work at my desk. On the nearby couch, my mom tackles a ten-piece jigsaw. After a lunch break, she flops onto the pillows to rest. From my office, I read aloud from writings she penned years before. Rosemary edits with spot-on accuracy and newfound insight.

"That sounds familiar," she says, dusting cobwebs off her own poems and stories.

My mom's nocturnal confusion reminds me of night-blooming cereus with its cactus barbs. Splendid, timeless beauty emerges among troublesome jabs. Tonight, the bedside commode looks suspicious to Rose.

"Does that thing have plumbing? I don't see a flusher."

"*C'est moi*, M'ma. I am your royal flusher."

Lost sensation in her left hand takes a philosophical turn. Elbow bent, palm toward her face, Rosemary opens and closes the numb fingers in bewilderment. "Hmm, dead." A parody on life, she waves goodbye to herself. "Dead," she repeats.

Trying to get up, her blood pressure plummets to 56/28 (normal is 120/80; dead is 0/0), yet she remains conscious. Only once as a paramedic did I witness someone remain alert with such a low BP.

> *An intoxicated teenager went through the plate glass window of an abandoned building and lay bleeding for days. Pedestrians heard his groans and called for help. Police used their Kel-Lites to break off guillotine shards of glass so I could enter more safely. After shooing away rats and roaches, I checked the boy's BP: 54/34. En route to the hospital, I raised his legs straight up to keep his vital organs infused.*

That boy was young and fit. Rosemary is neither.

Hospice nurses call her low BP many names—orthostatic hypotension, postural hypotension, diastolic dysfunction, congestive heart failure. It amounts to the same thing: Rosemary's ninety-year-old heart cannot keep up with her vibrant spirit. Body surrenders, but her patchwork mind persists.

"I feel like I'm in the wrong place. This bed makes me dizzy. It's ridiculous. If I can ever stay vertical without falling back down, remind me to look up the word 'risible.'"

Her BP also drops predictably when she bears down on the toilet. In the 1980s, before Okaloosa County earned advanced-life-support certification, we stimulated this vasovagal response in the field to treat hypertension (high BP). With no medications, we encouraged patients to bear down.

Rosemary sits on the toilet. While she does her business, her head rests on my belly in case she faints. It happens often.

This month's stroke, coupled with the nursing home bump on her head, dropped her daily function to one-year-old level. In addition to right peripheral blindness, she has all three types of apraxia—the inability to coordinate bodily functions. Speech apraxia interferes with her recollection of words and their meaning. She knows the word "sit" but forgets what it means. Ideomotor apraxia prevents her from imitating function. Shown how to feed herself, spoon in hand, all she can do is tap the table. She's forgotten how to use a chair, toilet paper, blankets . . . The worst is ideational apraxia. Rosemary cannot figure out the sequence of functions necessary to eat a meal, use the toilet, or get into bed. Books mystify her; she cannot discern their purpose. But she still enjoys it when Robert reads aloud to her from Rumi poetry, Michio Kaku physics, or Kantian philosophy.

"Thanks for the adult, intellectual conversation," she tells him.

She hears her stomach grumble, echoed by a threatening overcast sky. "Either I need to rain or that cloud needs to burp." Looking around the room, her hapless eyes don't settle. Unable to focus, she speaks in a nervous, troubled tone. "I can't do. I, I feel . . . insecure."

My soul aches for her. I recall Temple Grandin's pressure box to ease tension for people with autism. I cradle my mother a firm hug. She feels frail, tiny, and perishable. "Does this help, Ma?"

"Ah, that's better."

She melts into my arms: another precious moment embosses on my heart.

Later in the evening, she keeps wringing her numb left hand. "This one is an isolated island . . . missing. I guess it's only natural that missing islands are isolated." Her eyes scan the room for some semblance of reality, but fail to focus.

"What's up, Ma?"

"My! What a plethora of this and that." Confused resignation slackens her shoulders.

Robert notices her glum expression and asks what's on her mind.

"Hair, just hair," is all she says, settling into bed. "This is a nice place to sprawl."

She tries to identify who is speaking. "Your face looks jigsaw, in puzzled pieces, not quite together."

Tucked in, I chat to her in soothing nothingness until she dozes off.

Alert and awestruck with "sunup syndrome," Rosey sits in her wheelchair gazing out the window as if for the first time. "So still. It looks like the world went 'uaauh'" (unspellable, gentle inhale thrill). "Life is holding its breath, waiting to see what happens." She observes our tiny family unit.

"What are the three of us for?" Suddenly, she scrambles to her feet, struggling to walk. Urgent. "Is this south, this direction? . . . I need south."

"How far south, Mom? South America?"

"That's too far."

"Too far from what?"

"Too far from north," she chuckles as my phone rings. It's Pat . . . calling her from south Florida.

After the pleasant phone call, Rose urgently needs the bathroom. Her head against my belly, she bears down and slumps over. I call for help from neighbors who established a network of volunteers. Nurse Joy, two doors down, and Andy from around the corner come to the rescue. Joy and I clean unconscious Rosemary. All three of us pack into the small bathroom and lower her to the bathmat. The seal on her third dirty diaper releases. Cleaned again, we roll Rosemary onto a sheet for a ride across the carpet to her room. Hoisted into bed, she responds.

"It's time to push a vital button that turns off my toes. B-b-brrrr."

Sounds like cold feet. I tuck her tootsies tight under blankets. She murmurs an almost imperceptible laugh.

One icy 1958 winter morning in Runnemede, Rosemary came dashing through the snow to our rescue. Headed for school, my second-grade sister and I, a kindergartener, fell on the frozen driveway. Beth helped me up and we reached the slick sidewalk, only to fall again, twice. The prospect of another six blocks unnerved me. I looked at our mother waving goodbye from the front door, like she always did. Seeing my desperation, she told us to stay put. Moments later, Mom rounded the corner from out back pulling Dad's big sled, off limits to kids. She loaded us aboard and headed for Bingham Elementary with the sure-footed confidence of a reindeer, gathering other children along the way. By the time we reached school, the sled was invisible beneath the mound of kids. The school bell was barely audible over our laughter.

This morning, my mother laughs at the nonsensical vision afforded by her nonfunctional eyes. Briefed on last night's episode, she attempts to write thank-you notes to our helpful neighbors.

"Do we have Winesaps? I need to bake a pie before the apples pass their prime." Along with her scribbled gratitude, I leave neighbors delicious thoughts of her desire to bake them pie.

Rose still tries to read. By the time she deciphers a large-print word, she cannot recall why. The effort does not faze her. She forgets her attempt to read.

In a futile effort to help her sleep, the hospice physician—who never set eyes on Rosemary—prescribes assorted pharmaceuticals: Melatonin, Seroquel, Benadryl, Compazine . . . Nothing helps; she's up every few hours. Caring for my mother is like being a first-time parent. Never again will I take for granted the sheer bliss of uninterrupted sleep. Keepsake moments strengthen my perseverance. Good times inoculate against surrender during brutal challenges. Our ludicrous routine repeats hourly as follows:

Rosemary fumbles, unable to find her way out from the covers.

"I have to pee."

I hop to my feet. "Sit up, Mom . . . swing your legs around."

She forgets how, so I raise her. She loses equilibrium as her blood pressure drops.

"Oh, dizzy. The world is spinning." She leans on me to avoid fainting. We linger in that precious pose, her head against me. I stroke her hair for a minute until she stabilizes.

"Stand up, Mom." She hugs me as I raise her. We pivot to the commode, right beside the bed. "Hold on." I place her right hand on the commode rail. "Turn, Ma." This part of our dance confuses her. My arthritic thumbs wrestle to pull down her pants and diaper. Unlatching her left hand from my waist, I place it on the other commode rail and inch her onto the seat. She sighs with relief.

"Oh, is this a toilet? How convenient," she says and dribbles.

"Pee some more, Mom." She cannot tell when her bladder is empty due to peripheral neuropathy, dementia, or who knows what.

Mom: "I already went."

Me: "Go some more."

She does so, pauses, and then a little more. Her fumble for toilet paper tells me she's done.

Wiped, diapered, PJ pants up, I tuck her in bed to rest up for the next round.

Raised during tough times, Rosemary took conscientious shopping to meticulous lengths. Before mass-produced disposables overflowed current-day waste sites, tattered clothes became diapers, sanitary pads, and hankies. Laundered, reused until threadbare, cloth then became rags. The same cloth diaper-changing pad was used for dozens of baby bottoms over three generations.

Rosemary canned food as her mother and Grossmom had done. Rose made modeling clay, baked fresh bread, dipped candles, and repurposed empty tins for cooking brown bread. After baked, she opened the other end too and pushed the molasses-rich delicacy out in portions, cutting each slice to perfection.

Thrifty and efficient, Rosemary's economical shopping grew into a conscientious art form. S&H Green Stamps, coupons, and elaborate grocery lists were her stocks-in-trade. On a first-name basis, she haggled with the bread man, milkman, butcher, tomato man, and local produce vendors. Mom knew every farm stand in South Jersey along our travel routes. She wasted nothing. Like Gandhi, she used pencils down to nubs. Garbage went to local pig farmers. Lights were never, ever left on. Instead of Christmas wrapping paper and bows, she put each of her children's gifts into a box, wrapped in brick chimney paper. Coffee grounds fertilized yard plants. Remnant soap bars went into a container of water that formed a slimy concoction we called "snot"—a precursor to liquid hand soap. And Rosemary limited herself to three squares of toilet paper per wipe followed by thorough, snotty-soap hand washing.

After changing my mother's diaper, we clean our hands with disposable wipes. "Stand up, Mom." She struggles to rotate. The back of her knees against the mattress, I instruct her to sit down.

"Where? I can't find the bed."

"Right here." I pat the mattress hard, making vibrations against her legs.

Christmas 1956 "chimney box" gifts

"I don't know how." Rosey's voice implores, her small child self helpless without detailed directions.

"Sit down, Mom." I pause while she figures out what the words mean and how to comply. "Here's your pillow." I pat it hard so she can zero in. Gradually, her cheek makes contact but her head hovers above the pillow, neck rigid. She forgets how to relax. "Bend your knees, Ma. Slide your feet under." I toss the covers over her. "Goodnight, Mom." Hair over her ears the way she likes, I kiss her forehead. "You're in bed. You can relax." She melts into the pillow, and then surprises me.

Reaching up, she pats my cheek. "Thank you, dear." An early sunray lights my mother's tender expression. The monotonous routine ends with eternal love.

I crawl back in bed and hold my mother's hand. She squeezes mine in return until her grasp releases with sleep. I doze off, dreaming about her cooking. Aromas of Mom's spaghetti sauce bubbling on the stove, nut loaf cake rising in the oven, and the scent of fresh-squeezed lemons fill my sleepy senses.

Before the strokes, Rosemary hosted several gatherings a month—birthdays, church highway cleanups, reunions, Singers of United Lands, and neighbors for holiday meals. She also baked food for the homeless shelter. When the nine-foot-long dining table was not set for a feast, its surface was a social magnet for jigsaw puzzles, card matches, and Scrabble games.

Renegade pages of Rosemary's recipe books escaped their binding from extensive use. She made heart-shaped wedding anniversary cakes, Easter Bunny cakes with weeping jellybean eyes, and conifer-shaped cakes for Christmas and Earth Day. Cookie cutters served year-round to liven up lunch sandwiches. Nothing wasted, leftover crust became breadcrumbs. She stored baker's dozen cookie batches for unexpected guests. People dreamed of my mom's apple pie, chocolate éclairs, cream puffs, pistachio cake, whiskey cake, and her signature cinnamon buns (see Appendix for recipe).

Rose took great pleasure in feeding others. She enjoyed eating, too, but remained so active that she never became overweight. A self-critic, every dish she made could stand improvement, according to her taste. She cherished good recipes, paying tribute

Gram makes cookie-cutter sandwiches

to their source: Nancy's fruit pie, Aunt Jenny's nut loaf, "Maggie's Muck" (a Guam Chamorro dish), and Aunt Ruth's pie crust with its secret ingredient (vinegar).

Rose preferred basics over gourmet. Before Rosemary's strokes, she was leery of the license I took in the kitchen. Whenever I prepared her meals, I braced myself for her rebuke.

It has become a pleasure to cook for my mom. Each platter elicits her accolades.

"Oh, my! How wonderful." She marvels at a simple bowl of butternut squash soup and licks the spoon clean. "That was lovely. Good chow."

Meal enthusiasm is not reflected in the tiny portions she consumes. Tipping the scale at 109, her weight keeps dropping. "Would you like some more?" I always ask.

Rosey surfaces with an Oliver Twist request, "More?" Just as fast, sedate Rosemary quells the desire. "No, thank you. That was just fine." For how little she eats, her gratitude is piercing.

Hospice brings a gait belt to help us hold her when she walks. Fastened around her waist, it lasts a short minute before she manages to remove the thing and hands it over.

"I don't know where this belongs." The convenient handle departs with the nurse.

No sooner do I sit down to relax than she calls for help.

"I'm trying to make everything zero, but it doesn't matter now."

I surmise she needs to use the toilet. Either the sensation passed or she wet her diaper. I check. It's the former.

She looks exhausted. I encourage her to lie down.

"Which way is down?" she asks in all sincerity.

A pillow held against her cheek, she relaxes into it. In partnership with gravity, I lower the pillow and the rest of her follows. Peaceful, she listens to transcendentalism lectures of Emerson, Thoreau, Dickinson, and Whitman. People she understands, not so her own bodily functions.

But Rosemary never stops trying to make sense of things. Her thoughts bounce topic-to-topic, like ping-pong balls on a trampoline.

I wouldn't mind getting up early in the morning if it didn't happen so early . . . It used to seem like we had all the people in the world in our family . . . Is humanity serving a useful purpose? . . . Mmmm, Wise potato chips . . . I'm so glad potatoes were invented . . . Am I in New England? . . . Maine or Massachusetts, one of those 'Ma' states?

Perhaps due to a urinary tract infection or advancing dementia, she is up every twenty minutes now. Urinalysis lab work shows a high white blood cell count, yet no infection. I don't understand, and no one explains. Nor does hospice provide effective palliative treatment.

Caregiver fatigue drains Robert and me. We get sick and run fevers. Recuperation demands sleep. We hire the only sitter willing to stay overnight. Insurance does not cover in-home costs. $100 buys us a night's rest. Twice, I check on my mother and the sitter. All is well.

We seek advice on Rosemary's constant need to get in and out of bed all night. Unable to comprehend the severity of her pain and short-term memory loss, a hospice nurse assumes the patient's brain is giving false signals and suggests I "train Rosemary to sleep longer and use the toilet less often." It makes no sense. My mother has obvious urinary retention and no capacity to learn anything. At wit's end, I try all lights off at night. It has no effect. Rose is unaware if the room is pitch dark or fully lit. I try to explain the bladder training suggestion to my mother. She doesn't understand either.

"My bladder always shares its longings with me. Of course, we've known each other a long time."

Rose is so frail that sometimes we cannot tell if she is alive. Robert and I stare at her, trying to detect the gentle rise and fall of breathing. This happens often. We find it easier to spot movement in her animated feet. Even asleep, they wiggle, flex, and squirm as if in private conversation with each other.

Rosemary never met her Aunt "Deda." Albertina Philomena Josephina Schwab had rheumatic fever as a child. Left with St. Vitus Dance—a chorea nervous system disorder manifested in non-purposeful movement—Deda's feet fidgeted the rest of her life. One year married, her weakened heart could not withstand giving birth and she died at age twenty.

Rosemary is still kicking. Her dancing feet pay tribute to Deda. Sensing her own end drawing near, Rose sings a tearful, "You Keep Coming

Back Like a Song" to those already departed: Dad, her friend Maggie, and the many people who enhanced her life. I assure her that, until her time comes, she is secure with us.

"We've gotcha, Mom, safe and sound."

"That's a real gotcha," she laughs, aware of the intense care she requires. Attempting to sort genuine recollections from fantasies, Rosemary confesses that she no longer trusts her own mind.

She fancies the notion that lost memories "already graduated. Once we die, I suspect our stray parts re-amalgamate, united with the mystic Whole." In post-death reverie, Rosemary gazes beyond her body, her bedroom, and the world we know.

A hospice nurse tells Rose to take a nice, deep breath.

"They're all nice," the patient retorts. She listens to the RN report on a medical staff meeting about Rosemary's bladder frequency—many suggestions, already tried. My mom pipes in with appreciation for the effort.

"Great minds work together."

Now Rosemary gets up to pee every ten minutes when awake and every hour at night. The invisible hospice doctor ups her meds and adds more—Detrol (tolterodine), Compazine, Baclofen, Motrin (ibuprofen). I could swear Rose gets more medication than food. Her weight's down to 106 pounds. Often, she sits on the commode unsuccessful, but must lie down before she faints. Another urinalysis confirms: no infection. Medications for bladder spasms prove useless. Hospice folks surmise that her dementia is constantly triggering her brain to think she needs to go. Her diapers are often moist but almost never soaked. Already unsteady, the added prescriptions worsen her balance. She falls daily.

Reclining, Rosey reaches out in the darkness, grips the bedside commode, and pleads with me.

"Mom, I need to pee. I can't find the toilet." She calls me Mom now.

"Sit up, Mom." I get close to assist her.

"Wait, I need to overcome gravity." She leans on me, goes limp and, slumps over. Hanging onto her, I distribute the pressure to avoid tearing her skin. My body against hers, I shove both of us against the bed. Her hands grasp the sheets.

Rose beseeches, "Where's the bed? I need the to-lie-down place."

Like a rote prayer, we do our step-by-step routine.

"You're touching it, Mom. Turn around. Sit down. Lie on your pillow. Right here. Bend your knees." I cover her and caress her forehead.

Exhausted, she sighs with relief and cuddles in . . . then hurries to get up with an overwhelming sense of urgency.

"It's nice and warm here in Guayaquil." Awakening elsewhere, she spells out the place for me and elaborates on its location. "South, south, Central America. So warm here."

The Internet shows no such place in Central America, and I shrug it off. This afternoon, I take my raging, arthritic joints for treatment. By incredible coincidence in the physical therapy waiting room, I meet an old woman and her translator daughter, both from Uruguay. Retrieving this morning's note from my pocket, I ask if they've ever heard of Guayaquil. The pair brighten and tell me it's in Ecuador—South America at the equator. No wonder Rosemary felt warm.

In the Gulf of Mexico, Hurricane Michael strengthens and aims our direction. We cannot prepare for the forecasted Category 3 storm while caring for Rosemary. Hospice arranges emergency shelter for her in a skilled nursing home, so we can deal with the looming weather.

In the driveway, Rosemary surprises us by getting from her wheelchair into the passenger seat of our SUV unaided. Her first time outdoors in ages, she seems revitalized. I offer to recline her seat, but she sits up the entire half hour drive inland. It's the longest she has been upright in weeks. Upon arrival, she hops into the wheelchair and gets settled in time for dinner. The hospice nurse and I watch in astonishment. Feeding herself, Rosemary scarfs down a full, adult portion meal. She is recuperating. It seems that last month's head injury she sustained at rehab had caused her setback. Was her sleeplessness worsened by the plethora of medications?

I request a doctor's order for a bed alarm. No need. This facility's staff put one on her bed and her wheelchair as well. All windows boarded for the storm, patients are oblivious to its approach. Rosemary forgets the hurricane, eager to socialize. She sits in a wheelchair and waves happily as we depart.

Old-time hurricanes like Betsy, Elena, Erin, Opal, and Ivan died down once they made landfall. Michael is a new breed. Earth's weather is on a rampage. Mother Nature seems bent on shaking loose our exploitive ways. Sustained winds surpass 150 mph as the brutal storm takes aim at our county. Before it hits, the monster veers east, just missing our area. All we get is a stiff, kite-flying breeze. Sixty miles away, forest and neighborhoods lay in ruin. The storm wreaks havoc across the full seventy-mile depth of the Panhandle, still Category 3 when it strikes Georgia. This is unprecedented hurricane behavior.

Once Michael's eye makes landfall a safe distance away, we dodge downed tree limbs and visit my mom. She is contented and able to sit in a wheelchair much of the day. The atmosphere sends her mind to the Children's Seashore Hospital where Dad coordinated VFW Christmas parties to bring a little cheer.

"Helping with these hospital parties is just fine, but I need to know if I'm an assistant or a patient."

For several days, Robert and I alternate hurricane clean up with trips to see Rose. On one visit, my mom observes a woman walk by wearing an air force uniform. Past and present superimpose in Rosemary's head.

"I can see this is a military hospital," Rosemary surmises, "but how long have I been in the navy? Am I a file clerk for the WAVES?"

Once a file clerk at N.W. Ayer and Son advertising company in Philadelphia, decades before that Rosemary had enlisted in the

US Navy's Women Accepted for Volunteer Emergency Service (WAVES). As World War II came to a close, she met my father and they married. Herman, a navy man, had just returned from service in Europe and the Panama Canal.

Ex-file clerk Rosemary returns home from the storm shelter placement. These past few days of respite, Robert and I cleared paths through hurricane-downed branches and nine-inch longleaf pine cones. Perched in her wheelchair eagerly await whatever comes next, my mom applauds our removal of remaining debris.

An unofficial post-hurricane protocol, people, grateful to have been spared, pitch in during disaster relief efforts. If not for Rosemary's care and our ages, we would offer meals and comfort. Community crisis response has a powerful healing effect.

Every twenty minutes, I help my mother to the bathroom. Her sore bottom indicates wet diapers left on too long at the nursing home, proof that she is better off with us. Paid care is no substitute for love. Some necessities require dedicated family. I ask my mom if she realizes how often she goes to the john.

"Just a different lifestyle," she replies.

During personal crisis, the occurrence of a widespread calamity at the same time bestows me with a secret sense of consolation. I join the masses in serendipitous suffering. Rosemary approaches death in tandem with vast storm devastation. Her failing body has unspoken solidarity with Hurricane Michael victims, especially the ravaged trees. I felt the same sense of communal misery when my brother died in 2001, right after the September 11 terror attacks. My individual grief has a habit of melding with collective trauma. Mourning harmonizes in sorrowful, minor chords.

Hindsight calculations upgrade Michael to Category 5. Before gauges at Tyndall Air Force Base blew away, they registered 208 mph winds. Northwest Florida terrain's 100-mile-wide assault zone looks strip mined. Lush landscape left scalped. Fallen trees pile into mountainous heaps. With no power and no functional hospitals in the strike zone, patients flood our direction in droves. No one need go through this alone.

October 2018 is traumatic for the Florida panhandle. Our local hospitals fill beyond capacity with hurricane-zone transfers. Beds line hallways. Traveling nurses arrive from across the country.

At the same time medical care is stretched to its limits, Rosemary's condition crescendos to its worst. My skeletal mother bears resemblance to storm-battered trees, clinging to life in vain. Sleep only happens in fitful spurts. Pain surges with fierce intensity. Devastated woodlands—and Rosemary—desperately hang on.

Severe lower back pain plagues Rose. Robert and I take turns massaging, but nothing helps. Due to the location over her kidneys, I suggest it might be pyelonephritis (kidney inflammation). Nurses speculate on costochondritis (rib joint inflammation), medication reactions, or gas. Rosemary's moaning intensifies.

Death doula Deborah gives the situation perspective: "It doesn't matter if she stubbed a toe. Do not allow her to suffer."

"I want my brain back," Rose groans. In fitful snatches of sleep, she maintains a grimace crying out all night for her son Martin and grandson Adam. A hospice nurse returns my 2:00 a.m. call and says to give Rosemary more muscle relaxer, ibuprofen, and Compazine. My mother's agony worsens. She's lost the ability sip through a straw. *Could it be a medication reaction or brain deterioration? Is this another relapse or her approaching end?* She cannot see well enough to identify anyone.

"Your voice is your same," she jumbles words, trying to make out who is speaking. Unable to decipher faces, she looks upward with suspicion. "That's not my ceiling. What's happened to me?"

"Eight strokes, Rose," Robert responds.

"Well, that's a bad habit," she replies in baffled wonder.

I encourage her to chew the food in her mouth. She looks puzzled. "One chew off and one chew on?"

I get the "Diddle Diddle Dumpling" nursery rhyme reference but cannot tell if she is joking or truly doesn't understand. No smile, I suspect the latter. She sits motionless with a mouthful of unchewed food. I fish it out with my finger so she won't choke.

A pair of hospice nurses arrives, one in training. The hurricane-ravaged panhandle is short-staffed. The seasoned RN has a habit of speaking baby talk to patients. It comes across as condescending and ridiculous. Brought to her attention, the nurse tries to refrain but reverts back. After I brief her on my mother's misery, the woman turns to Rosemary in a jovial, saccharin tone.

"Hi, Wosemawy. How would you desquabe yoa wevel of pain?"

My weary mom looks at the nurse with an expression that either means *What's wrong with this poor gal* or *What on Earth is she asking?* After contemplating the question, Rose responds with a question, "OUCH?"

Laughing along with her comrade, the baby talker tries for more clarity. Words drip from her lips like high fructose corn syrup.

"Ouuch wike a bee sting or childburff?"

"Twins, both at once." My mother looks deadpan at the women.

Rose had a straightforward approach to children. She spoke with expression, but none of that belittling baby talk. Nor did she simplify her vocabulary. Rosemary's eloquence wrapped young people in fond respect.

Kindergarten teachers marveled at the verbal skills of Rosemary's children. We knew Philadelphia meant City of Brotherly Love, and the plant winding around our living room posts was philodendron, meaning lover of trees. Our mother did not foist Greek roots or scholastic lessons on us. Rosemary's fount of language simply flowed.

Learning the names of colors at age three, I asked my mother to identify the yellow-green hue of our kitchen chairs. "Chartreuse," she said, peeling potatoes. Each combination, tint, and shade had its own name, she explained as a pot boiled. Like Helen Keller realizing water had a name, my eyes opened and ears perked. I grabbed the family Crayola box and she read more color names to me: periwinkle, mauve, fuchsia, cobalt, robin's egg, maroon, indigo, amber . . . That nonchalant chat colored my world forever. But in Rosemary's mind, the most miraculous maternal feat she accomplished was teaching her children to tie their shoelaces.

The baby talk nurse cannot reconcile Rosemary's distress with her witty childbirth analogy. The RN contacts the hospice doctor but fails to relay the gravity of her patient's distress. The physician orders prescription-grade ibuprofen and tramadol—a synthetic, non-sedative anti-inflammatory opioid, not to be taken with the antipsychotic Seroquel they've had her on. The nurses leave. My head spins. And Rosemary moans in pain.

A menagerie of medications fills her room. I sort them into four piles: to be taken, discontinued, kept on hand, and those to counter the effects of others. Absolutely nothing eases her pain.

People possess mixed bags of competence and shortcomings. Like everyone, hospice staff members have good and bad days. The most professional sometimes fall short. And on occasion, less capable workers render quality care. Not the case on this particular night.

Rosemary writhes in agony. A graveyard shift nurse returns my desperate plea for help. The drowsy RN mentions her need for coffee. On the way over, she gets lost and calls for directions, twice. Upon arrival, as if middle-of-the-night house calls are casual social get-togethers, the nurse chats with me, her back to my mother's intractable pain. Despite negative urinalysis results, the nurse rightly appraises Rose's frequent toilet visits as something amiss in her urinary tract. Nothing to offer, the ill-equipped RN improvises, collecting another urine specimen with our unsterile bathroom cup between Rosemary's legs.

The nurse mentions coffee again, seemingly hinting for me to brew a pot. She departs with the contaminated cup of urine. Alone again, I cradle my wailing mother. Fond memories quell the bitter aftertaste of ineffectual hospice care.

Young mother Rosemary devised an endearing morning ritual. Whoever woke up first prepared coffee for the family and served it to everyone in bed. Effects of caffeine on children went unaddressed. In an era before automatic timers, we awoke to the aroma of coffee, oblivious that Mom had already been up to brew the pot. Even six-year-old Marty carried a heavy tray of hot mugs upstairs for everyone, the brown brew sloshing as he walked bedroom to bedroom. The ritual held lasting charm. Like a family code, we knew one another's coffee preferences and greeted each day with a gesture of kindness.

Ten-codes for radio transmissions—as we used during my paramedic years—apply on this day. It so happens that the date, 10/18, is the emergency code for urgent response. Two hellish accounts follow of an early morning ordeal that lasted a brief forever. The first focuses on Rosemary's encoded effort to communicate her dilemma. The second shares the same experience from my caregiver perspective. Hospice service is free and, on this godforsaken night, we get our money's worth.

At midnight, Rosemary sits on the commode without results and mumbles to herself.

"Seconds of life go by." Back in bed, she immediately tries to get up again but is too dizzy and lies back down. Up again, she fidgets and writhes on the makeshift toilet without results. Back in bed for a few seconds, she screams.

"Oh Chris, hurry, hurry." Incoherent distress overwhelms her. She blares gut-wrenching bellows: "90, 90! Hurry!"

"What is it, Mom? Are you in pain? Do you need to pee?"

"90, 90, 90," she wails at the top of her lungs, pauses, then screeches, "Ahhh, 90! Say it, 90!"

"90!" I say, hoping to appease her. "What hurts? Is it your back?"

"Hurry, hurry. Oh Chris, please—90, 90, 90!" Screaming, she tries to get up again. I help her onto the commode, to bed . . . Up. Down. Up. Rocking in excruciating pain, she shrieks with inarticulate desperation, "90!" After an eternity measured in minutes, she urinates a tiny trickle and the decibel level of her howls diminishes to a haunting holler. "80." After a pause, she pees a little more. "70, 70, 70." Her countdown in increments of 10 continues as she battles for relief. As if she is the rope in a tug-of-war, bladder and blood pressure drag her in and out of bed. With each diminishing number, her pitch subdues. "60—50—40." She hovers back and forth at 50-40. Each successful sprinkle, I wipe her, pull up her diaper and pajama bottoms, then put her to bed before she faints . . . until the pain forces her back onto the commode, wailing as the countdown continues.

At 30 she relaxes. Tucked in bed, she utters in a mild moan tapering off to a whisper. "29, 28, 27 . . . " At 22 she dozes off.

The caregiving nightmare version begins as I catapult from bed to my mother's gut-wrenching bellows.

"Oh, Chris, hurry, hurry. 90, 90!"

My husband—whose heart condition never stops him from lending a hand—remains in bed at the other end of the hallway despite Rosemary's screams. I am certain he hears her. Anyone passing by outside could hear this amplified madness. Knowing Robert would be with us if he could, my concern expands to *his* well-being, as well. Later, he confesses he felt helpless, unable to cope with the sheer insanity of the situation.

Hospice makes matters worse. I dial for help. To reach an on-call person assigned to render aid after hours, the system requires steps be followed to the letter. After speed dialing, I wait through a recorded message that I can now recite by heart. My mother's screams pierce the air. When a hospice operator answers, callers must provide their name, relationship to the patient, patient's name, the situation, and a callback number. Then, the voice repeats everything stated, literally spelling out every detail. After confirming that R-O-S-E-M-A-R-Y is the correct spelling, and yes, it is one word, I am told to hang up. Within a few minutes, a triage nurse—somewhere in the country—calls back to evaluate the situation. If deemed worthy, I am told to hang up and wait again. Triage briefs a local nurse whose callback takes up to twenty minutes. Meanwhile, poor Rosemary screams. Holding the phone with one hand, I transfer her on and off the commode, pulling her pants and diaper on and off. Luddites leery of new technology, we are ill-equipped for use of this, our first smartphone. I don't dare use the speaker button for fear of hanging up by mistake and having to start over.

Still on hold, I fail to pull her pajamas down enough, and she wets them. I grab clean pants from another set and do a one-handed change. The resulting outfit of two clashing owl patterns underscores the night's macabre torment.

At 2:00 a.m., the local hospice nurse calls with outright annoyance. If she must come, it will take over an hour for her to arrive. She highlights the inconvenience with details about her personal affairs, attempting (successfully) to dissuade my desire for her service.

"Nothing I could do 'cept sit with y'all." The RN considers another prescription, but adds that the nearest open pharmacy is over an hour away. I can barely manage to get my mother to and from bed, let alone to the car and drive three hours, round trip. The nurse hears the frantic counting and asks if it is Rosemary "making all that fuss."

"YES," I reply, trying to help my mother back onto the commode. The Velcro on my hand splint snags on Rose's mismatched pajamas and jerks my arthritic thumb. My mother lets out an ear-piercing scream for the both of us. I tell the ineffectual nurse that what we need is her advice.

"You could call 9-1-1," she suggests, precisely what hospice orientation directs *not* to do. "Maybe EMS can start an IV or something," the nurse speculates as I give up on her, say goodbye, and hang up.

With both hands free to hold my mom, I hug her and try to comprehend what she is experiencing. As a paramedic I witnessed plenty—childbirth, amputations, heart attacks, traumatic eviscerations—but this is worse. The only solace is in knowing that once this misery passes, she will forget it ever happened.

Racking my brain for anyone else I can call this time of night, I remember the smartphone has a video feature. As she calls out "80" in her countdown, I record footage to later show someone who may know what is happening. Up and down from bed, she urinates a tiny bit and the countdown diminishes in intensity. As she hovers at 50-40, I grab the phone and film another short clip. Once she reaches 30, she goes limp with exhaustion. Shell-shocked, after hours of the ordeal, the two of us hold hands beside each other in bed. The torture relinquishes its grip and her moans fade to whimpers. "29, 28, 27 . . . 22."

Once my mom is asleep, I rush to check on my husband. Asleep. Rosemary and Robert are both asleep. Smack-dab between them in the hallway, I wonder if it was all a nightmare. Later, my husband, hospice, and film footage confirm the reality of her dreadful ordeal.

At daybreak, Rosemary's matter-of-fact demeanor assures me the trauma has passed, along with her recollection of what she went through. Her eyes are dark, bottomless ponds.

"If I'd said it out loud, I'd remember it." She utters in a calm tone, reminiscent of a good-natured sports announcer. Sincere nonsense words, not found in any dictionary, fill the air. I write "gemtrix" and "gemfree" to add to our collection of invented words on the Scrabble game lid. Definitions will wait until later.

For this morning's routine, I follow her lead, improvising our conversation, thankful for the pain-free dialogue. Her higher-pitched voice announces Rosey's emergence, tickled pink just to be alive. I bask in her jubilation.

"You do remember now why I remember, don't you? Isn't that a wonderful remembery?" Her snicker explodes into uproarious laughter. "I'll be darned," she chortles. "It's time I walk upon the ark, forever and ever." This over-the-moon atmosphere lasts hours. She laughs and sings, then dozes. Eyes closed, a big grin forms, and the hilarity continues. "Ha, ha, ha, black." Rose serenades anyone in hearing range with "Accentuate the Positive."

Hospice aide Latavia arrives. Efficient and caring, the woman gets Rosemary to the edge of the bed and brushes hair from my mother's face. The gal then bear-hugs Rose and hoists her up. "Hold on to me, Mrs. Baker."

"Latch on to the affirmative," sings my mother, her arms around the burly woman's neck. Merrily hooting her way to the wheelchair, Rosey exclaims, "Oh my, it's so wonderful. Everybody can add their own verse!"

A nurse shows up and we put Robert's Velcro back brace through the front wheelchair bars to keep Rose from falling out . . . or flying away in her euphoria. Everyone joins the laughter, conducted by my mom's cheerfulness. I sigh with relief that she is not suffering.

Too dizzy, Rosemary slumps, and the aide puts her back in bed.

"Two heads are better than one," Mom tells me. "Yours and mine." Her pupils dilated from meds, she also converses with others not present.

I try in vain to convey to the nurse the severity of Rosemary's suffering last night. But my mother's current, chipper disposition makes last night's horror unbelievable. The RN charts the patient's vital signs without acknowledgement or suggestion, should it happen again.

Shortly after the hospice workers leave, Rose whispers in surprise, "I'll be darned. I think I'm becoming angry. When is common sense supposed to come up?"

Counting to herself, she grabs the bedside toilet paper roll, and weight-lifts it like a dumbbell. Up and down, she explains with annoyed determination that the roll pumps air, so she won't drown or be drowned. Poised to pitch a purple fit, she hoists and scowls.

"Holy smokes," I interject, hoping levity offsets her sudden irritation.

She searches her blankets for the alleged smoke. Her glare targets the tissue box. She wants it gone. Aiming across the room, her mightiest hurl lands it on the floor beside her.

Back into the wheelchair I put her and scan the room for ways to offset her mysterious agitation. Everything I hand over gets a dismissive fling of rejection. Our trail to the living room litters with forsaken offerings. Rose snatches a hand-sized marble sculpture and rears back for a pitch. I confiscate it and park her in front of the piano. Mrs. B—as Marty's musician friends call her—plays B-flat with emphatic redundancy for several minutes.

"Her first piano concert," Robert and I commiserate. We slump stupefied in nearby chairs, like parents at an unrehearsed children's recital. Rosemary's fierce strikes on the key signify mounting fury. I scurry her to the kitchen for something soothing. Perhaps an orange. She loves the smell of citrus, and fruit seems harmless enough.

"Here you go, Mom. Take a whiff."

Inconsolable, she snatches the defenseless orange. Clutching it, her glower is as menacing as a mischievous puppy wrestling a stolen sock. Surely, she needs rest after last night's ordeal. Tucked back into bed, her ornery hands keep occupied the fruit, a Pandora's box she aims to open. From the photo blanket, a snapshot of her parents peers in her direction. I pray for them to keep watch over their wayward daughter while I park the wheelchair.

Rosemary casts aspersions at the orange. "Wet," she accuses. Fingernail gouges cover the surface. Pieces of peel scatter the bedspread, like a citrus battlefield. Holding the dribbling fruit overhead, gravity runs juice down her arms, under the pajama sleeves. Her parents' jovial smiles, dappled with bits of rind, grant me permission to take a moment. In fact, take five. *At least Rosemary's not in pain.*

Mess cleaned, bedding changed, I spy the closet door. Stuffed animals from our foster parenthood years may ease her volatility. Deep in the heap, I locate the scrawny, monkey-like teddy bear she made for us when we were kids. She swipes it from my hand, smiles with recognition, and then sends it careening past my face in airborne cartwheels. Midair, I catch the talisman of motherly love. To avoid a similar fate, I hide the rabbit she made for her newborn grandson (now almost 50) and hand her sturdier critters. Each one takes off in flight. Her fiendish grin gives me pause. *What other shenanigans await?* She grabs a defenseless bear and attempts to tear it limb from limb.

"Stop that," I demand, with instant pangs of remorse. Appalled by my mother's uncharacteristic malice, I am equally upset by my tone, reprimanding her like a naughty child.

She quits her bear attack but scans the room like trouble, looking for a place to happen. I remember her advice during saner years: *Hold disagreeable people's heads above water until they surface as human.* I sing her "Stormy Weather" while speed dialing hospice. Medication side effects suspected, they reshuffle the prescribed drugs and dosages.

By afternoon, Rosemary's agitation surrenders to nausea. She vomits bile until her stomach is empty and continues to dry heave. Hospice orders Haldol; Robert picks it up from the pharmacy. Dosage instructions, in tiny script four lines long, wrap around the pill bottle. As best we can decipher, it says take one or two. I give her one, leery of adverse effects. She cannot hold it down. A tele-nurse orders 25 mg Compazine suppositories, not to be confused with 10 mg oral Compazine "but the same level of medication," she explains in vain. The pharmacy has none; a special order takes days. Instead, promethazine (i.e., Phenergan) suppositories are ordered, only available at a distant pharmacy. Robert drives to get it. Lost, he calls six times for directions as I console my moaning, heaving mother. Phone in one hand, my other arm wraps around her and holds a basin under her chin.

The Haldol or combined medications cause tardive dyskinesia. Her body jerks in violent twitches. She dozes momentarily, awakened in agony but cannot say what hurts.

A compassionate neighbor, Shew, stops by to lend a hand. Arms open, she sits beside Rosemary on the bed. Rose leans into the calming embrace, only for an instant. Pain flings Rosemary across the bed like a possessed rag doll.

At nightfall, she needs to urinate but cannot. Every few minutes, she is up and down without results. Perhaps due to brain damage or peripheral neuropathy, her bladder refuses to release. I suggest she coughs. Nothing. Hospice offers no helpful solution. Later, she lets loose and overflows her adult diaper.

The volume of patients transferred from post-Hurricane Michael strike zone overburdens local medical systems. A capable, out-of-state hospice nurse suggests we hire sitters more often. Worth every dollar, professional caregiver Cari with her Brooklyn accent reads Rosemary her favorite books, plays Mom's music, chats like a fond friend, and tidies up.

"She sounds like home," South Jersey born-and-raised Rose smiles.

I seize the free time to hire carpet cleaners, a prudent expense since Mom falls often and must wait on the floor until help arrives. A family-owned cleaning company truck pulls up. The courteous owner treats Rosemary with respectful kindness.

Next-door neighbor Harmony checks on us and asks permission for her children, five-year-old August and three-year-old Amelia, to climb Grandma Rose's magnolia tree around the corner. They also hope to climb Robert's spiral staircase sculpture, "Double Helix." The welcome sound of children's laughter brings refreshing diversion.

First, sitter Cari stays with Rosemary while Robert and I relax over lunch at the Aegean Restaurant. Then we stop to check Rosemary's house. Harmony's husband Dan arrives with their children to climb the old-growth magnolia. Once upon a time, eighty-two-year-old Rosemary and her two-year-old great-granddaughter Kayla "climbed" the massive, low-flung bough together. While Robert and I neaten Mom's yard, Dan hoists his kids onto the big limb, shadows of past climbers by their sides.

My mom awakens alert the next morning at 8:00 a.m. She recognizes me and knows her name. Invigorated, we head outside. Rosemary in her wheelchair ponders metamorphosis as a caterpillar sojourns up her sleeve.

Her neck has given her grief since the rehab fall a year ago. But today she declines our massage offers. "Don't touch. I think it's contagious. Wash your hands well; cover your face. I'm afraid it might spread."

The traveling nurse returns. She listens with concern about Rosemary's deteriorating condition. Her soothing touch as she tends to my mother eases our frazzled nerves.

Rosemary is calm until evening. Then the moaning resumes with unintelligible mention of umbrellas. *Is it lame humor or fraught with significance?* We'll never know.

Anticipating another dreadful night, I call hospice. The weekend nurse happens to be nearby, at the local hospital, but cannot come. We feel abandoned by the hospice system. Much later, resentment vanquishes when I find out the poor nurse was in the ER for a personal matter—having a stroke!

All night, abdominal and back pains slash Rosemary's vitality. No sense calling hospice. I am left alone to guess what she needs. *Maybe it's her hiatal hernia or GERD. Will medication help or will adverse effects worsen her distress?* Options for nausea are Compazine (pills or suppositories) or Phenergan, which produce muscle spasms. *If her problem is constipation, will Tramadol 25 to 50 mg for muscle spasms counter the bad effect of Phenergan or make her GI pain worse?* Haldol for agitation inflicts fierce twitching. Her suffering worsens. *Maybe Gaviscon for gas.*

Nothing helps. I agonize along with my mother.

I am not a chemist, nurse, or pharmacist. Nor am I a functional paramedic any longer—medically retired with a broken neck. Not so young or fit myself, I am a daughter watching my mother succumb to disease. My sleep-starved brain runs marathons on the hamster wheel spinning in my skull. *What can I do to alleviate her misery? Is the torment from dementia, strokes, medication side effects, unnamed disease, the natural aging process, or a plague of combined forces? Maybe her pajamas are uncomfortable, something I can fix.* But a fresh set doesn't help. I pray for my dad and brother to let me know what is best for her, unsure what that means anymore.

All night long, the clock glares the hour. She is up at ten, eleven until one, again at three, and four to six. Cries of pain pour from her lips like blood from my gaping heart. Free-flow bellows declare her agony. In rhythm with her moans, my fingers caress her wavy hair.

At daybreak, neighbor Dan brings his kids to visit. Grandma Rose struggles into her wheelchair, grinning as playful children prance about. But it only lasts a minute before pain doubles her over. The kids go outside to climb Robert's *Double Helix* spiral staircase. Rosey wishes she could join them but can only catch glimpses of the fun from her bedroom window.

Hospice nurse Dave arrives in time to help get Rosemary in bed. The children flit back in to show their father the secret passageway in the hall closet outside Rosemary's bedroom. The entry is cluttered with stuffed animals, tossed in a haphazard hurry when she went berserk. Five-year-old August observes Nurse Dave's evaluation of Rosemary's cognitive function. Afterward, the clever boy brings stuffed animals to Gramma Rose. Imitating the mental exam, he holds them up one by one and asks if she can identify the animal. He applauds her ability to distinguish the teddy bear from the polar bear.

My mother's momentary joy evaporates with pangs of pain. At first, the nurse suggests anti-gas meds. But Rosemary's intractable torment convinces him to obtain a morphine order. He tries to communicate with her, but she cannot hear.

"What? My ears are ringing."

"Don't answer." His lighthearted quip breaks the suffering spell.

"Mother Nature hates a smart ass," she rejoins.

Her body wants to say uncle but her mind has other ideas. No matter how bad things get, Rosemary is determined to laugh her way out.

Good fortune prevails. Every two months, Medicare requires hospice to determine if patients' conditions have improved, plateaued, or worsened. Only the latter remain eligible. After the past week's odyssey of agony, the timing is impeccable.

A highly experienced nurse practitioner evaluates Rosemary. I show the woman videos of 10/18. She immediately identifies the malady as "neurogenic bladder," caused by, among other things, strokes. Finally, someone understands the symptoms Rosemary has endured since the fourth stroke when she had to cough in order to pee. The practitioner orders Neurontin (gabapentin) and an in-home abdominal ultrasound. "The least we can do after all Rosemary's been through." With that, the woman departs.

Robert drives to pick up the prescription. Rosemary steals out of bed and finds her way to the bathroom. I find her, pants down, sitting on her walker, parked in the shower stall for lack of space. I roll the walker to the toilet and pivot her onto the proper place. Once finished, she collapses.

"Oh, help, help."

Her back arches rigid with a grand mal seizure. Extremities stiffen as violent convulsions thrash her about. Head turned sharp left, her eyes gaze extreme left. My paramedic knowledge kicks in with foreboding: a convulsive gaze deviates toward the afflicted side of a brain injury. This purports a pending left-brain stroke, destined to debilitate the more functional right half of her body. The seizing intensifies. I buffer her body with mine so she won't bash against the unyielding doorjamb while I phone for help.

The convulsion subsides. Cradled in my arms, she goes deadweight limp. We await aid for an eternity of minutes. I shake from the strain, about to lose my grip. Then all at once, I sense my brother's arms supporting us. Whether Marty is here in spirit or just my imagination is irrelevant. His comfort is real. The tremble abates, and my awestruck soul rejoices.

Neighbor Dan arrives to help at the same time Robert returns from the pharmacy. Dan scoops Rose into his arms with the tenderness of a loving grandson and carries her flaccid body to bed.

Revived, semiconscious Rosemary manages to speak. "What a pain in the ass."

She takes her first dose of Neurontin, which coincidentally also treats seizures. Snuggled down with a prayer for sleep and a "Too Ra Loo Ra Loo Ral" lullaby, my mom ekes out a smile and blows a kiss.

When we were little, Mom demonstrated fun ways other cultures and species kiss. We fish-kissed in repetitive pursed puckers. Eyelashes batted against each other's cheeks for butterfly kisses. And Ma told us that people exchange Eskimo kisses by rubbing noses, to avoid frozen lips near the frigid North Pole.

I later learned that Eskimo kiss folklore stems from Inuit nuzzling called kunik.[14] New Zealand Māori have a similar sharing-of-souls ritual, pressing noses and foreheads together in a salutation called hongi.[15] Mom's various kisses left us gratified that every people and species express compassion.

I kiss my mother goodnight . . . again. At 10:00 p.m., she stands beside the bed.

"That leg feels funny," she says.

I give her the minimum dose of Haldol, hoping it helps her relax without side effects. Ten minutes later, she's standing again.

"What's the matter, Ma?"

"Why? I don't know." Her delicate Rosey voice emits surprise from my withered mom's lips. She settles again for fifteen minutes, then . . .

"Should I be getting up? Why is it so dark?"

"It's night, Ma. Time to sleep." She settles for a minute.

"My left leg is twitchy. It won't say what it wants."

Thinking her skin is dry, I rub her leg with lotion, and she relaxes for five minutes.

"My left leg is asleep. It doesn't want to go to sleep." For an hour she thrashes. Stands up. Sits down. Up. Down. She stretches like a jogger at a marathon starting line. I give her more Haldol.

Rosemary announces the arrival of midnight. "Is it going to keep going to sleep in here?" She tries to convey insomnia. For an hour she passes gas, long, impressive flatulence that would do the brass section of an orchestra proud. It's been days since her last bowel movement, so the relief diminishes anxiety for both of us as she dozes off.

If I were on a pharmaceutical-naming committee, I would suggest descriptive references to ailments or parts of the body they serve. Haldol would be agitatol. Morphine could be MoreDream. And if someone invented a wonder drug to revive failing mental faculties, I'd call it the Rosary, to honor my mom and as an answer to prayers. Three sleepless nights pass. Rosemary's punishing back pain inflicts relentless torment. Hospice juggles medications, unsure of the source of her distress. They guess muscle spasms, gas, restlessness, or infections that tests refute. One nurse insists Rosemary's urinary frequency is mental agitation. Without seeing the patient, a nurse supervisor discontinues the Neurontin, increases the Haldol, and, once again, insists Rose needs bladder training. The repugnant advice implies we indulge my mother's delusion by allowing her up so often to pee. At best, the idea is absurd since she lacks short-term memory for learning. Worse, it insinuates attention-seeking behavior. *My mother deserves compassionate relief, not armchair speculations from afar.*

"That's not right." Rosemary's pronouncement silences crickets outside her window. "My left hand is numb. My body's playing tricks. It's trying to leave without me."

For hours, she marches. Bedside to commode, up, down, up, complaining of leg and back pain. Too tired to keep pace, I hold her hand or pajama shirttail to detect if she starts to fall. Her voice merges with my dreams, a cornucopia of non sequiturs. Exhausted, I only recall disjointed phrases between snatches of snooze: "Why are legs?" "It's important . . ." and a distinct, "I wish to write a letter to my sister Dolly."

About 2:00 a.m., holding her pajama tail, my arm lifts off the bed in midair. Rosemary stands atop the commode. Frail health has yet to overcome her youthful, tree-climbing agility.

Following my upwardly mobile arm, I exclaim, "What are you doing, Mom?"

"I need to climb this ladder."

Jolted from sleep, I guide her to safety. Rationality serves no purpose. "Looks really steep, Ma. Better come to bed and rest first."

GPS was nonexistent and Okaloosa County had no 9-1-1 system when I first started work. Paramedics pulled 24-on/24-off shifts, a red phone in our quarters. Sound asleep, on the first ring, we sprang into action. Slipping into shoes and uniform smock, we determined the nature of the emergency, conveyed first aid instructions for panic-stricken callers, and consulted hard copy street maps. God help patients on any of the five Circle Drives. EMS shared a radio frequency with the water and sewer department, so cross communication was common. Talk of leaky

water mains and fractured femurs overlapped.

From 3:00 to 5:00 a.m., zzzzzzz. A noteworthy two hours straight of sleep passes. Granddaughter-in-law Melissa arrives with the sun. Still recovering from brain surgery, her scalp glows with a promising crown of sunrise stubble. Unsteady on her feet, she parks her walker beside Rosemary's. Hero of the day, she sits with Grandma Rose to give us a break. My mother dictates a letter to her oldest sister—who died two decades ago. Melissa transcribes. Then Rosemary recopies it onto a hand-painted note card she received for her birthday.

It reads: "Dear Dolly, Here I am committing the murderous act of writing a letter, just to prove that people still can do such things. The best invention in the world is trees." She mentions beautiful Shalimar weather, the overhead fan, and her owl pajamas, then adds, "My numb left hand annoys, and my right hand has a snooty expression." I save the letter for Dolly's branch of our family.

Evening descends, and Rosemary gives herself a status check. "I'm to the point where I don't know when I need something or when I've arrived."

Medications for pain, nausea, bladder, and seizures tend to reduce my mother to one-word grunts. Drugs intended for relief steal her vitality. Today would have been my parents' sixty-ninth wedding anniversary. For the first time since their marriage, Rosemary is oblivious to the date.

By remarkable coincidence, a young couple scheduled their wedding for today at Shoal Sanctuary. We were supposed to host the venue. Instead, Robert stays home with Rosemary—safely asleep in bed—while I make a quick appearance. The wedding couple assures me the nature preserve pleases them. I snap a few pictures of the bridal party and return home.

Robert frets in a dither. No sooner had I left than he heard the front door and thought I had forgotten something. Instead, he found Rose trying to leave. He helped her flop into a nearby rocking chair. It takes all our might to get her slumped, exhausted form into the wheelchair and back to bed. Robert and I stagger to the couch. Instantly, we hear commotion and find her on the bedroom floor. Bedrails have proven useless. With every ounce of strength, we get her back to bed, hurting all three of us in the process.

At nightfall, Rosemary announces, "My neck's not nice. Help me out of these elbows, please. My neck is tangled." Transferred onto the commode, she says, "I have to pee."

"Go ahead, Mom. You're on the pot."

Puzzled, she shoves her hand between her legs. "Wet."

Cleaned up, Rosemary grows alert, eager to greet the day . . . still hours away. I take her to the couch, drape my legs across her lap to prevent her from falling, and rest until sunrise.

Morning finds us still on the couch. Rosemary emerges from slumber with a wacky expression. She scrutinizes the day ahead, then wavers. "Things are mighty peculiar. Life's getting complicated. I must fulfill an obligation."

I suggest she write a note to her lifelong friend Pat. "You can thank her for her steadfast dedication during your dementia."

Rose latches onto the idea, but first something distracts her.

"My nose needs a drink," she sputters, catches a tossed tissue midair, and gives a hearty blow. "This sounds like an Irish tradition, secure in our seats."

No idea what that means. I clear medications off her sewing machine cabinet surface so it can serve as a letter-writing desk.

Situated in the wheelchair, Rose waves her pen like a flag, then leans in to write. My hands on either side of the paper prevent mars on the wooden surface. Tens of thousands of letters penned over her lifetime (I did the math), this turns out to be her last one. Unable to get comfortable, she sighs, "I wish I could accomplish bed." Back she goes, tucked in once more.

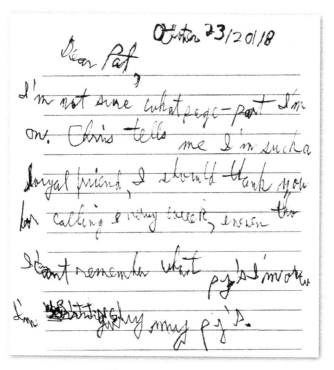

Rosemary's last letter

Before mailing the missive, I type it verbatim and add an attempted interpretation.

October 23/ 20/18

Dear Pat,

I'm not sure what page-part I'm on. Chris tells me I'm such a loyal friend, I should thank you for calling every week, even tho I don't remember what pjs I'm or why. I'm writing why my pjs.

Translation: Although confused, she appreciates Pat's loyalty and weekly calls, but doesn't remember them . . . and is distracted by her owl-print pajamas, and wonders why she's wearing them during the day.

Suddenly rambunctious, Rose squirms with urgency. "I need to decide what it is I need to do before I do it. I need to communicate. I'm not sure if I can interpret things right. I need to go somewhere and push something. If I just push it, I'm not sure I can do it."

Constipation? Or is death calling her name? After a futile bathroom break, I bring lunch and a laxative.

Seated on the bedside, legs dangling, childlike Rosey emerges with a big grin. Feet swing back and forth as she sips soup.

"Oh, I know this. I've had it before. It tastes like lunch." She reaches beneath the table and thumps her palm. "And this is the underside of lunch."

What a relief to see her cheerful. I share some exciting news. Aunt Pat plans to visit in a few weeks.

"Electric joy," Rosey replies. Her smile could light New York City.

A pleasant hospice volunteer, Gladys, visits with Rosemary for a few hours so I can sleep. Descendants of the same era, the two women chat about olden days.

Refreshed, I return and kiss my mother's cheek with infinite gratitude for the brief break. Volunteers are godsends.

The next day's suffering, Rosemary speaks through clenched teeth. "I suppose it's flattering to acknowledge that we're alive."

Robert tries to distract her from the pain with a tale of Dostoyevsky's epilepsy.

"Whenever the Russian philosopher took a nap, he wore a cautionary note that he was asleep and not to bury him." Rose's son-in-law leaves the room with a final comment. "I'm about to nap so don't bury me."

"You're safe, long as you don't start smelling bad," she calls back.

Robert out of sight, Rosemary's gurgling belly summons young Rosey's curiosity. "With all the rumblings of stomachs, I wonder if there are any duplicate sounds or if digestive noises are like snowflakes."

Well enough to sit in her wheelchair, she joins me in my office. But dizziness saps her pleasure. Her whispered plea for help sounds my red-phone alarm.

"Hang on, Mom." She hugs me as I transfer her onto the couch. Barely making it, she flops over with her head on the pillows, feet still on the floor. I ask if she wants them up.

"Just shove them in a file drawer."

Legs lifted, her feet dangle over the armrest. She flops catawampus, a grounded angel, her post-life passport pending. With a long exhale and aura-lit smile, she contemplates her circumstances.

"I wish to all the older people as nice a closing to their lives."

By evening, Rosemary's left leg swells, hot and red. Medical advisors speculate it is due to a clogged lymphatic duct, either from inactivity or a thrombosis. But they do nothing to alleviate her discomfort. The restless up-and-down marathon continues. She cannot specify what causes her distress: bladder, bowels, swollen leg, or something else.

Come morning, the mobile ultrasound arrives. The sonographer scans Rosemary's belly. The efficient technician approaches the patient with indifference. The machine peers into Rose's abdomen; the busy tech looks right through Rosemary as well. My mother does as she is told in silence. For someone in her presence to remain unmoved wrenches my heart. The tech departs. Inside myself, I cry. My translucent mother exists more elsewhere than here.

For breakfast, I feed my mom oatmeal with prunes.

Gazing out the window, her senses of taste and sight intermingle. "What a delicious taste of the countryside. Who could have imagined waking up to savory flowers?"

In her wheelchair parked by the open door, she absorbs sunlight while I garden.

"I love the gentle breeze dancing the leaves," says Rose.

She used to disdain "wafting gusts of pollen" and called people who opened windows "fresh air fiends."

Twelve-year-old great-granddaughter Kayla calls from her home in San Francisco and mentions hummingbirds outside her window.

"I'm glad they learned to hum," says Grandma Rose. After the call, she sits perched on her bedside. Her stomach gurgles; she surveys the surroundings for the source of the creaking digestion noise. "Do I hear a door opening?"

Morphine-topped dementia thwarts salient thought. Searching for clues to her worldly existence, Rosemary wonders, "Do I have a little girl? School-aged?" "Am I in high school?" She extends her arm and nearly falls. "I need that yellow lid to put on the jar. Where's my mustard? Where's my mothered?"

Her swollen left leg hampers her ability to bear weight. Transfers from bed to wheelchair to commode present greater risk. A hospice nurse witnesses Rosemary's distress and increases the morphine from every four to every two hours. Volunteer Gladys visits again. She and Rosemary converse merrily in the simple pleasure of each other's company.

Evening arrives. Flickering LED candles in the West Wing offer just enough light to get her to and from the commode. A hygienic sentry of hand wipes stands atop the bureau. For easy access, a long shoelace tied to the bedrail strings through a toilet paper roll, and hooks to the commode arm. The torn paper end dangles like an off-balance tightrope walker about to fall, hanging on for dear life.

Fitful, exhausted Rosemary zombies through the nights, dragged out of bed by her relentless bladder. Haldol, Baclofen, and morphine fail to subdue the misery. With calisthenic contortions, she twists backward to grasp her lower back. In the minimal light, we catch each other's eyes. She stares at me as if into oncoming headlights. Agony short-circuits her brain. She dissociates. But motherly concern overrides the torment. Unaware she's referring to herself, Rosemary beseeches in a third-person plea.

"Is your mom okay, Chris?"

No, Mom. You're suffering and I don't know how to help. Please, someone tell me what to do.

Her body longs to relinquish its duty. "Oh my, my ears are ringing in the hereafter. I wanna shiver."

A hospice nurse sees for herself Rosemary's dreadful discomfort and increases the morphine dosage yet again. I grab another blanket, eager to do something, anything to relieve her distress.

"I think I'm done trying to talk," my mother utters. "Rock-a-bye . . . hush-a-bye . . . bye-bye."

A phone call interrupts Rosemary's effort to vacate her bodily premises. It's Pat, who sensed her friend's distress. I hold the receiver to my mother's ear.

"I can't, can't the phone," breathless Rose stammers. Pain and heart failure impede her slightest exertion. It takes Herculean effort for her to get in and out of bed, more so to communicate. Rosemary is unable to converse, *maybe never again.*

After a snooze, "sunup syndrome" relocates Rose's voice, and she sucks in almost adequate amounts of air to ramble. Gasps and grins enliven her speech:

> Bugling is tough. Breathing (inhale), can't. Not that easy. One way or another (inhale), I have to get past the bugling. (Inhale.) Humanity needs perspective. We need to play well together, (inhale) in tune. Different instruments, sure. (Inhale.) Not everybody wants a horn. Violins, maybe. (Inhale.) But, for God's sake (inhale), at least try to breathe together. (Inhale) We do, don't we? Tommy Dorsey, I think played both (inhale)—trombone too. Guess he could breathe. It's tough going, but (inhale) worth every breath. All we can do is hope to (inhale) add our own notes to the mix. Not easy. (Inhale.) But do it right and

(inhale), TA DUM, orchestra. Otherwise, we're just tooting in the wind (exhale).

Another grueling night. Rosemary finally empties her bladder. I am too tired to dump the pot into the toilet this time. Early morning, on the commode again, she tries to get up. Her hands push hard against the armrests as she struggles to rise, and the commode tips backward. I catch her, but the pot topples. Its contents dump down the bureau, onto the just-cleaned carpet.

I dial the national hospice triage nurse. This one is proficient. After explaining the situation, she tells me to hand my mother the phone. Rather than transfer our dilemma to the local nurse, the clever woman keeps Rose occupied in bed while I clean. It is just the leg up I need. Dresser drawers removed and cleaned, prop about the room drying. Rags and cleaners pile into chaos. It looks like a bomb went off. I stack the last drawer before tackling the soggy carpet. In my peripheral vision, I catch Rosemary kicking off her covers.

I yell loud enough for the nurse on the other end of the line to hear, "Stay in bed, Mom."

On cue, the RN redirects Rosemary to tuck herself in. Pillows form a fortress around her.

The next day, the carpet cleaners return to spiffy her room again. Tubes snake from their truck, propping the door ajar. No problem, the weather is nice. But a fly follows them in and hovers above Rosemary.

An unexpected surge of fury seizes me. Lava courses through my veins. Pent-up outrage and anguish over my mother's predicament take aim at the tiny insect.

"Don't you dare!" I scold, shaking my finger at the fly's nose. Radiation of my glare sends the varmint fleeing. My seething overreaction surprises me. Sleep-starved, I could swear the flighty trespasser looks back with a flummoxed expression on its itsy-bitsy face and begs the question: "What the heck, lady?"

Refocused on the task at hand lowers my nuclear temperature. To stabilize the commode better, I set the front legs one notch shorter than the back. That angle makes it easier for Rosemary to dismount. For good measure, duct tape in front prevents the pail from sliding forward. The workmen depart, followed by the shooed fly in hasty retreat.

While Mom naps, I contemplate my explosive reaction to the insect. It wasn't just her need for rest. The reason for my macabre dramatics dawns on me. I'd envisioned the creature as a mini-Grim Reaper, here to dine on my mother before her final breath.

At noon, an intolerant nurse arrives with an accusatory tone. Why was the Neurontin discontinued? She puts my mom back on the medication and notes that Rosemary has developed an arrhythmia. Her poor heart struggles from sleepless, night-after-night yoyoing and day-after-day medication shifts.

"Thank you, dear." Mom takes my face in both hands. Frustration melts away. She appears fully aware, for all she's worth. Our eyes meet a moment longer. The mutual gaze reminds me of the Zulu salutation *Sawubona*, "I see you." Midway in the commode to bed transfer, we bask in an extra-long hug.

"In case I don't see you again, ta-ta," she lilts.

One October morning, the clock reads 4:00 a.m. as she jostles from bed. She slept nearly all night! Refreshed and rejuvenated, "sunup syndrome" sighs resound, better than percolating coffee. But happiness takes a sudden nosedive. Something unexplainable is wrong.

"Oh, oh, my tree limb." She searches her stifled vocabulary for words. "I can't think . . . what it's called. My trunk-foot. Oh damn." Then, in a productive cough of a shout, she yells, "OUCH. There. I've given it a name. Now I don't want to think about it anymore."

Without another word, she takes the pain in stride. It's what people do. We cope. Be it dementia, brain cancer, or furious weather, we adapt, until the fatal end.

Rosemary's life divides into intermittent thirds—1/3 sleep, 1/3 pain, and 1/3 bliss. But the division is not evenly distributed. Glee whizzes by fast enough to emit sonic booms with resonant echoes of laughter. Rest comes in erratic, fitful snoozes, interrupted by plagues of pain. Rosemary suffers eternities.

Mind over matter, Mom. I massage her sore thigh, swollen twice the size of her other one. The skin is taut. *Come to think of it, a few days before my dad died, his leg swelled in the same freakish manner.* I deliver a kiss to my mother's cheek.

"Puf," is all she manages to utter. Another dose of morphine and she nods off, hopefully to pleasant, pain-free places.

Rosemary sleeps like a bear in winter. Hour upon hour passes. We check often, unsure if she is still alive. Robert and I exchange silent shrugs. Her telltale toes wiggle, and we relax. The photo-imprinted blanket enshrouds her. She rests in the peaceful company of herself, all ages.[16]

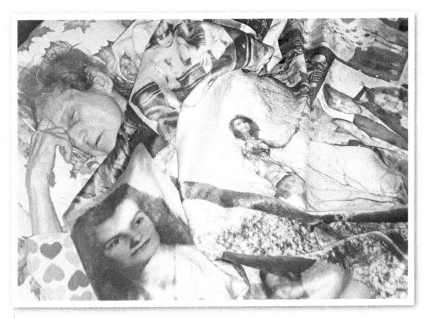

Rosemary of all ages

Late afternoon, Rosemary awakens bright-eyed. Voice strong, she sounds herself. Her resilience inches along like a determined caterpillar, spied by a hungry bird. For the moment, the morphine and haloperidol keep her pain-free and chipper.

Touching one of Robert's granite sculptures, Rose regards the piece and surmises, "It's a beautiful work. 'Earth without art is just e h,'" she quotes. The critical thought necessary for aesthetic appreciation breaks the caregiving grind for a moment of spectacular reprieve.

Critical thinking lessons erupted in one-minute bursts during 1960s TV commercials. Mundane evenings, our family zoned out in front of the television. Glued to the tube, channel options were 3, 6, and 10-- NBC, ABC, and CBS respectively. Back then—before public airwaves were sold to corporate interests—the FCC's Fairness Doctrine strived for honest, balanced broadcasting. We'd settle down to absorb whatever news aired or sing along with Mitch Miller, Lawrence Welk, and the Smothers Brothers. Our casual postures merged into a single organism. Heads rested on laps, elbows intertwined, hands flopped slack. Our dog Charlie's chin rested on any nearby extremity. The only disturbance to the bodily mass was to improve reception as someone adjusted the horizontal hold button or the antenna.

Commercials were another story. One-minute intermissions broke the hypnotic spell. Adrenaline rushed. After mad dashes to the kitchen or upstairs to the john, we returned with snacks or slid down the banister before the show resumed.

The fun part of commercial breaks came when everyone remained to scrutinize product pitches. Our parents lampooned nonsense, passed off as fact. Those minute-long lessons taught us to distinguish merits and absurdities. Two booby prize commercials were a breakfast cereal hawked as only for real men and a cigarette brand aimed at liberated women. Thereafter, if a guy revved his hotrod engine or a woman feigned sophistication with a butt hanging off her lip, we sang the marketing jingles in sarcastic jest.

Those spring-into-action breaks conditioned me for future years as a paramedic. Whenever the EMS red phone rang, abrupt, life-and-death adrenalin rushes became second nature.

Mirthful Rosemary adopts a new mantra: "A couple more days." *Precognition or fantasy firings of damaged brain? It's anyone's guess.* Her voice chimes with anticipation.

The sad emptiness I had anticipated with my mother's dementia never transpired. Rosemary's effervescence has seen to that. *Cherish every last moment,* I tell myself. *Record every pithy comment, witticism, and epiphany.* But necessary chores distract my attention. Mom joins me for brief spurts while I clean the commode, pay bills, and do laundry. Seated in her wheelchair, she holds a banana, but I must direct it toward her mouth. She helps pair socks until dizziness slumps her over. I move the freshly folded, banana-smeared laundry and prop up her legs. She slumps further, reminiscent of her great-granddaughter's melting ice cream improv. Rushing my mother into bed, stacked laundry topples to the floor along with the banana peel. All the while, she expounds with jubilant insight. Multi-layered meanings of life exude from her in crystal clarity. I snuggle her under the covers as she dozes off.

Confident I'll recall her astounding remarks, I pause to put the clean-ish clothes away. Then, pen in hand, I cannot recall a single word. I vow to be more attentive. *A pad of paper by the bed should suffice.*

"Mischief Night" in New Jersey, Halloween Eve brings a few disreputable hours of pranks and vandalism. In Florida, Rosey converses with people not present. Her angelic, one-sided dialogue halts around midnight. She complains of a headache and her entire right side goes limp.

Lights on, she appears completely blind, her skin hot and pulse racing. I remove her blankets, consoled by the leaf-print sheets we bought for my brother when he was sent home to die. I encourage her to imagine an afterlife reunion. She laughs as if floating on cloud nine. After twenty minutes, her right-side function returns and vision resumes its minimal level. *Only a ministroke*, I assure myself.

As the crisis ends, she celebrates in unspoken awareness, apparent in her dancing eyes, fidgety toes, and secret snickers. *What's happening, Mom? Why do you keep reviving for more agony? Are you pleased to be alive, or enthralled with your near-death sojourns?*

The wee hours become heavenly as a veil lifts. Rosemary makes remarkable sense. An ancient shepherd staring into the night sky, she connects the stars into meaningful pictures. Truths unfold. Souls, past and present, intermingle. Primal forces guide her journey, no compass needed. Awestruck, she exalts relationships—molecular, interpersonal, and cosmic. Although my mother is lost in her worn-out body and brain, I envision Rosemary at home in the universe.

Half asleep in dim lighting, I locate the notepad and pencil on the nightstand to preserve her spirited escapade. Page upon page, I transcribe. Laughter punctuates her astounding oration. Insights illuminate the crisp darkness, like cobalt blue Christmas lights of her youth.

Exhausted, I nod off, only to be reawakened by her chortles. Her enthusiasm infuses me with sufficient stamina to keep writing. She settles down, her hand on mine, and I treasure the significance of its warmth, knowing it won't last much longer. I doze off, gratified. My notes immortalize Rosemary's peeks into the near-death beyond.

At daybreak, I am baffled to find the notepad completely blank. Was it a dream? The orange pencil rests beside the orange syringe for administering her oral medications, and I realize my mistake. In the muted light, I grabbed the wrong implement. Pencil in hand, I attempt to recall what she said. Nothing. Her prophetic proclamation lost forever.

An unbelievable blunder

My mom interrupts, placing a succinct cap on her beautiful mind. "My little regulator in the head doesn't wanna anymore."

Seven ups and downs from the commode last night proved non-productive. Hospice nurse Penny finally decides it is time for Rosemary to have an indwelling catheter. After relentless unkind tricks by her bladder, a Foley tube is an ideal Halloween treat. Her distended bladder relinquishes 700 ccs of retained urine. *Ouch!* Afterward, the nurse rolls Rosemary over in bed and asks where she is most comfortable.

"South Jersey," my mother replies without hesitation. In a merry voice, Rosey adds, "I don't know how it can be wrong. Everywhere faces the right direction."

The nurse leaves, and I brush my mom's hair out of her face, careful to cover her ears.

"Ahhh, what could be more pleasant than having your head stroked," she purrs.

Memories of all the strokes that poor cranium has endured coax my fingers through her wavy hair. *If only I could preserve her radiance.*

A grin flits across her face. "My, oh my. Cars certainly have short legs."

I give my mom a kiss and head toward the kitchen and get dinner cooking.

She stops me with a casual question and comment. "Coming back later? I won't be here."

"Where're ya going this time, Mom?" *Another soul excursion to a different state, country, planet, or dimension?* I smile to myself.

"Somewhere else. On the roof. Anywhere but here." She seems poised with anticipation. All aboard for multifaceted Rosemary, Rose, Mrs. B . . . and little Rosey.

Lacey-brain musings combined with medication cocktails make it hard to fathom the gravity of her words as she dozes off.

Slumber, that inexplicable intermission from consciousness, evolves in stages. Typical toddlers struggle to stay awake, not wanting to miss a single curious moment. Baby Rosemary's appetite for play only surrendered under the influence of her pop's bedtime stories and her mother's lullabies. Reaching Rosemary's hormonal teens, what was once confinement became a haven. She loitered in bed to pilfer a few more winks before school. Next, the romance of marriage transformed her mattress into an adult exercise mat. A hardworking middle-aged woman, she snatched snoozes on any cushioned surface. In the 1960s, I sketched my exhausted mom catching some shut-eye.

Attitudes toward sleep evolve with age

As it was in the beginning, Rosemary's bed becomes a trap. More than I can possibly foresee, her premonition comes true. The only escape from the tedium of dying is for her to accept life's limited-time offer and vacate the worn-out body that pins her down. My mother waves Happy Halloween with her right hand, the most functional one. Although unsure where she is going, Rose knows she won't be here anymore. Lovingly, I film her nonchalant utterance of what turns out to be her final words.

"Factoid years."

STROKE 9

THE LAST LIGHT OF "FACTOID YEARS"

Entreaty

The fluttering leaves of autumn
Briefly lift as golden hands
In silent supplication
To the One who understands.
For what can they be pleading
As toward the earth they're hurled?
They beg of The Great Healer
to aid the suffering world.
– ROSEMARY, CIRCA 1960S

IN THE KITCHEN ON ALL HALLOW'S EVE, I prepare a quick supper before sunset brings trick-or-treaters hearkening at our door. While I prepare to moor my mother with food, she hoists anchor and sets sail. Entering the bedroom carrying a dinner tray, adorned with a tiny ceramic jack-o'-lantern, I find Rosemary unresponsive, but breathing. Her entire right side is flaccid. A major stroke, as she foretold minutes earlier.

After her goodbye wave, Life's Coach benched her from consciousness.

Only her bodily shell remains, stuck on autopilot. The anatomy persists by sheer habit. Like a cruel Halloween trick, she's trapped in limbo, no sign of her endearing presence on this side, and no eternal light of release on the other. Rosemary's ghost chases after the sinking sun.

Eyes glaze with a ghoulish miasma shading her windows to the world. Sightless orbs bob in their sockets. The right side surrenders to gravity. A threadbare handkerchief—her father's shirttail in a previous life—peeks from a half-open nightstand drawer. Like the tattered relic, my mother's once useful mind has disintegrated into more holes than viable material. Rosemary's spirit ventures onward: only a remnant beating heart remains. No one is home inside to speak, see, swallow, or answer to her name.

Like the boy who cried wolf, brushes with death have occurred so often that it's hard to believe this one's conclusive insinuation. Exhaustion and sleep deprivation muffle the blow of my mom's mortality. She has endured agony sufficient to level an army and bounced back elated. Reality penetrates my skull in ripples, then waves of contractions. The same surges as a pending birth, the countdown to death shifts from months and weeks to hours and breaths.

Rosemary's slow tiptoe toward death formed cognitive dissonance. Professor Pauline Boss of the University of Minnesota named it "ambiguous loss."[17] Paradoxical thoughts vie for attention. Rosemary's body persists, yet she has gone. Present, yet elsewhere. Worldly bonds sever, yet hold firm. Impossibly frail yet influential, she's a portrait of powerful vulnerability—an oxymoron clarified by research professor Brené Brown.[18] A Buddhist adage that's puzzled me for years starts to make sense. *Life is too short; we must proceed very slowly.* Rosemary has done just that.

Surely Rosemary would have died many times over, could she comprehend her circumstances. Corrosive acidic suffering fails to erode her body's iron grip on life. Like it or not, Rosemary's repeated defiance of death attests to the tenacity of survival instinct. Layer by layer, strokes peel her away like an onion. Still, she declines death's relentless invitations.

The last animated extremity Rosemary possesses, her numb left hand makes feeble attempts to rub her face in response to itchy side effects of morphine and gabapentin. I worry she'll snag her frail facial skin, and put on jewelers' glasses to trim her fingernails. A visitor notices my arthritic attempt and takes charge. The final manicure cut accidentally goes beyond the thumbnail. Her hand retracts in momentary reflex as blood dots the sheet. I grab the frayed hankie to cover the wound while the apologetic helper locates a Band-Aid. I assure the woman that if Rose could speak, she would convince her that the kindness outweighs a minor cut. Rosemary leaves again for some distant elsewhere.

My mother's life has been a blessing to those who love her. I sense an immeasurable loss to the world, especially those who never met Rosemary. Overhead, a sound draws my attention. The scurry above reminds me of her comment about going up on the roof. A squirrel scampers across and leaps to the magnolia outside her window.

Hospice delivers a hospital bed along with an alternating mattress pump designed to alleviate pressure. Next-door neighbor Dan arrives, accompanied by his children. Daddy Dan helps Robert rearrange the West Wing to accommodate the additional bed. Once the room is situated, the men reconvene at the other end of the house for guy talk, leaving me with two preschoolers and my dying mother. Questions about Grandma Rose pour from the bright kids. I rush across the house to seek their father's input. Dan assures me that he trusts my judgment. Back at my mom's bedside, I switch from caregiver to kindergarten teacher.

"What's that yellow stuff?" Five-year-old August points to the Foley bag.

"It's pee," I tell him. "Grandma Rose is too weak to use the bathroom."

"How's does she get it into the bag?"

"Through a tube," is enough information.

"Why won't Gwamma Wose open ho eyeeez?" Three-year-old Amelia frowns, disappointed.

"She's too tired," I explain. "And she's blind now, so her eyes don't work."

"Does blind mean she can't see?" August sounds anxious.

"Yes, but she doesn't need to see anymore."

He lifts an eyelid for reassurance that the eyeball remains intact.

"Her eyes can't focus anymore," I tell the boy as I soothe the eyelid shut.

"Can she hear us?"

"Maybe. And your voices sound like music to her."

"Can Gwamma Wose hold ouwa heends?" asks Amelia.

"No, but you can hold her hands if you like."

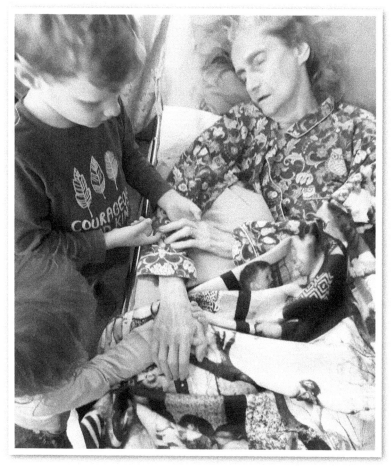

You can hold Gramma Rose's hands, if you like

Always punctual, nurse's aide Latavia shows up at 8:30 a.m. sharp and bathes "Mrs. Rosemary." Although seven months pregnant, the woman has the strength, energy, and know-how to safely hoist my mother's withered body. Head to toe, Latavia cleans my mom with a kindness I imagine she bestows on her own grandmother. In bed, she shampoos Rose's hair with soothing strokes. Experience tells her this will be the last bath, last visit. Wet sheets changed, the kindhearted woman combs a tight bun to crown Rosemary's head. Before leaving, Latavia positions unresponsive Rosemary like royalty perched on a throne of pillows.

Every two hours, as I did for Marty, I roll her body to prevent bedsores. It's all I know to do for our family's unpretentious, ever-loving matriarch. Moving the swollen leg elicits a faint groan. *Does rubbing it with lotion soothe or make matters worse?* This stroke could be the result of an embolism from a leg thrombosis. As nature takes its course with Rosemary, hospice is insufficient, overwhelmed by Hurricane Michael aftermath. Her left hand no longer attempts to scratch. Toes cease their telltale dance.

If life came with musical accompaniment, Rosemary's exit would intermingle the angelic crescendo of Barber's "Adagio for Strings" with Mancini's "Baby Elephant Walk." Saint-Saens' "The Swan"—played on a theremin by Clara Rockmore—would befit this between time.

After years of care, I am at a loss for what my mother needs. The prophetic truth she spoke two days ago assures me she is not here, not in this spent body. She has taken flight. Perhaps in a holding pattern, Rosemary circles overhead, waiting for life to let her go.

Night descends. I utter assurances into the vacuous room. "I'm here, Mom." *Is it better if I hold your limp right hand or the numb left one? Do my kisses somehow reach you? Is your right or left cheek more receptive?* Unresponsive, either way.

Her body lacks the gumption to cough. After minutes of indifferent effort, a loud, low groan escapes her lips in a long exhale. She stops breathing; I hold my breath, too. Her face turns to colorless slate. I touch a cold, skeletal hand. Then I rise to awaken Robert. Just as I reach the doorway, lifelong reflexive respiration kicks back in with a slow, apathetic breath.

Deprived of air, a healthy person revives with fast, deep breaths to replenish lost oxygen and eliminate CO^2. Not so with agonal breathing near the end. Respiration resumes with indifference, out of habit rather than need. Transfixed, I watch her chest rise and fall. *How many times must my poor mom die?*

Helpless resignation deflates my spirit. Nothing to do for her, I turn off the light and zombie down the hallway, until . . . A sudden resuscitative energy fills my lungs. My dead, six-foot-three brother's embrace uplifts me. Edna St. Vincent Millay described this in her poem "Renascence": "I know not how such things can be—I breathed my soul back into me."[19] Revived by Marty, I rush back to our mother and plant myself beside her. Raspy breaths syncopate with the intermittent mattress pump, the noise of brake release when a semi-tractor comes to a dead stop. I stroke her forehead, strain to hear, longing for her sigh.

Kindness from others warms the frigid vigil. Words, any words, soothe like a fresh breeze over a stagnant quagmire. Cousin Linda phones from New Jersey. Friends Shew and Deb inquire. Caregiver Cari plays songs from Rosemary's list—"We'll Meet Again," "You'll Never Walk Alone," and "Till the End of Time." My godmother, Aunt Pat, tearfully cancels her planned visit. Her encouragement these past years has been the greatest gift a godchild could receive.

Neighbor Sharilyn brings a hug and a banana loaf. Under the circumstances, the savory baked good comforts like my mother's cinnamon buns. Sharilyn lauds Rosemary: "a brilliant, joyful lady of poetic words and a jubilant voice."

Daughter Mary calls to say she's flying here from her home in Maryland (our grandkids call the state "Mommyland"). Although it's their anniversary, she and her husband Mark agree for Mary to come help us with Grandma Rose. Until their offer, we did not realize how much we need family support right now.

❧

November third, Rosemary's Eveready body lacks the energy to clear her throat. But her morphine refill is delayed by a hospice clerical error. Nurses, who quadrupled the dosage, neglected to inform the physician.

"Wish I could cough for you, Mom." From the pond next door, frog croaks echo Rosemary's labored breathing. Prescribed in combination, morphine alleviates pain and respiratory distress, Ativan (lorazepam) calms anxiety, and Atropine dries throat secretions. Crush the pills with mortar and pestle, add the last morphine drops, and aspirate the mixture into the orange syringe—the one I mistook for a pencil on Halloween. I squirt the cocktail between her cheek and gum. Thankfully, it absorbs without incident. Her cough gradually calms.

The medications cannot dampen her survival instinct. Bodily function clings to the fallacy that the object of life is to keep living. Schopenhauer disparaged this insatiable "will" as a blind, perpetual force of nature.[20] Contradictory to the bleak philosopher, what has kept Rosemary going is her joy, even in the face of intractable pain. But no resource is limitless, certainly not life as we know it. For vegetative Rose, each breath is a futile habit postponing the inevitable.

"It's okay, Mom. Relax into it. Watch for Dad." I speak to her empty form, spurn any residual compulsion to hold on. "A welcoming committee of loving people from your past awaits your arrival," I reassure the both of us.

Barely there, the crescent moon fades from sight. Darkness recedes to another dawning day. On the wall, the world atlas traces her years of mind travel. Post-it flags wave to me. *Where does your consciousness drift now, Ma?*

Her final words, "factoid years," console me as I nod off beside her barely breathing shell and dream she escapes. This deplorable condition only imprisons her "factoid" existence. Rosemary's spirit travels on magnificent out-of-body adventures. In Audubon, New Jersey, she visits "240" and climbs her willow. Unanchored by temporal hold, she glides over Ireland, the birthplace of her father's people. Her soul wanders Konstanz, the German/Swiss border town where her maternal grandparents hailed. Like a captive bird released after a lifetime encaged, my mom circles over the Bodensee (Lake Constance), then follows the Rhine River downstream. She lingers at the majestic Rhine Falls; its mighty roar in joyful, harmonic play with her tinnitus. The bird's-eye river view leads Rosemary across Europe to where the North Sea welcomes the rising sun.

At 8:00 a.m., I hear Robert saying his morning prayers in time to physical therapy exercises.

"How long can your daughter stay?" I ask him. "When is Mary's return flight?"

"She doesn't know. It's a one-way ticket."

The thought brings me memories of my close-knit family in South Jersey. "Maybe we can keep her and lure Mark down."

A big grin forms between my husband's snow-white mustache and beard.

Death hovers over Rosemary, as much a weight as a wait. We adapt to the suffocating interval between alive and not. Stuck. Trapped. We pray for release, hers and ours alike. Mom told stories of people asphyxiated in the 1919 Boston molasses flood. Heaviness envelops us. We acclimate, taking the smothering tension in stride, unnoticed . . . until it lifts.

At 11:00 a.m., Mary arrives. Just knowing she cares enough to be here makes the intensity manageable. Mary helps sort Gramma Rose's clothes. We keep only flexible socks and shirts, useful apparel with a diaper, catheter, and gigantic swollen leg. We save a few keepsake outfits and donate the rest to Hurricane Michael survivors. The storm could have hit here. There, but by the grace of God, go any of us.

My lover-of-trees mother's pending death tangles with reports of Hurricane Michael's destruction. Official calculations of almost 17 million devastated acres put the forest death toll at an unfathomable hundred million trees.[21] Endangered Torreya yew saplings lay crushed under debris. Woodlands lay slashed as if by a seventy-mile-wide machete.

Tree climber Rosemary dwindles in sympathy with the dying forest.

Cousins Erika and Kip come with their five children to pay their last respects. The three youngest bring homemade cards. "The littles" scuff their feet and look away, unsure how to cope. Then they do what comes naturally and surround their unresponsive Aunt Rosie with stuffed animals from the closet. Like the *E.T.* movie closet scene, bears, seals, and a swan encircle my mother. The teen boys shuffle in the doorway, in need of a plausible escape or sense of purpose. I ask them to reconnect the toilet flusher, dismantled when Aunt Rose was active. Erika and Mary roll my flaccid mom on her side. Five-year-old Aiven helps her mother comb Aunt Rosie's hair before the cousins depart.

At 2:00 p.m., Rosemary starts moaning, loud and prolonged. We can only guess that her distress is from the swollen leg that resembles an overripe melon about to pop. The well-loved Chaplain Charlie from hospice sees her suffering and summons help. Nurse Sheila does a top-notch job of patient care and family guidance. She takes Rose's vital signs. Blood oxygen saturation is at fifty-eight compared to the normal 90 – 100 percent. Together, we change my mom's diaper and Sheila checks her vitals again. O2 has dropped to fifty. Nurse supervisor Debbie arrives to offer parting hugs. The two RNs concur a prognosis of hours and decide the alternating pressure mattress is sufficient. No need to turn Rosemary any longer.

At 3:00 p.m., our neighbors stop over with their children. The chatter of youth is a sweet reprieve from the mattress cycling noise, solemn adult voices, and Rosemary's ear-piercing silence. Five-year-old August questions an inconceivable detail of dying. His tone is incredulous. "Grandma Rose sleeps *all* the time? Day *and* night?" Hands on his hips, the skeptic challenges, "What about naps?"

Night falls. Except for the flickering LED candles, the house is still. Death doula Deborah arrives to hold vigil with us. Her common-sense whispers of reassurance and confident composure set a reassuring tone of fortitude. She keeps constant watch, whispers loving encouragement, and monitors Rosemary's respirations. At 1:50 a.m., Deborah detects the short, shallow breaths of pending death. The two of us say our goodbyes and then awaken Robert and Mary.

Attempts by Rosemary's body to depart life stuck, like trying to exit a revolving door in constant motion. Over the course of nine strokes, centrifugal force spun bits of her conscious self away. *But where is away?* Years of near-deaths conditioned me to expect another revival. Not this time. Entropy prevails. In the wee hours of November 4, with tremendous relief similar to giving birth, but the opposite, Rosemary Jane Baker dies.

Never to go again like the old man's clock, her time of death chimes one last idiosyncrasy. After a long exhale, my mother's pulse ceases and the clock strikes 2 a.m. . . . No, make that 1:00 a.m. on the precision atomic clock, the exact moment daylight saving time ends. A classic Rosemary-style coincidence.

"Mom?"

ONWARD:

ROSEMARY, DEAD OR ALIVE?

DEFINING DEATH

AFTER LIFE CARE

POSTMORTEM PLANS
(AND REALITIES)

A Toast
To the many far-flung
friends and family members
who pretty much are now strangers:
Though fate has made us less acquainted,
I salute the fact that you exist!
– ROSEMARY, 2014

POSTMORTEM CARE

THE STORY OF ROSEMARY CONTINUES for her survivors in a world without her and for herself in whatever comes next. Wishing Rosemary a fond farewell, we decide not to notify hospice of her death until dawn. Everyone functions better after a restful night's sleep.

Postmortem care is designed for solemn efficiency. The process is *supposed* to work something like this: A hospice nurse arrives and officially pronounces death. Since Rosemary donated her body to science, the nurse contacts MedCure, a medical science program. A local funeral home transports the body to a teaching hospital for educational research. Several weeks later, they ship the cremated remains back to family—the process is streamlined and MedCure absorbs all costs.

Reality is quite another story. A blunder on our part: we forgot to consider dressing Rosemary in appropriate attire. Her planned formal wedding-and-funeral dress only made sense if she had wanted an open casket service. It would be cumbersome with the catheter, and discarded by the mortician or teaching hospital. She wears a diaper and the top half of her favorite owl pajamas. Knowing Rose, she would have wanted the PJ set kept intact. That means removing the top and redressing her in an expendable shirt, a task easier done before rigor mortis. Like dressing a stiff doll, we maneuver unyielding arms through sleeves. Garb changed, we know Rosemary would approve our practicality.

At sunrise, I contact yesterday's well-prepared hospice nurse who left her cell phone number. En route, she is redirected to a living patient and must transfer Rosemary's death to Nurse B, who is out of the loop. While awaiting the woman's arrival, I notify MedCure, and the intake person discovers hospice neglected to date the paperwork. By the time Nurse B arrives and officially pronounces death, it is 9:00 a.m., eight hours after the fact.

Murphy's Law reigns throughout the bureaucratic procedure. But it doesn't bother us in the slightest; we are relieved Rosemary's misery is over. The absurdity would have rolled her on the floor laughing. For us, postmortem blunders hold an element of Zen release, like untangling knots.

Hospice Nurse B plants herself in the living room and takes root for hours with her cell phone, laptop, and muffled paperwork frustration. The rest of us head to the kitchen. Reminiscent of my father's Christmas morning tradition of fresh-squeezed orange juice, we toast my mother with Florida's finest nectar. Awaiting the mortician, we meander in and out of Rosemary's bedroom. Many calls and emails later, the RN decides to finish the forms at the office. Acclimating to life without Rosemary, we share stories, take calls, sip tea, and allow the circumstance to gel. In the words of poet philosopher, David Whyte, "The conversation of reality oscillates from loss to celebration."[22]

Disentanglement from caregiving continues. Each mundane chore relaxes my urgent sense of responsibility. The hospice nurse guides disposal of leftover medications. Combined in a plastic bag, the colorful assortment of pills, capsules, and liquid looks festive. Add detergent and water. Mash until the rainbow mixture dissolves into grayish sludge. Double brown bag and throw away. In our disposable society, "away" is some landfill or trash-laden barge, ashes to ashes, meds to mush.

MedCure sends two men from a funeral home in Pensacola, over an hour away. Lost en route, they request directions from navigation-challenged Nurse B—the same nightshift RN who lost her way here more often than not. The solemn duo eventually arrives and wheels in a gurney. Everyone remarks on the statuesque beauty of Rosemary. Her face appears neither human nor mannequin. Her ninety-year-old skin is smooth, wrinkle-free, and luminescent bronze, the color of a radiant sunset. Unlike ancient Egyptians who mummified dead pharaohs to preserve their remains, I have no qualm parting with my mother's corpse, confident that she left days before, just as she said.

Instead of a body bag, the morticians wrap her stiff cadaver in sheets and cover it with a cobalt blue comforter. *Nice touch, her favorite color.* As they roll her out the door, one wheel crushes a garden sand dollar. The men apologize profusely. No need, I assure them. With legendary significance, the minor misstep sets free tiny "doves" inside the shell. We wave goodbye, and the hearse drives away.

ROSEMARY JANE BAKER

Confident in love eternal, I imagine my mother surrounded by her people. Rosemary's spirit is free to catch up with her parts already promoted. Reunited with her fondest memories, her beautiful qualities, including those unrealized, and with her cantankerous left hand, she has joined the

Rosemary, with wings by artist Sonyia McSwain

big family reunion ever after. Mom and Dad are together, with Marty and every kind person who touched their lives.

To honor my remarkable mother, rather than black, I wear her keepsake clothes and sense her embrace. Grateful to have lived long enough to appreciate her, I am equally grateful she lived long enough for me to let her know.

Rosemary's warm hugs remain embedded in her long sleeves. Although dead, her kindness lingers. Her extraordinary, yet subtle influences hold strong. Surely, along with every other well-loved person, I am one of the wealthiest people on Earth to have had such fine parents. Sharing the wealth is only fitting. No epitaph, no funeral, no tears or coffin for Rosemary. Instead, the turning of these pages celebrates her life.

Mortal Consolation

A few weeks later—at the noteworthy hour of 2:00 a.m., Rosemary's actual time of death—I gaze out the West Wing window. In contrast to an otherwise bleak night, the following affirmations arise with the full moon.

Pain coaxes us more willingly to the grave. Death's misery comes from resistance. Accepting our bodies as temporary containers eases the process. When life grow unbearable, people possess a remarkable ability to let go. Severe illnesses and injuries force the decision to either struggle or surrender.

During my paramedic years, I witnessed patients calmly relinquish their lives. A child after a car crash, a teen who drowned while saving her friend, an elder with a ruptured aneurysm . . . despite medical intervention, these people relaxed into death.

Failure-to-thrive babies succumb in peaceful surrender. Abused infants with no smile left in them let go of life. A two-year-old, safe from harm, lost the gumption to breathe. And sometimes, healthy babies fall asleep, never to reawaken.

Welcoming death occurs in close relationships when one partner dies and the bereft mate follows soon after, so common it earned the name "widowhood effect." An evacuated elderly couple survived Hurricane Opal in their car under Brooks Bridge, their island home destroyed. Rosemary took them in until emergency housing became available. Then, with no electricity, no air conditioning in temperatures over 100oF, the husband perished from heat stroke. His healthy, grieving wife died days later. Decrepit seniors eventually greet death like a kind friend. None of this happened with Rosemary; she lost the capacity to connect the dots.

REGRETS

Unassuaged by wonderful memories, grueling details of Rosemary's final years haunt me, stored away until time allowed permission to face them. Catching a nap on her West Wing bed, I roll over and my hand brushes the stiff edge of a throw pillow. Although fully aware she is dead, I mistake it for her skeletal body and let out an involuntary shriek. *I hope no one heard.* My cringe vaporizes and breaks the dam that held back years of horror. On my cell phone screen, an animated likeness of my mother stares at me; the perplexed expression turns out to be my own reflection. Outdoors, I gaze upward through pines, seeking clues to the grand scheme. Chicken Little style, the sky looks ready to fall flat on its face. *Get a grip*, I chastise myself.

Sufficient sleep refreshes me with "sunup syndrome" clarity, but taints with survivor guilt. If only I had called abuse registry with every rehab negligence infraction. I wish I had reported the lecherous minister to police right away; church authorities could not defrock him because no ministerial credentials were found—despite years at the pulpit, AALA officials concluded that the man was an imposter. On 10/18, I should have done as the half-hearted hospice nurse advised and called 9-1-1; EMS would have relieved my mother's torment. Knowing hospice night shift inadequacies, I wish I always called during day shift. If only I'd weaned my mother off excessive pharmaceuticals with their grueling adverse effects.

I bemoan how my busy-living duties distracted my attention from her busy-dying visions. If I believed her Halloween premonition, I would have held her in my arms, cherished her final moments of conscious life, and soothed her way, piquing her curiosity with questions: "How can you tell it's time, Mom? Who do you see? Is it Dad, Grossmom, Marty?" Watching the film footage of her pending departure, I seek signs. Her voice sounds nonchalant and blithe, quintessential Rosemary. Even so, the video reveals a widening distance between us. While I speak of our next meal, she readies herself for the ultimate exit.

Two months after her death, my mother's abdominal ultrasound results arrive. The findings knock me off my feet, aghast. A prominent pancreatic head indicated inflammation or other abnormalities. Her liver displayed a suspicious speckled pattern. Both kidneys, covered in lesions, exceed the criteria for simple cysts. Malignant neoplasm not excluded. Trivialized and treated as restless agitation, undiagnosed cancer appears the likely cause of her excruciating back pain and bladder issues. What an appalling way for dear Rosemary to die.

To break my guilty ruminations, I contact MedCure for answers, but no autopsy per se was performed. The hospice agency welcomes my suggestions at their group meeting. Members say they don't know how I coped for so long with Rosemary's level of need. I raise the issue of prompt, adequate pain relief. We discuss improvements in after-hours care. Encourage family advocates to join team meetings. Ask caregivers to film unexplained behavior so hospice staff see for themselves and provide appropriate palliative care.

Still plagued by guilt, I try Rosemary's language gymnastics. Think of words that make sense, no matter what vowel is used. My cerebral exercise leads to pit pot pat pet put . . . and dispels my self-flogging. On impulse at the grocery spice aisle, I spot a conciliatory bottle and purchase the six-ounce herb container for its label: "Rosemary leaves."

GRIEF'S GRACE

Rosemary's death leaves contradictory solace and heartache. Tight bonds unravel at their own pace. The angst of loss serves its invaluable purpose as fond and dreadful memories alternate unbidden. Their intensity disrupts routines turned obsolete. The A/C switches on in the night; I startle from sleep to aid my mother. Grief intercedes: Rosemary is gone. Healing continues to adopt a new normalcy. I doze off again, cradled in lullabies my mother sang.

Near-death pioneer Elizabeth Kübler-Ross's stages of grief occur in unpredictable, nonsequential spurts. My professional training as a paramedic, mental health counselor, and Crisis Hotline counselor sketched the basic map of grief. My personal caregiving of precious, dying loved ones painted the vivid, Grand Canyon depth of grief in hues that defy comprehension. I came to realize this: the speed of demise, the depth of the relationship, and its shared impact with others influence how survivors adapt. Sorrow eased as my caregiver fatigue abated, relieved that Rosemary finally rests in peace. A single word strengthened my resolve. The Korean term *Han* has no English interpretation. I first heard it explained on a *West Wing* television episode named after the word.[23] *Han* reconciles intense anguish with far-reaching hope. Losing someone dear brings sorrow too deep for tears. Contradictory grief and relief created whiplash. But *han* looked beyond Rosemary's departure with confidence in her influence on the world and promise of her continued consciousness ever after.

The unexpected death of my brother to brain cancer embedded shards of glass in open-heart wounds. The slow-motion death of Rosemary inflicted pricks of anguish spread over calendars. Whether sudden or drawn out, the promise of eventual "closure" is a myth. Neither the lowering of a solitary coffin nor scattered ashes can prevent ghostly memories, triggered by reminders and milestones. Nor should it. Coming to terms with what once *was*, healing happens in jolts of readjustment. People who knew Rosemary became most important to me. We celebrated her. The same with my brother. Over the years, Marty Parties formed to honor him. Closure would cease the sorrow but also stunt fond memories. Honoring Rosemary affirms her contributions rippling over the world, no big splash.

Rosemary stories filled the void left by her absence. Years of goodbyes had allowed lighthearted Rosey another chance at life. Her glee reminded me of Benoit Mandelbrot's contagious elation when he first discovered fractals.[24] Adults in touch with their unscathed, youthful awe make the world a more pleasant place. With thoughts of peace on Earth, I shared my mother's cinnamon bun recipe. No one ever asked until she died; Aunt Rosie always provided.

Harmony with Nature

For survivors, postmortem care continues beyond bereavement. Existential questions beg for answers. Rosemary seasoned her intuitive reverence for nature with scientific curiosity and religion mysticism. Her insights she penned into poems, stories, and quotables. One parent-to-parent suggestion raised cordial discussions to pithy levels: "To make a person more than whole, first stimulate the sense of soul."

Earning a religious studies degree, I found gratifying connections between scientific empiricism and religious sensibilities. The Law of the Conservation of Matter from classic Greek physics reflects the Sanatana dharma religious concept of śūnya. Misinterpreted as emptiness, it actually means quite the opposite; both reflect complete fulfillment. Nothing disappears; it transforms. Like Rosemary's dementia, as her brain emptied, sneak previews of otherworldly realms literally raised her spirit. As her physical body weighed anchor, her soul set sail. Neither created nor destroyed, matter and energy simply transform.[25] Life could not exist without death. Conception did not create Rosemary, nor did death destroy her. Through death's uncanny passageway, her spirited energy ventured onward, beyond the fringes of understanding.

Worn and torn, all that remained was an empty body, marred by life. Like Rosemary's Tupperware that she had scrawled on in permanent ink, her weathered container once held her vital soul. Death released that essential element, leaving behind her marred, empty container.

Rosemary's gleeful reactions as dementia dipped her toes over the edge of apparent oblivion provided me ample assurance of a joyous afterlife. Described by near-death experiencers, the ultimate homecoming reunifies everyone with all-encompassing Love.

The most misunderstood, watered-down word, *love* is our immortal core. "To love is to fathom infinity," I read on a fortune cookie message, of all places. By any name, if God is love, then that essence of Rosemary is what advanced beyond the grave. Her capacity to love was her transcendent puzzle piece, the biblical "image of God within" and Taoism's

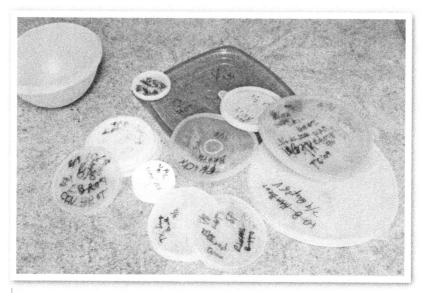

Life leaves indelible marks on our containers

Wu Chi eternal energy. Sacred Upanishads scripture says we are all incarnations of God. The ultimate realm called nirvana in Buddhism and Sanatana Dharma, parallels the heaven of Christianity and Islam, and the comforting afterlife my brother, Martin, called "Hug Heaven." Compassion flexes heart muscles in preparation for afterlife.

Mom was driving a carload of family down South Jersey's Black Horse Pike. I was a teen riding in the back seat. All at once, she pulled to the curb. A speeding car had splashed through a mud puddle and drenched an old Black woman waiting at the bus stop. Mom offered her a ride home, and we all shifted onto laps to make room. During the long, twenty-minute ride to the woman's house, everyone sat in awkward silence. I always wished I'd said something kind, or better yet, funny. Only Rosemary was at ease, confident in her spur-of-the-moment decision.

In Rosemary's mind, leaving that drenched woman would have been a sin, a missed opportunity for human decency. Mom said we create our own hell whenever we fall short. But regardless of misdeeds, her motto was try, try again.

The last line of the Beatles song "The End" sings of love in give-and-take proportions. From thimbleful to buckets, if kindness increases our postmortem transcendence, then Rosemary's cup runneth over. At senior fitness class—an easier-going replacement for Zumba—dancing to Shaggy's "Only Love," I imagine exchanging immortal hugs with my mother, brother, father, and everyone who has passed. Stepping to the beat, the lyrics conjure souls dancing at some hyperspace realm, beyond current comprehension.

AFTERLIFE SPECULATIONS

AS FAR AS THE EYE CAN SEE, AND THEN SOME

Fossil
The body I wear conceals the real me . . .
Years added growth-rings like a tree.
Resin-wrapped over the ages,
now, my amber-embedded mummy
reemerges from carapace.
But in what altered place?
– ROSEMARY, 1983

A MEANINGFUL PANDEMIC COINCIDENCE

HANDWASHING DOZENS OF TIMES a day during our chrysalis time-out for the COVID-19 pandemic, I recalled my mother's October 2018 warning about contagion, handwashing, and covered faces. *Did her addled mind receive premonitions?* A year before the germ-gone-global, it seems Rosemary's departed brain cells opened portals to broadened awareness.

In early 2021, a life-threatening pandemic twist of fate literally took my breath away and enhanced my afterlife perspective. Hours after my first (and last) COVID-19 vaccine, I stopped breathing and became cyanotic. The grueling part of dying was relinquishing my will to breathe. Once I realized breathing was impossible, I mouthed, "I love you," to my terrified husband and waved goodbye. No longer struggling, dying felt exactly like falling asleep, and I came to realize why. The first thing we do upon birth is breathe. From then on, our chest rises and falls without a thought. Breaking that lifelong rhythm is a transformative, material-to-spiritual adjustment. My mother's 1996 "Birthday Blessing" poem prioritizes what matters most, and it isn't death: "Take lots of pleasure from lots of *things*, but mostly savor the *love* life brings."

After being revived by paramedics, their treatment wore off, and I stopped breathing again. They scurried me to one hospital, and then another. Physicians surmised it was an inflammatory autoimmune reaction to the messenger RNA inoculation.

Transient global amnesia (TGA) left me only disjointed memories of the ordeal. Although disappointed to have no near-death recollection of seeing my mom, dad, brother, or anyone past, my glimpse of eternity left me awestruck. Like my mother's lost hand sensation, my TGA occurred while my consciousness was elsewhere, on the far side of death's door.

Afterward, I remained around the bend, slowly reacquainting myself in brief spurts of worldly awareness. I thought our middle-aged son was still a teen. A man I mistook for a TV talk show host (ER remote neurologist) asked the date. I could only recall "lots of twos." Robert says I repeated myself incessantly, in loops—just as Rosemary had done. My poor husband agonized that I might stay that way the rest of my life.

A jaw-dropping headache set in, like my brother's description of his level-ten pain after brain surgery. To endure, I followed his lead and immersed myself in the loving energy I sensed to and from others, both living and dead. Like Marty, despite the physical agony, all was well.

The headache simulated a brick with razor-sharp points rapidly rolling around in my skull, jabbing my Jell-O brain matter. As I recuperated, the brick's tumble cycle slowed, and its points dulled. It then progressed to aseptic meningitis.

I cannot say how long anything lasted. Hours? Days? Months? The medical term for this glimpse of timelessness is dyschronometria. Clocks, calendars, and numbers lost their meaning. Asked when something happened, I stammered. Aphasia left me unable to decipher questions, much less formulate answers. My short-circuited brain threw off mental sparks, but none connected. Dreams and reality meshed. Thinking my brother had died, I was astonished to find it was true. Like Marty, my hearing intensified. Spoon taps on a bowl went through me like an F-35 jet. I had to wear industrial earmuffs. On an amusing note, I heard in harmony. Everything, even my own voice.

MRIs, spinal taps, and two hospitals later, I was released from the COVID-riddled facilities. My wherewithal gradually returned, but life moved too fast for my battered brain to process. Thoughts bounced in my skull like giddy hieroglyphics. This is where pure fascination kicked in. Unable to speak well or keep up with conversations, intense concentration proved exhausting. Futile effort temporarily blew my brain circuits. Thoughts on hold, my consciousness cradled me in waves of utter tranquility that stretched to infinity. I tarried in the biblical (Philippians 4:7) "peace that passeth understanding" I'd sung about in childhood. Truly an indescribably amazing, immortal realm![26]

That pandemic event deepened my insight into life, love, dementia, brain damage, death, and afterlife. I am grateful for enhanced understanding of what my mother and brother went through. Thoughts became more fluid, less often evaporating, the way moisture transforms into clouds. Words sometimes elude me, like Rosemary's lost hand sensation and Aunt Jenny's dress. Irretrievable. And yet, most importantly, *all was well*.

Only scattered memories stuck of 2021 and I continue to adapt. Unable to effectively handle my daily care, I cut off my thigh-length hair. During conversations, my eyes dart trying to keep pace, searching for appropriate responses. Recognizing my brain lapses, Robert jokes, "Pay it no mind," and fills in discussion voids. As I regain my worldly footing, the other-worldly experience dissipates.

By summer 2022—after Russia waged war against its southeastern neighbor—I had recovered sufficiently for us to host a Ukrainian family struggling to learn English. Their eyes scanned the room seeking the right words. I empathized with them . . . and all the more with Rosemary.

Symptoms surface now and then, especially in sundowner evenings. But "sunup syndrome" clears my mind. Death's trial run bestowed gifts. Dying felt familiar, the same path of illness, injury, or simply falling asleep. That magnificent, infinite tranquility that I experienced, I also remembered from infancy. Residual tinnitus, time perplexity, and sensory delays opened peeks into pre-birth/post-life existence. I wonder if the beyond is glimpsed via mathematics and physics in terms of hyperspace. The way warmth subdues cold and compassion overcomes apathy, my vital essence animates my body. Cold, apathy, and death are voids; warmth, compassion, and our loving consciousness are real. Morbidity only exists on this side of death. For now, life holds wonder. Every aspect is miraculous. Said best in this inspired quote of unknown origin: "We are not human beings having a spiritual experience. We are spiritual beings having a human experience."[27]

Out-of-body and near-death experiences (NDEs) assure me that love is eternal. On ever-fewer occasions, I perceive the infinite splendor of cosmic consciousness. Science tracks brain locations where dysfunctions occur; spirituality traces where lost abilities go. Physics explains the physical here and now. Afterlife "spiritics" explains timelessness in terms of infinite, multi-dimensional, loving energy.

My feet planted more firmly in the transient present, I reacclimate. Amazed by life's wonders. Simple things dazzle me: pencils and erasers, conference calls with people across the globe, and lungs that know precisely what to do with air.

A practicality from my pandemic complication occurred to family. If I had died, generations of memorabilia inherited from Rosemary may have ended up at Goodwill. We sent out an APB to relatives.

Six cousins came to collect our ancestral treasures—naturalization papers, twenty-six photo albums dating back to the Civil War era, framed portraits pre-dating World War I, Rosemary's handwritten genealogy . . . all placed in the loving hands of people who adored their auntie. My life simplified, I resolve not to allow possessions to own me.

One near-death detail—too embarrassing to mention until better understood—was seeing my life flash before my eyes. Where others view events, I saw a ridiculous, rapid succession of clothes. It began with infant sleep sacks and knitted booties, then toddler pinafores, and onward to frilly dresses. At this point, I began to recognize outfits made by my mother, Granny, and Aunt Annie. Footwear increased in size from Mary Janes to saddle shoes, then penny loafers. Creolins, camisoles, swimwear, and on to my teen wardrobe. It made no sense; I have little interest in fashion or what is considered vogue. I couldn't imagine the significance of this materialistic runway show.

Then I remembered a foster care caseworker who questioned why I dressed the kids up. It seemed only natural to me. My pandemic ordeal finally answered why. I associated apparel with love. Although many childhood outfits were hand-me-downs from my big sister, every thread contained TLC. Dressing our children, foster children, and later my dying mother was an outward expression of my love for them. Carefully selected, colorful attire proclaimed to the world: "This person is precious."

First breath to last, humanity trods, fellow travelers all. The pandemic fiasco left me with everyone's-in-this-together comfort, the same solidarity I experienced as my brother died just after the 9/11 attacks, and again as my mother died along with Hurricane Michael deforestation. Aging toward death, the climate-altered biosphere aims to put humanity in its place. Mother Earth always nurtures our species' rises and consoles our falls. During worrisome times, Rosemary consoled with the Persian adage, "This too shall pass."

My broadened afterlife view found another upside to death. Along with the decay of our worn-out carcass, flaws wither away. During life, Rosemary embraced others, warts and all. It is gratifying to regard warts—of any kind—as mortal. Confirmed by others' NDE accounts, death vanquishes every imperfection, physical, psychological, and spiritual alike. Regrets, misgivings, bitterness, ineptitudes, and rage disappear forever. In cleansing waves, Rosemary's strokes washed away her blunders and self-condemnation until none survived.

OH MOTHER, WHERE ART THOU?

Rosemary once said, "Scrape the gray matter, and people usually discover their covert, philosophical itch." While life grounds us, broader awareness catches our attention time and again. Deaths of my mother and brother, along with my near-death, pandemic experience, left me scratching my head in amazement over what awaits. Like dandelion seeds on the wind that know not their destination, my spirit soars.

Afterlife speculations of Rosemary, my brother, and I follow as springboards for conversation. Connecting the dots, I see those living in the twenty-first century as pioneers, on the cusp of a major paradigm shift. Expanding comprehension is coming to recognize consciousness as immortal. *Until now*, science dismissed afterlife prospects as unreliable, unverifiable, and lacking in empirical evidence. Likewise, fundamentalist orthodoxies have discounted NDE details that threaten church authority. Now, serious NDE research is springing up throughout the world—such as compiled in the Bigelow Institute papers and affirmed by the spiritual enlightenment of NDEs, even fervent atheists and naysayer physicians. Although details vary, all have this in common: bodily life is mortal; consciousness—also known as the spirit, our loving energy, the image of God within—is eternal.

Dandelions: Winds of Change" by Christy Draper

After my cousin Eddie drowned at age four, I kept my thoughts about death to my six-year-old self. Busy living, it was easy to deflect my fears of being buried in a box like Eddie, or incinerated into ashes like Aunt Pearl, or—the ultimate dogmatic dread—eternally burned in hell for infractions. Following adult examples, I learned to take every breath for granted, my mortality relegated to some distant future.

Now, thanks to the combination of NDEs, social media, and a personal pandemic eye-opener, I have come to recognize death as nature's passageway to the magnificent beyond. Questioning life's meaning, I find answers in sneak previews. Seasonal changes, metamorphoses, connect-the-dots coincidences, and gorgeous fractal patterns piece together a mosaic of infinite beauty. Rejuvenating sleep provides nightly rehearsals for dying. Laws of physics assure me that, upon death, our mortal bodies enrich the soil and nourish the trees while our immortal consciousness continues onward. Clues abound for what became of Rosemary, and what awaits us all.

For linguist Noam Chomsky, language is humanity's distinguishing feature.[28] Words capture ideas. They share kindness, fling accusations, or ponder questions. Vocabulary corrals experiences, emotions, and thoughts, thus expanding imaginations to unknown realms of other planets, alternate dimensions, and afterlife. Rosemary's observations between worlds lacked empirical answers. Even so, the tension created intrigue, weaving a thread of thrill through her final years. Farther back, in April 2003, Mom wrote to me about her vivid sense of "awareness, too often in fleeting moments, before blundering along in the stream of goings-on." By necessity, communication efforts anchor us to life. According to NDE survivors, the post-life realm's wordless telepathy eliminates misunderstanding.

Linguist and priest Paul van Buren devised a clever model of language that puts afterlife speculations in their place.[29] Van Buren saw common words as central, readily defined for everyday use. Expressions more subject to interpretation are farther from the core. Indescribable experiences surpass the bounds of language. During brief *Rosemary moments* of ineffable comprehension, her transcendent experiences fell "over the edge" into inexpressible wordlessness.

To wrap my head around van Buren's concept, I found my brother's old Frisbee and labeled it with the language model to toss the idea around, literally and figuratively. Simple words with consensus clarity appear on the disc's center, words like "chair," "book," and "house." Words more subject to interpretation like "love," "superstring theory," "home," and those my mom and I devised during Scrabble games, balance along the Frisbee edge. "God" names and death euphemisms such as "deceased," "mortal," "dearly departed," and "afterlife" express awareness over the rim of comprehension. Feet on the ground, thoughts reach out to catch incomprehensible experiences with words—like those of my mom with dementia, my brother's post-death "Hug Heaven," and my pandemic NDE. The language Frisbee has become my model of existence. A mortal life disc, beyond its edges is the immortal pre-birth/post-death realm.

Closing in on death, Rosemary struggled with language. Organized thought gave way. Pre-stroke Rosemary had a rational approach to jigsaw puzzles. She linked edges, then grouped by color, themes, and shapes. Each stroke eliminated steps as her perception broadened beyond mortal boundaries. Dementia vanquished her urge to organize. Classifications became superfluous. Last to go was the sense of negative and positive space, vital to fitting round-pegged nubs into appropriate holes. Instead, she ran her hands through the mounds. Simply holding a piece between her thumb and forefinger, she marveled at its singularity. "Life zips by," said Rosemary. "We must pause in appreciation, lest we miss it."

Death's bad reputation comes from the transition from material to spiritual existence. Grief and dust-to-dust bodily decay magnify fears. Middle-aged Rosemary buried our dead dog Charlie under the oak tree, watered with her tears. Yet fond memories of the wag-tail pooch continued to greet us. A decade later, working as a paramedic and an assistant to the local medical examiner put me face-to-face with post-death decomposition on *this* side. What sharp contrast to sublime near-death survivors' descriptions of an entryway rather than a trap door. The growing NDE volume provides rational expectations for a splendid afterlife. Our body simply sheds, the way lizards leave spent skin. Old flesh sloughs off, like worn-out clothes, says the Dalai Lama.[30] We are more than organic matter wandering around in bags of flesh. The rough part is the coming and going, as Rosemary did repeatedly.

Years ago in the hospital corridor, a patient located me by my paramedic uniform and thanked me for reviving him from cardiac arrest. He said dying was hard, but death was a breeze. It left him fearless, fulfilled, and curious. From his pocket, he pulled a golf ball, bounced it on the floor, and headed off to meet with friends on the course, his eyes open for purposeful pursuits until his final fatality.

CURIOSITY

At a 1990s New Orleans conference on autism, keynote speaker Temple Grandin—the renowned Colorado State professor of animal science—told how cows' curiosity overcomes their fear. In a circuitous manner, Grandin's research opened a path for creative dying. Curiosity led awestruck Rosemary onward in wonder.

Drawn by curiosity, even staunch sciences and radical faiths find it hard to resist the enigma of NDEs. But no one needs to be an expert or devout follower to appreciate contributions of both approaches. Under the spell of dementia, Rosemary no longer "churned the hours away in a rut of routine, hoping for a smooth existence, and not useless clabber." Fascination led her onward.

Quantum mechanics researchers at Max Planck Institute for Physics in Munich concurred that after bodies die, the soul continues in the infinite beyond. Here and now is just at the material level, according to Hans-Peter Dürr.[31] Life's punchline is that we cannot know firsthand what's on the other side until our time comes. Until then, we decide for ourselves what constitutes reasonable conjecture or mere wishful thinking. DNA from our parents coupled with personal experiences forges our unique outlook. Life's adventure would be pointless if everyone agreed on everything. Each person's perspective counts. Natural world mysteries sparked Rosemary's afterlife curiosity.

When my cousin Eddie died, I eavesdropped on adults discussing death and "the naked truth." At age six, my conjecture envisioned God taking a shower in a claw-foot tub, surrounded by a circular, opaque curtain full of pinholes. Each of my relatives could only spy through one hole, peeping into mysteries not meant for view. Similar to the story of blind men describing an elephant from their limited vantage points, the Naked Truth remained unfathomable. The only way toward understanding is to share perspectives. Death notions vary as much as the people who form them. Sharing promotes comfort and awe.

> End-of-life speculations form from our unique experiences. Listening to NDE survivor stories, I anticipate continued existence with past loved ones, colors beyond the rainbow's palette, and ancient trees like the one in James Cameron's 2009 movie *Avatar*. The greatest graduation gift will be understanding life's meaning. A Hebrew proverb says infants know the secrets of the universe until the angel Gabriel kisses newborns' foreheads, and they forget upon birth.[32] NDEs assure that the clarity left behind at birth reawakens upon death. At long last, we'll comprehend the Big Picture. Everything makes perfect sense again, to Rosemary and all who have died.

Our linear perception of time serves the lifelong practical purpose of keeping things from happening all at once. "Now" and "then" rivet our consciousness to living. Is afterlife timeless? Ironically, only time will tell. As the end nears, convenient clocks and calendars lose their sway. A few weeks before Einstein's death in 1955, he recognized time as an apparition, writing that the distinction between past, present, and future is only a stubbornly persistent illusion.[33]

Approaching death, Rosemary described glimpses of infinity and recognized herself as all ages at once. "Now I'm four and full of playful spunk. I'm also an old broad, looking forward."

Self-identity, another lifelong condition, puts us at odds with one another. After my father's death, Mom lost her role as a wife and signed a postcard to me, "Mom, Rose, whoever." Western culture places great emphasis on individuality. In contrast, the Japanese word for "self," *jibun*, meaning "shared life space" reflects interconnected balance between self and others, crucial to social harmony.[34] This broader view[35] permeates my preverbal memories. As a baby, I did not distinguish between myself and my big, two-years-older sister until I learned to talk.

Entering and departing life, functional MRIs of infants and elders with dementia find evidence of a broader sense of identity.[36] At her beginning and end, young Rosey and ninety-year-old Rosemary spoke of her expansive quintessence. Throughout life, due to our one-of-a-kind DNA and experiences, unique differences take root. Even so, we yearn for togetherness, to mind-meld and see eye-to-eye in that forgotten interconnectedness that Plato called "unus mundus," Teilhard de Chardin's "noosphere."[37] Longing to belong draws people together in friendship, marriage, and community, echoes of our spiritual interdependence.[38]

THE CYCLE OF LIFE

Western and Eastern religions bump heads over the concept of rein-carnation—the Divine recycling of souls in birth/life/death succession. Religious followers who anticipate a final judgement reject the idea, while those able to recall past lives accept the natural cycle. The thought of Rosey reborn cheers me. But reincarnation also appeals to me for less honorable reason. As a coping strategy, I fantasize deplorable people reincarnated as rocks, with ample time to reconsider their woeful ways. Loathsome lifestyles call for rock reincarnation time-out, not as punitive, but for extensive contemplation.

Rocks contain Earth's stories,[39] a fine place to set a spell for reflection, reincarnated or not. On occasion, I too need time-out as a rock to recollect myself. Reflective breaks—*yutori* in Japanese—soothe troubled hearts and curtail misconduct. Reincarnation, time-out, or a quick breather all provide chances to reestablish our balance. Done well, compassion extends to every person, pebble, and mountain.

ROSEMARY'S AFTERLIFE THOUGHTS

Rosemary's final words, "factoid years," beg deciphering. This side of death, reality jumbles into piled jigsaw puzzle pieces with only hints of the Big Picture. I take comfort in neurotheology research that shows as life concludes, pieces fall into place and understanding expands.[40] A 2023 study found evidence of heightened "conscious-like" brain activity at the time of death.[41] Losing her grip on fragmented factoids of living, my mother's awareness broadened. Her eyes opened to a simple truth: Death is an illusion. On the hereafter side of death's portal, Rosemary as a whole is greater than the sum of her parts.

From the game closet, I dust off our Scrabble lid. Inside, I add definitions to my mom's mystery 10/18 words, based on her final phrase, "factoid years." Rosemary's incongruous word *gemtricks* means life's illusions, the jokes reality plays. And her term *gemfree* means the sweeping bliss of death as it releases our gem-like, loving consciousness—the image of God within—from the factoid years of our lifetime.

A major influence on Rosemary's concept of afterlife grew from her sense of alienation, being far younger than her sisters and shunned by her brothers. Rosemary empathized with alienated people. She experienced the loneliness of isolation in third grade. Awkwardly aware of her exceptional wisdom, she deemed her esoteric intellect "impractical." Family gatherings eliminated such barriers; everyone connected without exception. Reunions formed Rosemary's spiritual cathedral, a place of unbreakable bonds that anchored her afterlife beliefs.[42] Approaching death, egocentrism lost its hold as her comprehension of who's who transformed into us all.

"Is your mother okay, Chris?" she asked me about herself.

Vantage points on post-death existence (or nonexistence) vary person-to-person. Rosemary's view of death found the notion of a period at the end of life's sentence incongruous. For her, the belief that life is the totality of existence is self-limiting.

"We are more than coincidental chemistry and random neurological patterns," Rose stated once while debating an ardent nihilist.

Her afterlife view developed from premonitions and mystical experiences of her dead Grossmom, then expanded with her out-of-body dementia travels. Connecting the dots of my mother's life, her yearning to belong painted her post-death vision of a happily-ever-after reunion.

Like an ancient tree growing in rich Jersey soil, Rosemary's afterlife beliefs were rooted in nature. Awe-inspired by Thoreau and Emerson, walks through the forest assured her of purposeful energy at work. Nature's counterbalancing persists in creation/destruction, evolution/ entropy, isolation/unity.

"All-consuming black holes surely lead to ever-evolving white holes," Rosemary deduced. The fabric of existence that interconnects yin and yang complements applies to us, no less than anything else. Physicist Brian Greene calls the constant negotiations of kindness/ indifference, generosity/greed, birth/death, "the entropic two-step"[43] (although "evolution/entropy two-step" sounds more balanced). When awful things happened, Rosemary found comfort in the idea that, and I quote, "Everything comes back into balance eventually, whether or not we witness it in our lifetime."

At a visceral level, she interpreted the physics theory of *entanglement* in terms of compassion. Mom and I agreed that the German-to-English translation of the word "entanglement" was flawed. Conversations with our German friends—artist Stephan Scherer[44] and physician Karl Michael Dürr (son of Munich's Max Plunck Institute for Physics president, Hans-Peter Dürr)[45]—convinced us that "enfolded" or "intertwined" elicits better understanding of the dynamics. In terms of relationships, love thrives regardless of separation, even beyond the grave. Everything is interrelated. "Heaven"—by any name—opens its symbolic pearly gates to all.

MARTY'S AFTERLIFE THOUGHTS

After my mother's death, I began cleaning out her garage, shredding old tax and medical records. The last bin rewarded my tedious work. The plastic, snap-lid container held decades of cards and letters, a treasure trove of personal exchanges with loved ones. Rummaging through her keepsake correspondences, I found a 1980 birthday card to her from my brother Marty that convinced me of the wholesome effect afterlife speculations can have on a person's outlook. He expressed enchantment over a movie he saw at the International Tournée Animation in Philadelphia. I located the film, *Sunbeam*, on YouTube. Hearing the lighthearted theme song, "What's at the Top of a Sunbeam," I immediately realized Marty had kept it stored in his subconscious as his metaphor for death. Three decades later, diagnosed with terminal brain cancer, he envisioned death as depicted in the film, climbing a golden ladder to a high dive and jumping off. It's doubtful he recalled the song's influence. Marty told me that, although the leap would be scary, he was confident it would be joyful. Filed away in my brother's brain, the alluring depiction resurfaced when the time arrived for him to vacate his body.

Discovering what prompted Marty's view of death, puzzle pieces fell into place for me. The revelation from that old birthday card granted me absolution. While my brother blunged toward death, my paramedic skills helped ease his way. The best parting gift I had to offer him under horrific circumstances was medical care, a practical expression of love.

MY AFTERLIFE THOUGHTS

Marty's death metaphor inspired me to consider how my own views of death and afterlife took shape. The pandemic ordeal, my paramedic career, out-of-body adventures like those my mother conveyed, mathematics of advanced dimensions, and near-death experiences fused with my broad religious, scientific, and cultural understandings. Interdenominational churches our parents sent us kids to on Sundays put love central in my mind. And clever sci-fi television programs like the first *Outer Limits* episode "One Step Beyond,"[46] with its spine-tingling theremin accompaniment to unexplained mysteries, and Rod Serling's *Twilight Zone* introduction put positive spins on curious phenomena. Intrigue, not fear, tops my sundae of unanswered afterlife questions.

My metaphor for afterlife tilts Einstein's theory of special relativity in a metaphysical direction. E=mc2 in plain English means energy (E) equals mass (m) going really fast (c2, the conversion factor for the speed of light squared). I imagine our pre-birth /post-death spirits as pure energy unconstrained by material existence. Slowed to an infinitesimal speed brings us into a state of bodily mass, the measure of our living being. Rather than projectors, our brains are receivers of energy signals. Slow motion heightens detailed awareness.

One such intense recollection during my paramedic years was when a truck totaled my ambulance. Rendering aid to a critical patient en route to the hospital, my adrenaline was already high. Topped off with the crash that broke my neck, vivid slow-motion memories hearken back to Einstein's equation. Increased adrenaline raised the amount of memory tape my brain used to record great detail. During life, we experience the nature of existence, sometimes with meticulous acuity.

Reading through my mother's poems, essays, and short stories, I realize *she* is the primary inspiration for my concepts of life, death, and afterlife. Although non-religious in any formal, church member sense, Rosemary acquired what Oxford philosophy poet David Whyte calls "spirituality by osmosis."[47] Like Longfellow and Muir, she recognized God in nature. Akin to the Dalai Lama's teachings,[48] kindness was her religion. And as theologian Paul Tillich defined God,[49] Rosemary's self-transcendent reverence for nature was the ground of all being. Unconditional love was her highest aspiration.

My mother's poems, essays, and short stories instilled me with abiding faith in human virtue and curiosity life's mysteries. In "Home" (1950s) and "Reunion Dream" (1986), she portrayed the afterlife as a serene gathering of family and friends. "It's Settled" (1991) pondered what to do with a corpse. "Fossil" (1983), "Metamorphosis" (1984), "Energy Eternal" (circa 2000), and "Recycling Eternal" (2013) mused over reincarnation and the physics of death. "Aging" (1988) contemplated spiritual revelations and out-of-body travel. Most gratifying to me, "Endless Churning" (1979) and "Dichotomy" (1991) envisioned love eternal. Rather than an absolutist authoritarian—as portrayed in the childhood story, "The Emperor's New Clothes"—the Naked Truth depicted in Rosemary's writing takes compassionate shape by sharing our viewpoints with one another. "God" *is* love.

AFTERLIFE INTRIGUE

The notion of death as oblivion suggests that humanity somehow evades basic laws of physics. Corroborated by a vast sea of NDE survivors, out-of-body experiences (OBEs) remind us that we exist without the confines of our physical flesh and bones. Back in eighth grade, my enthralled science teacher, Mr. Peterson, shared his fascination with Earth: "The Water Planet." Life-sustaining H_2O changes from ice, to liquid, to vapor, similar to the way our soul transforms from pre-birth, to life, to afterlife. Rosemary did not dissolve into nothingness. Her loving soul, and the souls of everyone past, continue in spirit. Death occurs like the ancient Tao master, Zhuangzi's dream: Just when the world seemed about to end, the caterpillar became a butterfly.[50]

Reality is overrated; sanity is a shallow trade-off. Rosemary did not "lose" her marbles; they migrated to eternity, ahead of her. Losing touch with her faculties gained her awareness of the realm from whence we come and go. She described her absent hand sensation as existing elsewhere, in a remarkable state of options.

I still sense glimpses of eternity's peaceful repose, but to a lesser degree as I regain functional footing. Rather than allow the incessant drone of residual tinnitus to pull a Smetana on me (i.e., the classical composer whose tragic deafness drove him mad), I imagine the electric hum as inadvertent eavesdropping on indecipherable, higher dimension chatter. Reminiscent of the Wildwood boardwalk mirror maze during my childhood, standing between front-and-back mirrors, my reflections stretch endlessly backward pre-birth and eternally forward post-death. Knocked for a loop by the COVID-19 ordeal, I comprehend love as an endless past reaching through me in the present and on into the future, forever.

Neither a unified field theory nor God can be pinned down with human language as if a noun, an object, or an entity. It's life's conundrum. The biggest questions remain unanswerable while in the throes of living. Regardless of what religious path we follow, if any, personalized quality afterlife allegories serve a purpose. My brother's golden ladder, my E=mc2 twist, and my mother's family reunion ever-after—depicted in Rosemary's customized Paradiso collage—ease the way when death ushers us onward.

From our first breath to our final exhale, momentous opportunities abound. Some nights at 2:00 a.m.—Rosemary's time of death—I look at the moon and practice Irish Aunt Sarah's bedtime tradition. Hands clenched, knuckles together, I tip my head in eternal awe and bid my mother a fond farewell . . . until we meet again.

*"Paradiso" 1868. Wood engraving. Gustave Doré (France, 1832–1883)
Published in Dante Alighieri's The Divine Comedy, Purgatory
& Paradise, Paradise Canto XXXI.*
(Superimposed with Rosemary's departed loved ones)

GIVING ROSEMARY
THE LAST WORD
"SHE STRIVED TO
BE PRACTICAL"

ROSEMARY TOOK HER VERBAL INTELLECT, lyrical heart, and extraordinary perception in stride, as inconsequential diversions from basic necessities. In her estimation, she lacked practicality. She most admired common sense, a dominant trait of her husband.

Herman knew his limitations and navigated within those parameters. Happening upon a traffic accident, he directed traffic until the police arrived. One summer at her parent's Avalon, New Jersey home, he spotted a rat at the entry, grabbed a stone, and knocked it dead from fifty feet away. Rosemary's face lit up whenever she shared stories of his sensible wherewithal.

My mother's smarts elbowed her in ethereal directions that she considered superfluous. Try as she might to plant her feet on solid ground,

Rosemary's consciousness soared. Hence, she penned this epitaph for herself: "She strived to be practical." Blind to her worth, she could not see the power her words had to pierce reality and lift spirits above the daily fray. Her cathartic presence held soul-mending sensibility. Thus, in the spirit of Socratic pragmatism, Rosemary's influence earned her a rightful place among the practical.

Reaching her sixties, "the end is nigh" took on a personal validity after my dad's death. Talk about practicality, she wrote her own eulogy. The love it shares abolishes all distinctions between now and then. Placed here, Rosemary gets the last word.

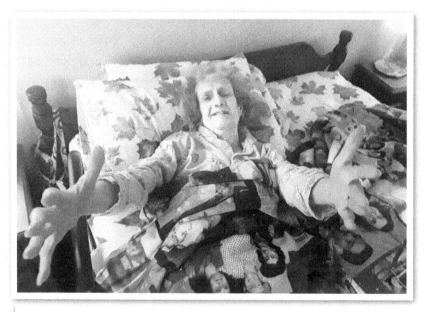

"Hugs are great because they're reciprocal."

DICHOTOMY

I don't mind. I don't mind
all the cares I'll leave behind.
Relationships that cause such stress.
Which course to follow's just a guess.
Needs to meet for all these souls.
Sorting problems, assets, goals.
Pain of spirit, body pain.
Leaving gives me much to gain.

But I will mind, I will mind
challenges I'll leave behind.
Folks I love and care about.
Helping some to sort things out.
The down that always swings to up.
To best the pain, just drain its cup.

So please don't mind. Don't you mind
when I've left you all behind.
Because, somehow, it all persists.
The troubles, triumphs, endless lists.
And though I go and long am gone,
for mine, my glow of love goes on.

APPENDIX

ROSEMARY'S RECIPE FOR CINNAMON BUNS

ROSEMARY'S SIGNATURE BUNS warmed many hearts over her 85+ years of baking. What better way to conclude than to pass on the tradition to readers who have now become acquainted with her? Optional extras and the directions she gave her children are included. For example, first gather all ingredients (in **bold** print for easy reading) to be sure nothing is missing. Line them up on the counter in order. Put each container away once used. Make your buns special by choosing whatever options you prefer. If you improvise, write it down in case it turns out delicious. Read the entire recipe before beginning. Several steps can be done in advance. Yields 16 to 24 buns, depending on width of cuts.

SWEET DOUGH WET INGREDIENTS:

- ½ cup **milk**, scalded
- 5 Tablespoons **sugar**
- 2 teaspoons **salt**
- 4 Tablespoons **butter**
- 1 envelope of **yeast** (expiration date matters)

- ½ cup warm **water**
- 1 tsp **sugar**
- 1 large **egg**

Sweet Dough Dry Ingredients:

- 3½ cups all-purpose **flour** (extra for dusting)
- (optional ¼ cup **nut meal**, replacement for ¼ cup flour)
- 1 teaspoon **nutmeg**
- 2 teaspoons **baking powder**
- (optional 1 teaspoon **cream of tartar**)
- (optional 1 teaspoon ground **cardamom**)
- Zest of 1 medium **lemon** (or **orange**)

Optional Ingredients:

- 2 cups of **fruit** (orange rind, lemon rind, fresh ginger, raisins, dried cherries)
- Fruit **marinade:**1 cup of coconut milk, orange juice, or cream sherry *Refrigerate dried fruits in jar of marinade overnight. On baking day, heat in saucepan until reduced (liquid evaporates). Cool. Reserve best ones for topping.*
- 1 cup cranberries
  (Note: Prepare fresh cranberries in advance, Jersey style. Cut each in half. Place in cool water. Pour off water to remove floating seeds. Repeat until no more seeds surface. Dry well. Freeze on cookie sheet. Transfer into freezer bag. Store in freezer for convenience whenever desired.)

Spread:

- 1 stick **butter**, melted
- (optional 1 Tablespoon **molasses** or **butterscotch schnapps**)
- 2 Tablespoons **sugar**

- 2 Tablespoons **cinnamon**
- 1 cup favorite **nuts, pecans, walnuts,** or **roasted almond** pieces
- **Topping:** two 9" square pans, two 9" round pans, or one 13"x 9" pan
- 1 stick **butter**
- 1 cup **brown sugar**
- (optional best-looking **fruits** and **nuts**)
- Dash of **water** or **maple syrup**

SWEET DOUGH INSTRUCTIONS:

1. Scald milk in saucepan. Melt in sugar, salt, and butter.

2. Remove from heat and set aside to cool.

3. Dissolve yeast in ½ cup water, lukewarm. Also set aside.

4. In large bowl, mix together all sweet dough dry ingredients.

5. In separate bowl, beat egg into bloomed yeast mixture. Add to cooled milk mixture.

6. Combine wet ingredients with dry to form dough. Knead 5–8 minutes until dough becomes smooth and elastic. Place in buttered bowl. Oil top. Cover with moist tea towel. Set in warm, not hot, oven to rise for an hour or two (or refrigerate up to three days in advance).

Roll and fill dough:

7. Dust flat surface with nutmeal or flour. Turn dough onto surface and dust top. Using a rolling pin, roll dough ¼ flat into a rectangle.

8. Melt butter (add optional molasses or butterscotch schnapps). Brush melted butter over entire dough surface to edges. Sprinkle cinnamon and sugar evenly, covering entire surface.

9. Reserve best fruit and nuts for topping. Scatter diced nuts and well-drained fruit evenly over dough. Roll dough onto itself

forming a tight snake. Tuck ends in to secure ingredients. Stretch and coax into an even width.

Topping (like Upside-Down Cake, the pan bottom becomes top)

10. Melt one stick of butter into baking pan. If using two pans, evenly distribute ingredients. Heat brown sugar into butter until dissolved. Add just enough water to disperse mixture evenly by tilting the pan. Arrange reserved best-looking fruits and nuts in pan bottom(s).

Slice and Bake

11. If using two pans, cut dough roll in half. Cut into even slices. Gently place buns into each pan, best side down and barely touching. Cover pan(s) with moist tea towel and place in warm (not hot) oven. Allow to rise until buns merge and cover pan bottom (one to three hours). Bake at 350 degrees for 30 minutes.

12. Share with those you love.

Share with those you love

BIBLIOGRAPHY

Beatles. "The End." *Abbey Road*. Apple Records, 1969.

Bitmango. Word Cookies! (Seongnam, South Korea: BitMango, 2016), video game.Berwick, Robert and Chomsky, Noam. *Why Only Us: Language and Evolution*. (Cambridge, MA: Mit Press, 2015).

Brown, Brené. "Strong Back, Soft Front, Wild Heart." *On Being*. National Public Radio. January 5, 2020.

Brown, Alice Cooke. "Six-Foot Lobsters and Foot-Long Oysters in the 17th Century." In *Early American Herb Recipes*. New York: Bonanza Book, 1966.

Burnford, Sheila. *The Incredible Journey*, 70. Boston: Little, Brown and Company, 1960.

Center for Disease Control and Prevention. "Leading Causes of Death." Accessed May 11, 2024. https://www.cdc.gov/nchs/fastats/leading-causes-of-death.html.

Coles, Robert; Komp, Diane; and Dittberner, Carol. "Children and God." (On Being with Krista Tippet, December 16, 2004) Accessed June 22, 2024, https://onbeing.org/programs/robert-coles-diane-komp-and-carol-dittberner-children-and-god/.

Dalai Lama, "The Dalai Lama describes the process of death." (Interview with Justin Brown, July 18, 2019 IdeaPod) Accessed July 3, 2024. https://ideapod.com/dalai-lama-explains-happens-die-can-prepared/.

Desu, Suki . "Translation and Meaning of 自分 (Jibun). Accessed June 23, 2024, https://skdesu.com › en.

Dürr, Karl Michael (emergency physician, son of Hans-Peter Dürr), discussion in Shalimar, FL, June 30, 2024.

Earle, Alice Morse. *Home Life in Colonial Days.* Chapter V: Food from Forest and Sea, 108-125. (Mass: Berkshire Traveller Press,1898, e-text 1974, 118). Accessed June 20, 2024, https://www.gutenberg.org/files/22675/22675-h/22675-h.htm

Elder, Jeff . "An 'Eskimo Kiss' is a Kunik, and Maybe Not What You Think." SouthCoast Today: Lifestyle. Accessed July 1, 2024, https://www.southcoasttoday.com/article/20050216/LIFE/302169966.

Ethereal theme. "A Year with Rilke," January 1, 2012, line 14 [Rainer Marie Rilke, "Earth, Isn't This What You Want?" *Ninth Duino Elegy, 1919*] Powered by Blogger. Accessed July 1, 2024, https://yearwithrilke.blogspot.com/2011/06/earth-isnt-this-what-you-want.html.

Gang Xu, Temenuzhka Mihaylova, Duan Li, Jimo Borjigin. "Surge of Neurophysiological Coupling and Connectivity of Gamma Oscillations in the Dying Human Brain," PNAS (Processing of the National Academy of Sciences, U.S.A.), May 1, 2023, 120 (19) e2216268120, Accessed July 1, 2024. https://doi.org/10.1073/pnas.2216268120

Greene, Brian. *Until the End of Time*. New York: Penguin Random House, 2020.

Hoffman, Donald. "The Case Against Reality." ZDoggMD, July 1, 2024. Podcast 1:52:39, Accessed July 1, 2024, 7:06-18:21, https://www.youtube.com/watch?v=dd6CQCbk2ro.

HuffPost, "Seven Cultures that Celebrate Aging and Respect their Elders." Life section, From Our Partners, Accessed July 1, 2024, https://www.huffpost.com/entry/what-other-cultures-can-teach_n_4834228

Kaplan, Robert. *The Nothing That Is: A Natural History of Zero*. Oxford: Oxford University Press, 1999.

Kent, Rockwell. The Complete Works of William Shakespeare, 743, "Hamlet" Act 1, scene 5. (Garden City, NY: Garden City Books, 1936).

Kimmerer, Robin Wall. *Gathering Moss: A Natural and Cultural History of Mosses*. Corvallis: Oregon State University Press, 2003.

Manning, Christel. "Facing Death without Religion: Secular Sources like Science Work Well for Meaning Making." *Harvard Divinity Bulletin: Beyond the Nones* (Autumn/Winter 2019): https://bulletin.hds.harvard.edu/facing-death-without-religion/

Martin, Sean. "Life after Death: Soul Continues on a Quantum Level—Scientists Reveal." Express. August 21, 2018, Accessed July 4, 2024, https://www.express.co.uk/news/science/1005845/life-after-death-what-happens-when-you-die-soul-quantum.

Meier, Basha. "The Hongi: Ritual and Ceremony in Everyday Life." New Earth University, NZ: New Earth. Accessed July 1, 2024, https://newearth.media/hongi-ritual-ceremony-everyday-life-new-zealand-traditional-maori-greeting/.

Millay, Edna St. Vincent "Renascence," *Collected Poems* (New York: Harper and Row, 1956, 12, lines 179–180)

Newberg, Andrew. "Spiritual Brain: Science and Religious Experience." *Great Courses*, No. 1682, 2012, DVD.

Paneru, Dilip; Cohen, Eliahu; Fickler, Robert; Boyd, Robert W.; and Karimi, Ebrahim. "Entanglement: Quantum or Classical?" November 6, 2019. Accessed July 4, 2024. https://arxiv.org/pdf/1911.02201.

Powers, Richard. Overstory. New York: W.W. Norton & Company, 2018, 320.

Putnam, Adam. "Agricultural Damages due to Hurricane Michael." *Capital Soup*. November 90, 2018. Accessed June 25, 2024, https://capitalsoup.com/2018/11/09/commissioner-adam-putnam-announces-estimated-1-5-billion-in-agricultural-damages-due-to-hurricane-michael/.

Quote Investigator. "We Are Not Human Beings Having a Spiritual Experience. We are Spiritual Beings Having a Human Experience." A quote often attributed to Pierre Teilhard de Chardin, the only found source is in motivational speaker Wayne W. Dyer's 1988, "A Letter to the Next Generation," (June 20, 2019) Accessed July 4, 2024. https://quoteinvestigator.com/2019/06/20/spiritual/.

Rilke, Rainer Marie. "Earth, Isn't This What You Want?" In *Ninth Duino Elegy* (line 14). 1919.

Scherer, Stephan J.M. (artist), discussion during Jarogera exhibition, Burgfarrnbach Castle, Fürth, Germany, August 11, 2000.

Shaggy. "Only Love." *Only Love*. (RED Associated Labels, 2015.)

Sorkin, Aaron. *The West Wing*. Season 5, episode 4, "Han." Directed by Christopher Misiano, performances by Martin Sheen, Peter Noah, and Paula Yoo. Aired October 22, 2003 on NBC, Warner Bros. Television.

Stevens, Leslie, director. "The Galaxy Being." *The Outer Limits*, season 1, episode 1, aired September 16, 1963, Daystar Productions.

Tandon, Ajay, Christopher J.L. Murray, Jeremy A. Lauer, and David B. Evans. "Measuring Overall Health System Performance for 191 Countries." World Health Organization, 2021. https://f.hubspotusercontent20.net/hubfs/2325471/Inspectorio_Dec2021/pdf/paper30.pdf.

Taylor, Jill Bolte. *My Stroke of Insight*. New York: Plume Books, 2008.

Tennant, Andy, director. *Ever After*. Produced by Mirelle Soria & Tracey Trench. Performed by Drew Barrymore. (Los Angeles: 20th Century Fox, 1998 film).

Tillich, Paul. My Search for Absolutes, 127. (New York: Simon & Schuster, 1967).

Van Buren, Paul. *The Edges of Language: An Essay in the Logic of Religion*. New York: Macmillan Company, 1972.

Whyte, David. "Seeking Language Large Enough." *On Being*, NPR radio (0:27 & 25:20-26:21), May 26, 2022 (50:34). Accessed website July 1, 2024 https://onbeing.org/programs/david-whyte-seeking-language-large-enough/.

Zeh, H. Dieter. The Physical Basis of the *Direction of Time*, (Springer-Verlag, Berlin and New York, 1989, Section: Epilogue, Quote, 149).

ENDNOTES

INTRODUCTION

1   Center for Disease Control and Prevention, "Leading Causes of Death." Accessed May 11, 2024. https://www.cdc.gov/nchs/fastats/leading-causes-of-death.htm.

STROKE 1: BACKWARD IN STEP, STANCE, AND STYLE

2   Alice Cooke Brown, "Six Foot Lobsters and Foot Long Oysters in the 17th Century," *Early American Herb Recipes*, (New York: Bonanza Book, 1966),105.

STROKE 4: THE CHILD WITHIN

3   ZDoggMD, "Donald Hoffman: The Case Against Reality," YouTube video, July 1, 2024, 7:06-18:21, https://www.youtube.com/watch?v=dd6CQCbk2ro.

STROKE 5: THE PIZZA RESUSCITATION

4   Ajay Tandon, Christopher J.L. Murray, Jeremy A. Lauer, and David B. Evans, "Measuring Overall Health System Performance for 191 Countries," World Health Organization, 2021, https://f.hubspotuser-content20.net/hubfs/2325471/Inspectorio_Dec2021/pdf/paper30.pdf

5   Sheila Burnford, *The Incredible Journey*, (Boston: Little, Brown and Company, 1960), 70.

6   Rockwell Kent, *The Complete Works of William Shakespeare*, "Hamlet," Act 1, scene 5, (Garden City, NY: Garden City Books, 1936).

7   Jill Bolte Taylor, *My Stroke of Insight* (New York: Plume Books, 2008).

CHAPTER 5-B: R.I.P. POSTPONED

8   *Ever After*, directed by Andy Tennant, director (Los Angeles: 20th Century Fox, 1998), film.

9   Lorenzo and Ruth, "Earth, Isn't This What You Want?" line 14 of *Ninth Duino Elegy* (1919), *A Year with Rilke,* blog, accessed July 1, 2024, https://yearwithrilke.blogspot.com/2011/06/earth-isnt-this-what-you-want.html.

10   Edward Moore, "Origen of Alexandria (185-254 C.E.)," Internet Encyclopedia of Philosophy, accessed July 4, 2024, https://iep.utm.edu/origen-of-alexandria/.

STROKE 6: BREATHTAKING, WE HATH A THOLE

11   "Seven Cultures that Celebrate Aging and Respect their Elders," HuffPost Life, Accessed July 1, 2024, https://www.huffpost.com/entry/what-other-cultures-can-teach_n_4834228.

12   BitMango, Word Cookies! (South Korea: BitMango, 2016), video game.

STROKE 7: AHA! HA-HA, AND AHHHH

13   Richard Powers, *Overstory* (New York: W. W. Norton & Company, 2018), 320.

STROKE 8: UNDRESSED REHEARSAL

14   Jeff Elder, "An 'Eskimo Kiss' is a Kunik, and Maybe Not What You Think," SouthCoast Today: Lifestyle, accessed July 1, 2024, https://www.southcoasttoday.com/article/20050216/LIFE/302169966.

15   Basha Meier, "The Hongi: Ritual and Ceremony," New Earth Media, September 29, 2016, https://newearth.media/hongi-ritual-ceremony-everyday-life-new-zealand-traditional-maori-greeting/.

16   David Whyte, "Seeking Language Large Enough," interviewed by Krista Tippet, *On Being,* NPR, updated May 26, 2022, audio, 50:34, https://onbeing.org/programs/david-whyte-seeking-language-large-enough/.

STROKE 9: LAST LIGHT OF FACTOID YEARS

17   Pauline Boss, "Ambiguous Loss and the Myth of Closure," interviewed by Kim Mills, *Speaking of Psychology,* American Psychological Association, accessed July 3, 2024, https://www.apa.org/news/podcasts/speaking-of-psychology/ambiguous-loss.

18   Brené Brown, "Strong Back, Soft Front, Wild Heart," *On Being*, National Public Radio, January 5, 2020. Accessed June 30, 2024, https://onbeing.org/programs/brene-brown-strong-back-soft-front-wild-heart/.

19   Edna St. Vincent Millay, *Renascence and Other Poems*, (New York: Harper and Row, 1956), lines 179–180, 12.

20   Mary Troxell, "Arthur Schopehnauer, 1788-1860," Internet Encyclopedia of Philosophy, accessed June 23, 2024, https://iep.utm.edu/schopenh/.

21   "Commissioner Adam Putnam Announces Estimated $1.5 Billion in Agricultural Damages Due to Hurricane Michael," Capital Soup. November 9, 2018, https://capitalsoup.com/2018/11/09/commissioner-adam-putnam-announces-estimated-1-5-billion-in-agricultural-damages-due-to-hurricane-michael/.

AFTER LIFE CARE, R.I.P.

22   David Whyte, IBID (3:56-4:23)

23   *The West Wing*, Season 5, episode 4, "Han," directed by Christopher Misiano, aired October 22, 2003, NBC, Warner Bros, television series.

24   Dilip Paneru, Eliahu Cohen, Robert Fickler, Robert W. Boyd, and Ebrahim Karimi, "Entanglement: Quantum or Classical?" November 6, 2019, paper, https://arxiv.org/pdf/1911.02201.

25   Robert Kaplan, *The Nothing That Is: A Natural History of Zero* (Oxford: Oxford University Press, 1999).

AFTERLIFE SPECULATIONS

26   ZDoggMD, IBID, (1:16:18-1:20:50)

27   You Are Not a Human Being Having a Spiritual Experience. You Are a Spiritual Being Having a Human Experience," Quote Investigator, June 20, 2019, https://quoteinvestigator.com/2019/06/20/spiritual/.

28   Robert Berwick and Noam Chomsky, *Why Only Us: Language and Evolution* (Cambridge, MA: Mit Press, 2015).

29   Paul Van Buren, *The Edges of Language: An Essay in the Logic of Religion* (New York: Macmillan Company, 1972).

30   Dalai Lama, "The Dalai Lama describes the process of death, interview with Justin Brown, *IdeaPod*, July 18, 2019, https://ideapod.com/dalai-lama-explains-happens-die-can-prepared/.

31   Sean Martin, "Life after Death: Soul Continues on a Quantum Level – Scientists Reveal," Express, August 21, 2018, https://www.express.co.uk/news/science/1005845/life-after-death-what-happens-when-you-die-soul-quantum.

32   Robert Coles, Diane Komp, and Carol Dittberner, "Children and God," interviewed by Krista Tippet, On Being, NPR, updated December 16, 2004, https://onbeing.org/programs/robert-coles-diane-komp-and-carol-dittberner-children-and-god/.

33   "The Distinction Between Past, Present, and Future is Only a Stubbornly Persistent Illusion," Quote Investigator, accessed July 1, 2024, https://quoteinvestigator.com/2024/03/18/stubborn-illusion/#daccfe67-685f-4e10-83f9-45494584e32.

34   Suki Desu. "Translation and Meaning of 自分 (Jibun). Accessed June 23, 2024, https://skdesu.com/en/meaning/%E8%87%AA%E5%88%86-jibun/.

35   Donald Hoffman, "Proof That Reality is an Illusion: The Mystery Beyond Space-Time," Know Thyself podcast E63 (2:02:42), André Duqum, Accessed July 2, 2024, https://www.youtube.com/watch?v=I7z26d8IsUc 47:34-54:2.

36   Andrew Newberg, "Spiritual Brain: Science and Religious Experience," Great Courses, 2012, No. 1682, DVD Disc 3.

37   Teilhard de Chardin, The Phenomenon of Man (New York: Haper & Row, 1955), 182.

38   Brené Brown, IBID.

39   Robin Wall Kimmerer, Gathering Moss: A Natural and Cultural History of Mosses (Corvallis, OR: Oregon State University Press, 2003), 271-C.

40   Andrew Newberg, IBID.

41   Gang Xu, Temenuzhka Mihaylova, Duan Li, Jimo Borjigin, "Surge of Neurophysiological Coupling and Connectivity of Gamma Oscillations in the Dying Human Brain," PNAS, accessed July 1, 2024,

https://doi.org/10.1073/pnas.2216268120.

42   Christel Manning, "Facing Death Without Religion: Secular Sources Like Science work Well for Meaning Making," Harvard Divinity Bulletin, accessed July 2, 2024, https://bulletin.hds.harvard.edu/facing-death-without-religion/

43   Brian Greene, *Until the End of Time* (New York: Penguin Random House, 2020).

44   Stephan J.M. Scherer (artist), discussion during Jarogera exhibition, Burgfarrnbach Castle, Fürth, Germany, August 11, 2000.

45   Karl Michael Dürr (emergency physician, son of Hans-Peter Dürr), discussion in Shalimar, FL, June 30, 2024.

46   Leslie Stevens, "The Galaxy Being," *The Outer Limits*, Season 1, episode 1, "The Galaxy Being," directed by Leslie Stevens, produced by Daystar Productions, aired September 16,1963, ABC, Daystar Studio Productions, television series.

47   David Whyte, IBID (3:56-4:23).

48   Dalai Lama, "The Dalai Lama: 'My religion is very simple. My religion is kindness,'" Socratic Method, accessed July 1, 2024, https://www.socratic-method.com/quote-meanings/dalai-lama-my-religion-is-very-simple-my-religion-is-kindness.

49   Paul Tillich. *My Search for Absolutes* (New York: Simon & Schuster, 1967), 127.

50   Zhuangzi, "Zhuangzi's 'Dream of the Butterfly: A Daoist Interpretation," Stanford Encyclopedia of Philosophy,'" accessed June 23, 2024, 49(4): 439-450, https://plato.stanford.edu/entries/zhuangzi/index.html.

ABOUT THE AUTHOR

CHRISTINA LARSON, ROSEMARY'S MIDDLE CHILD, was her mother's 24/7 caregiver for years. Before then, Larson was the first female paramedic in her county. She served as a registered mental health counselor, kindergarten and university psychology teacher, a foster parent for 145 children, a Foster Parent Association president, and was a delegate to the 1997 Mothers of Earth peace summit in Vienna. She holds a master's degree in psychology, bachelor's in religious studies, and AS Degree in Paramedics. Recipient of numerous outstanding performance honors and scholarships, she accepted a Top 10 Censored Stories award for grassroots coverage of depleted uranium exposure risks.

Larson and her husband own an award-winning ecotourism family forest, open to the public. Shoal Sanctuary Nature Preserve has seven miles of hiking and sculpture trails. Virtual visits and author insights available online **www.linktr.ee/christinalarson**.

Printed in the USA
CPSIA information can be obtained
at www.ICGtesting.com
JSHW010048101224
75129JS00001B/1